WRITING TO *Cuba*

ENVISIONING CUBA • LOUIS A. PÉREZ JR., EDITOR

WRITING TO

Cuba

Filibustering and Cuban Exiles in the United States

RODRIGO LAZO

The University of North Carolina Press • Chapel Hill and London

Designed by Heidi Perov
Set in Scala by Keystone Typesetting, Inc.

The paper in this book meets the guidelines for permanence
and durability of the Committee on Production Guidelines for
Book Longevity of the Council on Library Resources.

Library of Congress Cataloging-in-Publication Data
Lazo, Rodrigo.
   Writing to Cuba : filibustering and Cuban exiles in
the United States / Rodrigo Lazo.
       p. cm. — (Envisioning Cuba)
Includes bibliographical references and index.
ISBN 0-8078-2930-7 (cloth : alk. paper)
ISBN 0-8078-5594-4 (pbk. : alk. paper)
1. Cubans—United States—Politics and government—19th century.
2. Authors, Cuban—United States—Political activity—History—19th
century. 3. Exiles—United States—Political activity—History—19th
century. 4. Filibusters—Cuba—History—19th century. 5. United
States—Relations—Cuba. 6. Cuba—Relations—United States.
7. Cuba—History—1810–1899. 8. Cubans—United States—Intellectual
life—19th century. 9. Cuban newspapers—United States—History—
19th century. I. Title. II. Series.
E184.C97L39 2005
860.9′358′089687291073—dc22   2004019096

cloth   09 08 07 06 05   5 4 3 2 1
paper   09 08 07 06 05   5 4 3 2 1

CONTENTS

A section of photographs appears after p. 135.

PREFACE

"I respectfully submit my essay to the public, with a desire to be of some service to my fellow professors as well as to their pupils, and with the hope that I may meet their approbation," wrote Miguel T. Tolón in the preface to his book, *The Elementary Spanish Reader and Translator* (New York, 1853). The book consists of a series of exercises designed to acquaint English-language speakers with Spanish-language constructions and translation techniques. Tolón's reader, which guided students through a succession of themes (the Creation, a spring morning, Cuba, the Puritans) was one of numerous publishing efforts he undertook during almost nine years when he lived as an exile in New York. The *Spanish Reader* went through several editions, including one that appeared in 1905, no doubt as a result of interest in the Spanish language during the U.S. occupation of Cuba following the Spanish-Cuban-American War. Tolón's success in reaching language students through this book was an outgrowth of his work as a tutor of languages and as a journalist who published works in English, French, and Spanish. Like many of the exiles from Cuba that worked with him in the 1850s, Tolón believed it was important to cross from Spanish to English and back. In that spirit, I have written this book with the goal of contributing to the scholarship available on the history of writers of Latin American descent in the United States. The ongoing mass migration of Latin Americans to the United States is raising awareness of the long history of such movements. This book focuses on the growth of a community in which the publication of newspapers became an anchor for writers in exile.

While the primary concern of Tolón's *Spanish Reader* is learning to move from one language to another, I seek to cross another type of separation: area of study. (The two crossings are related.) This book began as a dissertation in "American literature." My focus on Cuba and the publication of texts intended to circulate both in the United States and on the island called for thinking beyond the physical borders of a nation-state and pushing past the conceptual limits of monolingualism. Many of the writers and writings discussed in this book had connections to two or more countries, and thus I argue that to analyze them within the confines of a nation-based approach to literary study is to miss the point of much of their work. I hope not only to add to the body of texts that people consider "American literature" but also to emphasize the importance of the U.S. theater of operations to a print culture that might otherwise be associated solely with Cuban studies. I hope readers find that *Writing to Cuba* addresses some of the concerns of the rapidly changing interdisciplinary areas of Latino/a studies, Latin American studies, and American studies.

Some of the names in this study will be new to readers unfamiliar with the history of Spanish-language publication in the United States. In keeping with Latin American customs, many of the writers and critics use two surnames, the first from the father and the second from the mother. In Cuba, sometimes people insert *y* (and) between the two parental surnames. For writers who are known by two surnames, such as Gaspar Betancourt Cisneros, I use both surnames after the first reference. Others, such as Cirilo Villaverde, use only one surname. In the case of Tolón, a central figure in this book, I have used the name under which he published in the 1840s and 1850s, Miguel T. Tolón, rather than adopting the convention of referring to him as Miguel Teurbe Tolón. In chapter 3, I discuss Tolón's use of names and why he was fond of his francophone surname. In relation to spelling and orthography of the Spanish language, I have brought nineteenth-century usage into accordance with contemporary conventions. This is most clear in the insertion of accents on Spanish words and names that at times were not accented in the original (e.g., López).

Whenever possible, I use previously published translations of Spanish-language writings. In most cases, however, I offer my own translations. Not a translator by training, I do not offer these as definitive translations. Instead, I attempt to convey the content of titles, lines, and passages to English-language readers. Every translation changes the original, and a translation of poetry, even if faithful to the words, may miss important dimensions of the original language. Unlike nineteenth-century translators, I do not create new meter and rhyme schemes. For anyone who prefers to see the original, I provide it for all poetry and lengthy prose passages, either directly next to the English translation or in the notes.

I send my love and gratitude to all of the people who helped me over the years. At the University of Maryland at College Park, I was challenged and nurtured by many faculty members. Robert S. Levine was an extraordinary dissertation director (he once returned a chapter in three days), an exemplary mentor, and a patient friend. He was there at the beginning, providing an initial bibliography about Cuba in the 1850s, and still listened patiently to my presentations of material from the book when it was almost finished.

Colleagues at Miami University of Ohio read chapter drafts and grant proposals. My sincere thanks to Alice Adams, Barry Chabot, Gregg Crane, Cheryl Johnson, Yvonne Keller, Kate McCullough, Susan Morgan, Rebecka Rutledge, Dianne Sadoff, and Keith Tuma. I have learned a lot from students at Miami, especially Karsten Piep, Michael Templeton, and Jennifer Harford Vargas. Miami provided a Summer Research Grant and travel money so that I could conduct research in Havana. The university also provided money to purchase illustrations.

My thanks to the National Endowment for the Humanities for a one-year fellowship that helped me complete the writing of the book.

I received early encouragement from Nicolás Kanellos and other scholars associated with the Recovering the U.S. Literary Heritage Project, especially Jerry Poyo, whose thoughts and scholarship provided an important guide. In 1997, while I was still a graduate student, the Recovery Project provided a grant so that I could travel to libraries to look for newspapers.

Sian Hunter, my editor at the University of North Carolina Press, took an early interest in the book and saw it through with great patience. The book owes its present form in part to the generous criticism of Louis Pérez Jr. I also thank the anonymous readers. For comments at various stages of the project, I thank Jonathan Auerbach, Virginia Bell, Kimberly N. Brown, Regina Harrison, Maria Karafilis, Kevin Meehan, Carla Peterson, Sangeeta Ray, and Elizabeth Renker. Ela Molina Morelock helped with proofreading.

Cheers to all librarians. At Miami, Ed Via helped find rare books and newspapers through interlibrary loan. Eliades Ignacio Acosta Matos, director of Biblioteca Nacional José Martí in Cuba, and the staff of the Sala Cubana were very generous with their time. I also thank the staffs at the Library of Congress, the Beinecke Rare Book and Manuscript Library, the Library Company of Philadelphia, the New York Public Library, the Wisconsin Historical Society, McKeldin Library at the University of Maryland, and the Duke University Rare Book, Manuscript, and Special Collections Library.

Parts of chapter 1 appeared originally in different form in *American Literary History*. Sections of chapter 5 appeared in *American Literature* and volume 3 of *Recovering the U.S. Hispanic Literary Heritage*. I thank Oxford University Press, Duke University Press, and Arte Público Press for their permission to reprint material.

My partner, Amy DePaul, provided the majority of our family's income during the first two years of my work on this project. Her labor and love contributed to this book. Gabriel and Francisco, my sons, shared their Halloween candy. Thanks go to my entire family and particularly to Martha Lazo DeLucca, Joe and Corinne DePaul, Bianca Ronquillo, and Vanessa Ronquillo. Long before I started this book, my mother, Grace Pombar, worked in the garment industry to raise me. Although we lived on a tight budget, she always had a little money for books. Gracias, Mama Yey.

WRITING TO *Cuba*

Introduction

On the Fourth of July, 1850, New York City saw the appearance of *El Horizonte*, a bilingual newspaper published and edited by Miguel T. Tolón, a poet and journalist from Matanzas, Cuba. The front page featured Tolón's "El Pobre Desterrado" (The poor exile), a poem that pronounced a desire to raise a "war cry" and take up arms for Cuba's liberty. On the same page, a Spanish-language article called for the establishment in Cuba of a republican government based "on the model of the United States, the archetype of all political constitutions conceived until now."[1] Another article, "The Fourth of July," appeared in English and Spanish versions on page 3, proclaiming, "Our hearts, too, swell with the glorious feelings of the sons of Washington;—yet the stifled and heart reviving groan of our country sounds louder than the cheers of the American people, and we deeply mourn amidst the rejoicing multitude."[2] "The Fourth of July" captured the contradictory tones of the newspaper, which was simultaneously optimistic about the dawn of a new future on the "horizon" and mournful about Cuba's status as a Spanish colony. While Tolón found common ground with the "sons of Washington" based on the search for a government in opposition to European colonialism, he also stepped away from the national U.S. celebration to note the different circumstances faced by Cubans on the island and in exile.

A forgotten part of print culture history, the inaugural issue of *El Horizonte* is marked by an uncanny sense of dislocation and raises a variety of questions. Why is an exiled writer known in Cuban literary history as one of the island's patriotic poets putting out a newspaper that praises the United States as a model republic? Who are his potential readers? What are the economic implications of the word "poor" to describe exiles? Does the publication of "El Pobre Desterrado" in a New York newspaper change the way we interpret a poem that has been anthologized in Cuba as a part of that country's national literature?[3] These questions, which return in various guises throughout this study, call for an analytical approach that takes into account both the U.S. context of publication and Cuban cultural influences on these texts. In turn, they prompt a reconsideration of the relationship between the publication of newspapers and other texts by Cuban exiles and historical events that brought them to U.S. cities in the mid–nineteenth century, giving rise to a community of writers who composed journalistic and literary pieces for readers in Cuba even as they grappled with the demands of life in the antebellum United States.

Tolón was among a cadre of Cuban exiles who settled in the United States in the late 1840s and 1850s to publish poems, newspaper articles, and pamphlets that were highly critical of the island's colonial government. Free from the limits imposed by censors in Cuba, these writers believed that the United States offered an opportune setting for publishing tracts that would persuade the Cuban population to rise against the colonial government on the island. Writing to Cuba, they also simultaneously tried to reach English- and Spanish-language readers in the United States. Some Cuban exiles called on the United States for help in ousting Spanish rule in Cuba and in installing a government based on reason and democratic participation. This turn to the United States is important to "El Pobre Desterrado," a poem that has been read as an inscription of the historical rupture created by exile and as a political adaptation of the Spanish romance featuring eroticized martyrdom.[4] The poem displays the voice of an exile explaining to a woman in the United States why his heart is committed to another place. Asking the woman to remember him when he is gone to fight for his country, the speaker envisions himself in the ranks of liberators on their native soil. On the front page of *El Horizonte*, the poem's language of republicanism and the U.S. Revolution resonate: Spain is despotic (*despótica España* and *el déspota osado*); the exile has a *patria*; he echoes Patrick Henry by calling for liberty or death (*Libre o morir*); and the U.S. woman is connected to a glorious eagle (*águila gloriosa*), which shelters the exile under its wings. In the United States, the poem proclaims, there is no room for the servility of colonial subjection. Thus, the literary performance of "El Pobre Desterrado" emerges within a print culture connected to both Cuba and the United States.

The dual influences of island colony and budding empire fueled the production of a dozen newspapers in New York and New Orleans between 1848 and the U.S. Civil War, including *La Verdad* (The truth) (New York, 1848–60), *El Mulato* (New York, 1854), and *El Eco de Cuba* (Cuba's echo) (New York, 1855). These newspapers, written largely in Spanish but sometimes containing English-language sections, were packed with polemical articles debating the future of Cuba and proposing strategies for organizing military attacks from the United States as well as an internal revolution on the island. The papers were produced by some of Cuba's most distinguished writers, among them Cirilo Villaverde (1812–94), Gaspar Betancourt Cisneros (1803–66), Pedro Santacilia (1826–1910), and Juan Clemente Zenea (1832–71). These writers remained in the United States for as long as several decades, working as activists and publishing revolutionary texts. Their newspapers were more than a venue for political journalism, as they contained poems, many of which were later collected in books such as Santacilia's *El Arpa del Proscripto* (The banished man's lyre) (1856), Tolón's *Leyendas Cubanas* (Cuban legends) (1856), and the anthology *El Laúd del Desterrado* (The exile's lute) (1858), all published in New York. In other cases, the work of writers led to nonfiction books such as Santacilia's historical study, *Lecciones Orales sobre la Historia de Cuba, Pronunciadas en el Ateneo Democrático Cubano de Nueva York* (Orations concerning the history of Cuba, delivered in New York's Democratic Cuban Athenaeum) (New Orleans, 1859).

During the nineteenth century, writers from Cuba published more than seventy newspapers in the United States. These newspapers varied dramatically in size, length of publication, and in the positions they took on the island's future and its relationship with the United States.[5] The best-known of the nineteenth-century Cuban exiles is José Martí (1853–95), a poet, essayist, and political operative who first arrived in New York in 1880, published his writings in newspapers, and worked tirelessly to build a coalition for Cuban independence until his death on the battlefield.[6] Martí's essay, "Our America," has become a staple in discussions of inter-American cultural studies in part because it articulates questions about power relations between the United States and what Martí calls "our America," the "romantic nations of the continent and the suffering islands of the sea" that endure European models of culture and economic control.[7] "Our America," as José David Saldívar argues, positions Martí "as a firm anti-imperialist who wrote about the emergent empire: 'I know the monster; I have lived in its entrails.' "[8] But decades before Martí developed his political program in the United States, his compatriots attempted to wield that "monster" to their benefit. By the time Martí arrived in New York, Cuban intellectuals had been publishing in the United States for more than fifty years and had failed in their efforts to rally the U.S. government and public to support their revolutionary efforts. Thus, the panorama that Martí confronted in the United States differed from that faced by writers in preceding decades.

In the mid–nineteenth century, Cuba's exiled writers were in many cases willing to embrace U.S. constitutional principles, if not the United States itself. They drew inspiration and political ideals from the writings of Thomas Paine, Thomas Jefferson, and Samuel Adams and from the U.S. Declaration of Independence. In addition to the content of U.S. revolutionary documents, exiles were captivated by the relationship between text and revolution exemplified by a pamphlet such as *Common Sense*. Their wish to recreate *el sentido común* for Cuba is an example of what Michael Warner describes as the "far-reaching impact both on the continent and in the New World" of the U.S. paper war waged by men of letters in the eighteenth century.[9] Of course, the historical and geographic circumstances differed for the revolutionary effort of the North American colonies in the 1770s and the Cuban exile anticolonial project in the mid–nineteenth century. Cubans attempted to reach from one country to another; consequently, their failure to oust Spain in the 1850s calls attention to the limits of a print culture that transcended national borders. I discuss in more detail throughout this book the particular challenges that Cubans faced in their publishing projects, emphasizing that difficulties were interconnected with a geopolitical battle between the declining Spanish empire and the expanding U.S. empire. While exiles looked back to the principles of the U.S. fight against monarchical colonialism, the U.S. government looked to expand its territorial holdings at the expense of populations in the West and even the Caribbean. Congress and several presidents debated what was then known as "the Cuba question"—namely, "Would Cuba join the Union?" Many Cuban exiles in the antebellum United States compromised on the possibility of full independence and democracy for the island and sought to replicate the type of slave-based society found in the United States. In turn, these exiles threw their support behind Manifest Destiny proponents who salivated at the thought of annexing Cuba.

A picture of anticolonial exiles supporting U.S. expansionism exemplifies the contradictions that emerged when Latin American intellectuals grappled with ideals in writings from the U.S. Revolution while witnessing the development of U.S. expansionism in the nineteenth century. Students of Latin American history are liable to find walls bearing the graffiti inscription "Yanqui go home" as well as letters of admiration to Washington. In the early nineteenth century, some Latin American intellectuals looked to the U.S. Declaration of Independence to develop their anticolonial fight against Spain. As early as 1812, the pseudonymous "El Amigo de Los Hombres" (The friend of men) published a Spanish-language pamphlet in Philadelphia praising "English America" among empires and nations that were successful because they "established liberty and brilliant prosperity."[10] This author was not alone. Many prominent Latin American intellectuals viewed geopolitics in the Americas not along a border dividing North from South but along an ideological and even natural difference between the Americas and Europe, particularly Spain.[11] In that sense, the separation of America as a hemisphere promoted by the Monroe Doctrine worked hand in hand with opposition to Spain in some sectors of Latin America.

The attitudes of Cubans toward the United States, as I show throughout this study, were neither monolithic nor static. As a culture of exile and print developed in the antebellum period, some Cubans adopted expansionist positions, while others challenged the ascendancy of the United States and its slave-based economy. Thus, while the dominant strain in writings by Cuban exiles during the antebellum period is pro–United States, heterogeneous and contradictory discourses circulated as a result of the complex relationships and political alliances prompted by U.S. expansionism and Spanish colonialism.

The defining movement for Cuban exiles in the antebellum period was a series of expeditions known as "filibustering." Before "filibuster" became common usage for a U.S. Senate legislative maneuver, the word was used pejoratively to disparage soldiers of fortune who attempted to seize parts of Latin America. From the Dutch *vrijbuiter*, or "freebooter," modified into the French *flibustier*, the Spanish *filibustero* became common in the seventeenth century as an epithet for pirates who plundered the Spanish West Indies. This sense of the filibuster as a criminal adventurer, one who seizes objects by force, infused the English "filibuster"—variously spelled "fillibuster," "filibustier," and "filibusterer"—in the antebellum United States.[12] In the 1850s, filibustering expeditions set out from the United States to Mexico, Nicaragua, and Ecuador, among other places, inspiring heated political debate, diplomatic exchanges, and a flurry of press coverage. Historians in both Latin America and the United States have studied in depth the diplomatic, military, and political implications of filibustering.[13] Robert May, for example, captures the contradictory responses to filibusters, who were viewed as pirates and usurpers of land but were also "worshipped as heroes by masses of people" who saw in the filibusters the romantic spirit of an age when the United States appeared destined to overtake the continent.[14] Critics of U.S. imperialism still view William Walker's expeditions to Central America as a defining moment in the sordid history of U.S. involvement in Latin America. "From then on," writes Eduardo Galeano, "invasions, interventions, bombardments, forced loans, and gun-point treaties followed one after the other."[15]

Galeano's reading of the filibuster as an Anglo-American invader of Latin America is at odds with the ways exiled Cubans conceived the *filibustero*. For Tolón, Villaverde, Zenea, and others, the *filibustero* was a symbol of exiles' determination to oust Spain from the island. While they called for the participation of the U.S. masses in the filibustering of Cuba, many Cubans identified themselves as *filibusteros* and presented their expeditions as examples of republican efforts to bring democracy and egalitarianism to the island. "El Filibustero" was the title of a poem and the name of a newspaper that attempted to dredge up support for filibustering expeditions to Cuba. Cuban writers believed that filibustering had both a textual and a military component; it was both a metaphor for the writer as activist and a historical movement. In turn, I deploy "filibustering" as a historically specific term that paves the way for conceiving the writers as *filibusteros* trying to take control of land. I use the term "*filibustero* newspapers" to refer to a handful of papers that overtly advocated support of filibustering expeditions, including *El Filibustero*, *La Verdad*, and the papers published by Tolón. Other papers published by Cubans during this period had more ambivalent positions toward filibustering, and still others outright rejected the U.S. annexation of Cuba.

My argument is not that Cuban *filibusteros* stepped outside of the ideological implications of filibustering as a U.S.-based movement. Most *filibusteros* compromised on the question of slavery in Cuba's future in an effort to build a military movement. Rather, I emphasize that the Cuban *filibustero* embodied the contradiction of protonationalist (Cuban) discourse and U.S. expansionism. In other words, the antimonarchical position of exiles was intertwined with the position of U.S. expansionists who relished the thought of roping Cuba into the Union. Why did some Cuban writers accept annexation as an option in the island's future? Historian Gerald Poyo argues that annexation was a calculated antinationalist solution based on economic and political necessities. Some of the exiles were slave owners who sought to protect their economic interests by having Cuba join the Union as a slave state. Exiles also believed that if Cuba became a U.S. state, it would not face the political upheavals that had shaken many independent Latin American nations.[16] As I show in chapter 2, annexation as an option for Cuba's future clashed with a sense among exiles that the people of Cuba and the island itself formed a distinct place with democratic rights. A careful reading of *filibustero* newspapers shows that for writers, a disjunction emerged between the hemispheric ambitions of the U.S. government and what *filibustero* writers believed America as a hemisphere meant for liberation movements. In other words, writers were inspired by America's promise of equality and freedom even as the United States instituted expansionistic military and economic practices at the expense of self-determination for indigenous and Latin American populations in the Americas. To reconcile the contradictions of opposing one empire while lining up behind another, Cuban exiles argued that Cuba's economy and public institutions would benefit from annexation.

The development of newspaper publication by Cubans in the United States can be traced back to a long-standing two-way flow of economic, political, and cultural exchange between the United States and the island. U.S. travelers and investors made their way to Cuba, and the island's intellectual and economic elite reciprocated in kind. In the first half of the nineteenth century, the U.S. became a major buyer of Cuban sugar and coffee as well as a provider of imports for the island. Investors from the United States in 1828 founded Cárdenas, which due to its demographic makeup became known as the "American city." Ten years later, engineers from the United States completed a fifty-one-mile railway between Havana and Güines, and locomotives as well as sugar machinery soon were among the U.S. imports flowing into Cuba. In 1826, U.S. vessels accounted for 783 of the 964 ships that visited the port of Havana. Meanwhile, Spanish economic participation on the island was diminishing.[17]

The economic exchange was intertwined with the U.S. government's desire for greater control over the island. As Louis Pérez notes, "North American designs on Cuba became a fixed feature of U.S. strategic objectives early in the nineteenth century."[18] Cuba presented a special set of conditions for U.S. foreign policy. Because it did not follow other Latin American countries in liberating itself from Spain in the 1820s, the island stood out as an anachronism, a territory out of sync with the twilight of colonialism in the Americas. Unlike other Latin American countries, Cuba did not abolish slavery early in the century, which placed it in a special parallel relation to the United States. Furthermore, the island's geographic position just south of Florida and jutting into the Gulf of Mexico drew the geopolitical interests of U.S. leaders. Considering Cuba's possible entry into the Union, Thomas Jefferson wrote to James Monroe in 1823, "I candidly confess, that I have ever looked on Cuba as the most interesting addition which could ever be made to our system of states."[19] By the 1840s, U.S. expansionists saw Cuba as a prize waiting to be taken. The United States had doubled in size in less than five years, having annexed Texas in 1845, acquired Oregon in 1846, and taken a portion of Mexico through the Treaty of Guadalupe Hidalgo in 1848. In the view of the *United States Magazine and Democratic Review*, Cuba was the next logical step following the U.S.-Mexico War: "The hardy character and indomitable enterprise manifested by the Americans in that war, pointed out at once the feasibility of employing a sufficient force to disenthral Cuba, and to allow, henceforth, the wealth of the island to accumulate within itself, to the enrichment of all classes."[20] By emphasizing the island's "wealth" and envisioning "enrichment," the magazine attempted to tap bilateral commercial interests. This type of desire for acquisition of the island's resources stretched all the way to the U.S. presidency; presidents James Polk

(1845–49), Franklin Pierce (1853–57), and James Buchanan (1857–61) all tried to purchase the island from Spain.[21]

In conjunction with growing political and economic exchanges between Cuba and the United States, a rise in the number of travelers going in both directions fueled the development of cultural connections. In the antebellum period, Cuba became a favored destination for the "invalid trade," the business of tourism for sick people who sought to improve their health under the island sun.[22] The invalids who traveled to Cuba during the 1830s included Sophia Peabody, a Salem, Massachusetts, painter who would go on to marry Nathaniel Hawthorne. During the two years she spent on a rural coffee plantation with the goal of improving her health, Peabody wrote detailed letters, an unpublished "Cuba Journal" that provides a prime example of the cultural-economic connections that took travelers and invalids to Cuba. She went there as a result of her sister Mary's employment as a tutor for the children of a U.S. family profiting from plantation labor. (Mary Peabody Mann would go on to write a novel about Cuba, *Juanita*, published posthumously in 1887.) The writings by the Peabody sisters were among dozens of nineteenth-century books and articles about Cuba that ranged in style and substance from the dreamy, orientalist vision of William Henry Hurlbert's *Gan-Eden; or, Pictures of Cuba* (1854) to the sardonic analysis and jaded tone of Julia Ward Howe's *A Trip to Cuba* (1860).[23] Hurlbert, for one, portrayed the island as a "garden of delight" offering exotic scenes: "India itself offers nothing more thoroughly strange to our eyes."[24] The use of words such as "strange" and "exotic" in these writings emphasizes the relativity of viewpoint in travel pieces, which were usually written by upper-class travelers and writers from New England.

The movement of people and the accompanying textual production went in two directions. When opponents of Cuba's colonial rule were forced into exile in the early part of the century, they chose the United States as one of their main destinations. After becoming involved in a plot to overthrow the government, poet José María Heredia made his way to the northeastern United States in 1823.[25] He visited Philadelphia, Niagara Falls, and George Washington's home in Virginia and then published a volume of poems, *Poesías* (New York, 1825). Priest and philosopher Félix Varela also settled in the Northeast and published *El Habanero* (1824–26), a pamphlet-size periodical that was banned by the Spanish government. Varela is also believed to be the author of an anonymous Spanish-language novel, *Jicoténcal* (Philadelphia, 1826).[26] Varela remained in the United States until his death in 1853, and his contributions there as a priest and writer were recognized when he was honored on a 1997 U.S. postage stamp. While Varela and Heredia are part of an exile intellectual tradition, Cubans also made their way to the north voluntarily for education and entertainment. The elite vacationed in the United States early in the nineteenth century and sent their children to U.S. schools.[27]

In the late 1840s and 1850s, concomitant with the filibustering expeditions led by General Narciso López, Cubans began arriving in large numbers, establishing the foundations of communities, and cementing a U.S.-based culture of newspaper publication. A series of events in the 1840s, including increased repression in Cuba and growing support among elite Cubans for annexation to the United States, created conditions that prompted a large number of Cubans to leave the island for U.S. cities even as the colonial government condemned other Cubans to exile. In 1844, Spanish authorities unleashed a reign of terror in response to a failed slave uprising that came to be known as the Conspiracy of la Escalera, named after the Spanish word for "ladder" because suspected collaborators were tied to ladders and flogged. A military commission condemned 78 people to death, imprisoned 1,292 collaborators, and exiled 400, and some historians estimate that hundreds died during torture.[28] Those executed publicly included poet Gabriel de la Concepción Valdez, better known as Plácido, whom I discuss in chapter 4. Authorities also imprisoned writers, and the censor banned, among other titles, the antislavery novel *Sab* by Gertrudis Gómez de Avellaneda, who was living in Europe at the time.[29]

La Escalera disrupted a literary and cultural movement to establish a discourse of Cubanness that had been building since the early 1830s. Writers connected to critic and literary impresario Domingo Delmonte had published a variety of texts, including antislavery poetry and an autobiographical piece by former slave Juan Francisco Manzano. Antonio Benítez Rojo argues that this cultural outpouring represented an attempt to manipulate, even as writers were manipulated by, a discourse of Cubanness that emerged in conjunction and in response to the rapid development of the sugar plantation as a site of power.[30] This movement, as Benítez Rojo notes, had an ambivalent relationship with "foreign intellectual circles" that included not only British abolitionists but also operatives in the U.S. State Department such as Alexander Everett.[31] In turn, Manzano's poems were published in London in 1840. As a result of these connections, writers turned to other countries following the repression of La Escalera. Writing to his friend Delmonte in 1844, Villaverde described the atmosphere in Cuba as so poisoned that two men who "cultivate letters" could not meet casually to discuss literature.[32] Imprisoned four years later for plotting against the government, Villaverde escaped from jail and settled in New York, where he lived until his death in 1894. In effect, La Escalera radicalized writers such as Villaverde and prompted them to look for places where they could produce political writing.

New York and New Orleans became publishing centers for writers who saw their work as connected to annexationist plotting and filibustering. In New York, the newspaper *La Verdad* began appearing in January 1848 as a voice of the Cuban Council, a coalition of revolutionaries and planters from the island who saw annexation to the United States as a viable option for separating from Spain. *La Verdad*, as I discuss in chapter 2, brought together U.S.-based supporters of Manifest Destiny, Cuban planters who backed annexation, and patriotic writers who supported filibustering as a military option for changing conditions in Cuba. But *La Verdad*'s support of annexation came under attack as exile circles drew writers with a variety of political positions, including abolitionists. By 1853, newspapers such as Villaverde's *El Independiente* called for an internal revolution on the island, de-emphasizing the importance of annexation. And not long thereafter, newspapers published in the United States began challenging one another on a series of issues, including the influence of Cuba's upper class and the acceptance of slavery in Cuba's future. To understand differences among the writers, I discuss each newspaper's platform and clarify its positions in relation to the politics of filibustering, U.S. expansionism, and slavery.

Most of the writers, editors, and publishers of these newspapers hailed from Cuba's intellectual elite. As educated Creoles—whites born on the island—these writers had distinct racial advantages in Cuba's slave society. In 1846, 36 percent of Cuba's population of 898,752 was made up of slaves, and another 16 percent were free colored.[33] With most of the population having little or no opportunity for an education, to be a published writer in Cuba in the 1840s and 1850s was a remarkable privilege. Some had made their marks by publishing literary pieces in Cuba: Villaverde in fiction, Tolón and Zenea in poetry, and Betancourt Cisneros in essays. In the United States, all four became newspaper writers and editors, and Villaverde went so far as to renounce fiction for some years because he questioned the efficacy of literary genres in bringing about revolution. This study, however, does not focus only on figures whose place in Cuban literary history is tied to fiction and poetry. I include lesser-known exiles who carved out a place in the U.S. publishing scene, including Francisco Agüero Estrada, printer José Mesa, and revolutionary journalist Juan Bellido de Luna. Ambrosio José Gonzales, a military man who fought with López in Cuba, published the pamphlet *Manifesto on Cuban Affairs Addressed to the People of the United States* (1853); planter Cristóbal Madan, the first president of the Cuban Council, published an economic treatise, *Llamamiento de la Isla de Cuba a la Nación Española* (An address from the island of Cuba to the Spanish nation) (1854).

Most of the newspapers' writers were men, and thus gender conventions and the development of revolutionary masculinity influenced their perspectives on filibustering and Cuba. To highlight the importance of gender to exile writing, I focus on the differences between the *filibusteros* and some of Cuba's major women poets who remained on the island or went to Europe. At the same time, I analyze the writing of Emilia Casanova de Villaverde, whose arrival in the United States during the filibustering fifties prompted a political development that culminated in her work as an activist during the 1860s and 1870s. My focus on a woman whose revolutionary writing work is slightly outside the period of this study is an attempt to question the marginal place of women in the newspapers and to shed a critical light on how textual production and activism were intertwined with masculinity. Vera Kutzinski argues that a self-effacement of masculinity in Cuban and other "Hispanic-American cultures" functions simultaneously with "an erasure of the female subject from critical discourses."[34] I attempt not only to critique this tendency but also to resist it by discussing women's writings, and I explore how masculine definitions of the *filibustero* were constituted historically in relation to writers' anxieties about their power (or lack thereof) in Cuban and U.S. societies.

In exile, many writers experienced contradictory social and class locations as the intellectual privilege they brought from Cuba and the political connections they developed in the United States clashed with the experience of poverty and U.S. racism. Many of the writers worked as language tutors and struggled to find money for their publications. While *La Verdad* was kept afloat by steady funding from Cuban planters who supported annexation, writers struggled to put out issues of fledgling publications. Mesa, for example, took a loss when he ventured to print and/or edit three independent newspapers. In the final issue of his *El Eco de Cuba*, Mesa told readers that working on newspapers had not brought him a single cent of profit. "On the contrary," he wrote, "they have been a burden on the pocket, in addition to taking up personal and work time."[35] Despite the economic challenges of putting out newspapers while trying to get by in a new country, Cubans developed connections in the highest circles of the U.S. government. Betancourt Cisneros and Jose Aniceto Iznaga, both of whom worked on *La Verdad*, met with President Polk in 1848, escorted to the White House by Senator Jefferson Davis of Mississippi.[36] During the height of enthusiasm for filibustering Cuba, exiles met with Robert E. Lee, Stephen Douglas, and Pierre Soulé. Some of these interactions were facilitated by the political operative who was closest to the exiles, John L. O'Sullivan, newspaper editor and prophet of Manifest Destiny. O'Sullivan, who was Critóbal Madan's brother-in-law, shared Cubans' belief in the connection between military filibustering and newspapers and helped organize filibustering expeditions.

The cultural, political, and economic connections that emerged in conjunction with the Cuban filibustering expeditions call attention to the depth and variety of Cuban exile experiences during the past two hundred years. Writers often referred to themselves as *cubanos*, but that self-identification as Cubans was not transparent; their desire to become Cuban in a governmentally sanctioned sense was heightened by the distance from home. Their publications attempted to connect "Cuban" identity with revolution and opposition to Spain. By bringing forth the way writers in exile articulate the nation as a desired ideal and a territorial reality, both present and absent from their immediate context, I challenge the belief that the nation is solely a local formation. At the same time, I emphasize that the nation was an important part of textual production and self-identification for Cuban exiles in the nineteenth century. Neither something to celebrate nor something to dismiss, the nation is the engine driving the distasteful alliances that developed in the mid–nineteenth century: filibustering brought together slaveholders in Cuba and the United States, northern U.S. expansionists, and soldiers of fortune. For some in that coalition, the nation (United States) provided a racist justification for the takeover of land. For other supporters of filibustering, the nation (Cuba) was the object of a desire that justified a compromise on the question of slavery.

More than a political end, Cuba was also a lost object for writers who mourned their distance from the island. Writers' references to Cuba were often intertwined with grief over distance from their relatives and a utopian desire for a future community based on equality. As Edward Said argues, exile can bring difficulty and opportunity simultaneously: "Exile is one of the saddest fates," Said writes in *Representations of the Intellectual*, describing a "median state" in which a person can neither fully integrate into the new setting nor let go of the old, "beset with half-involvements and half-detachments, nostalgic and sentimental on one level, an adept mimic or a secret outcast on another."[37] In *Culture and Imperialism*, Said points to another dimension of exile when describing his own experience: "belonging, as it were, to both sides of the imperial divide enables you to understand them more easily."[38] Exile, then, is an incomplete and unstable position, but it presents possibilities for individual and collective change. I use the phrase "Cuban exiles in the United States" because it emphasizes displacement and a shift in location. The writers in this study called themselves *desterrados*, deterritorialized people whose life experiences were intimately connected and disconnected to more than one country. While a common translation for *desterrado* is exile, the Spanish word has lexical and connotative dimensions that are not captured by the English. *Desterrado* emphasizes a tearing away from the land; thus, to be a Cuban *desterrado* destabilizes the association of territory and nation that has marked many of the seminal texts defining Cubanness. But the condition of exile created a longing for the connection to nation-territory; as a result, contemporary concepts that deemphasize the nation, such as borderlands, do not correspond to the historical vision of Cuban *desterrados*.[39] In turn, I have avoided contemporary ethnic labels, such as "Cuban American," that imply a more fluid sense of self and nation.[40]

To read these as writers solely of Cuba or solely as part of a U.S. tradition is to miss the multiple locations of writings that crossed languages, national borders, and sociocultural contexts. My goal is to recover the U.S. context of publication without integrating these texts solely into a narrative of U.S. traditions. *Writing to Cuba* is inspired by recent efforts in U.S. literary and cultural studies to examine the relationship of culture to U.S. imperialism by considering questions of nation formation vis-à-vis othered peoples and hemispheric debates over race and slavery, among other topics.[41] In some cases, moving beyond the nation can lead to incisive readings of how U.S.-based authors construct foreignness and both replicate and challenge cultural imperialism. A turn toward the analysis of imperialism in American studies, exemplified in the collection *Cultures of United States Imperialism*, emerged almost simultaneously with a scholarly project to recover and contextualize a history of writings by people of Latin American descent in the United States.[42] As Nicolás Kanellos notes, "Historically, the diverse ethnic groups that we conveniently lump together as 'Hispanics' or 'Latinos' created a literature even before the founding of the United States."[43] In response, Kanellos has led a monumental effort to gather and disseminate materials, making available through the Recovering the U.S. Hispanic Literary Heritage series numerous primary sources and critical studies that have called attention to a long history of publishing by people of Spanish and Latin American descent in North America.[44] In addition, scholars have published impressive studies of newspapers in the Southwest.[45] Notable recent books include Kirsten Silva Gruesz's far-ranging comparative study of cultural exchanges in the nineteenth-century United States. Calling "for a strong revision of literary-historical narratives of the U.S. national tradition that render the Latino presence ghostly and peripheral," Gruesz recaptures the ways in which writers of Latin American descent interacted with Anglo Americans and responded to a variety of social and political conflicts of the period.[46] Gruesz's reading of the past through the lens of Latino studies is likely to inspire other studies that employ a panethnic or multinational analysis. While the work of exiled Cuban writers is part of a broader history that could be retroactively read in panethnic terms, I emphasize the U.S.-Cuba connection to bring forth specificity in the political positions of writings and in the conditions of print culture. Whatever their sense of kinship with other Latin Americans, the writers in this study placed Cuba at the center of their texts.

Recovery work in the nineteenth century necessarily entails a tension between the particular conditions and affiliations of writers (in this case Cuban exiles) and the goals of contemporary analytical frameworks labeled Chicano/a, Latino/a, or Hispanic. As José Aranda shows, recovery work can bring forth heterogeneity in terms of class and political positions for groups that might otherwise be read as sharing a common social marginalization across centuries. Discussing the relationship of Chicano/a studies to writer María Amparo Ruiz de Burton, Aranda calls "for moving scholarship beyond counter-nationalist arguments that conceive Chicano/a culture and history in strict opposition to U.S. and Western cultures." Aranda insists "on the need to formulate histories and analyses that place some people of Mexican descent at the center of discourses more typically associated with Anglo America."[47] That type of discursive commonality is exemplified by the enthusiasm for annexation in some writings by Cuban exiles.

Writing to Cuba elucidates how exiles' texts displayed both Cuban protonationalism and the connections to Anglo-American expansionist politics and culture. With filibustering and the attendant politics of annexation at the center of textual production for exiles in the late 1840s and 1850s, both the United States and Cuba figure prominently in the writings considered here. I emphasize that recovery work, when considering publications by exiles and immigrants, needs to be attentive to the political arenas in writers' home countries as well as the United States. In U.S. cities throughout the nineteenth century, writers from Latin America took up periodical production to influence political opinion in their home countries.[48] As such, *Writing to Cuba* adopts a transnational approach that considers how writings relate to historical contingencies in more than one country. I seek to analyze how writings are influenced by and respond to more than one context. My use of "transnational" draws from the sociological examination of migrants whose economic, social, and cultural affiliations move from one country to another. In the contemporary period, for example, some workers who live in the United States retain families, political allegiances, and religious ties to their countries of origin.[49] Economic conditions, juridical relationships, and everyday experiences are not contained within national borders for people who can travel (with varying degrees of difficulty) from one place to another and back. Because present-day transnational studies tend to emphasize the interrelationship of commodity production and global capitalism, such studies usually focus on an economic subject, especially when that person is conceived as a migrant. John Carlos Rowe argues that contemporary transnational approaches have a tendency to separate new global trends from their histories, but he also warns against projecting terms such as "postcolonial" and "transnational," framed in the current crisis of capitalist exploitation, "too unilaterally onto the related but different histories that have given rise to such circumstances."[50] My use of "transnational," then, is specific to the notion of writing to Cuba from the United States, a process that takes into account audiences in an expanding nation-state and a colony where protonational sentiments circulated. I emphasize writing in its various forms as my primary object of study and thus use the term "transnational writing."

Transnational writing moved from the United States to Cuba and back as it went through the stages of composition, publication, and circulation. In other words, the texts were transnational not only in content but also in their production and dissemination. Print culture historian Robert Darnton uses the term "communications circuit" to describe a cycle that moves "from the author to the publisher (if the bookseller does not assume that role), the printer, the shipper, the bookseller, and the reader."[51] It is a cycle because the writer is also a reader. Darnton's model opens avenues for considering various manifestations of print, particularly newspapers and pamphlets, which are lighter than books and thus can be transported more easily from one nation to another. If the communications circuit through which transnational writing moves in the Americas were mapped, different parts of the cycle would exist in different countries. An article written in Cuba might be published in New York and read by someone in New Orleans. Or a poem that appears in New York might make its way aboard a ship sailing for Havana. This flow is not easy, and one of the challenges that Cuban exiles faced was how to move their texts through a transnational circuit that could be ruptured at various points.

The belief that texts printed in the United States could circulate in Cuba—the conceptual basis of transnational writing—came into conflict with the real impediments of how to transport the documents and make them available in a society where such texts were banned. The difficulties of circulating transnational writing hindered the revolutionary efficacy of publications. In the 1850s, texts did not circulate widely enough to prompt a revolution; the communications circuit was ruptured by censorship in Cuba and splintered by the multiple reading sites of transnational writing. Cuban exiles showed themselves to be more hopeful than realistic about the effects of both filibustering expeditions and their *filibustero* newspapers. As I subsequently discuss in more detail, efforts to filibuster Cuba both militarily and through writing failed to draw enough support from populations in Cuba and the United States to end Spanish rule.

Chapter 1, "*El Filibustero*: Symbol of the Battle for Cuba," establishes the conceptual premise for discussing transnational writing as a form of filibustering. I begin by providing an overview of the filibuster as a mid-nineteenth-century figure who embodied contradictions inherent in the U.S. mission to spread American, in the broader sense, republicanism throughout the hemisphere. Focusing on the newspaper *El Filibustero* and poems that appeared in transnational newspapers, I show how the *filibustero* as both a fighter and a symbol is important to understanding the connection between newspapers and other forms of writings by Cuban exiles, including poetry. I show that writers attempted to wage a war of words. I conclude the chapter by highlighting the irony of using the *filibustero* (which by definition does not have a territory) for an anticolonial battle and raise questions about writers' assumptions that they could take over the island and change governmental structures in Cuba by printing newspapers.

Chapter 2, "Annexation and Independence: Newspaper Wars and Transnational Cuba," provides an overview of the variety of newspapers, their connections to Cuban cultural contexts, and their adoption of U.S. print culture conditions. Through an analysis of *La Verdad*, I show how writers negotiated the politically loaded question of annexation and debated issues that concerned exile communities in New York and New Orleans. Although most exiles adopted a proannexation position, notions of "independence" circulated freely in the newspapers as writers conceived of the island as a separate territory from Spain. A reading of newspapers shows a dialogic process that led ultimately to a budding sense of Cuba as a distinct place and culture with its own people.

Chapter 3, "Men of Action: Revolutionary Masculinity and Women Writers," argues that men in exile developed a male-centered notion of a revolutionary fighter in part out of anxiety about how effective a man of letters could be in removing Spanish colonial rule from Cuba. In the wake of the death of *filibustero* Narciso López, writers promoted the notion that "men of action" would have to take over Cuba. In turn, these writers published a stream of poems valorizing General López as the ultimate revolutionary fighter. Given the gendered dimensions of the "man of action," I turn to Miguel T. Tolón's efforts to build a revolutionary movement that included women and compare poems by U.S.-based male writers to some of Cuba's women writers from the period. I then show that the ultimate woman of action was Emilia Casanova de Villaverde, a political activist who gained prominence in the late 1860s. Reading Casanova's letters to various leaders in the Americas, I argue that she came to embody the revolutionary agency sought by *filibusteros* in the 1850s.

Chapter 4, "*El Mulato*: Race, Land, and Labor in the Americas," focuses on the newspaper *El Mulato*, which ignited a debate over abolition among exiles. Looking at the way antebellum U.S. culture promoted a notion that filibustering and territorial rights were tied to race, I show that Cuban writers promoted a construction of island identity tied to a white Creole (*criollo*). But that construction prompted a handful of Cuban abolitionists to challenge the proslavery position; consequently, a different kind of man of action, *mulato* writer Plácido, emerged in both Cuban and U.S. letters as a new revolutionary martyr for the cause of abolition and racial equality. I conclude the chapter with a reading of *El Negro Mártir*, an anonymous serialized novella published in *El Mulato*.

Chapter 5, "A *Filibustero*'s Novel: *Cecilia Valdés* and a Memory of Nation," brings together the various issues presented in the previous chapters—filibustering, the man of action, gendered conceptions of Cuba, and debates about slavery—by considering the transnational dimensions of one of Cuba's canonical nineteenth-century novels. I read Villaverde's *Cecilia Valdés o La Loma del Angel* (New York, 1882) as an attempt to seize the territory of the Cuban nation when it appears that the military battle for the island has been lost. By considering Villaverde's work as a *filibustero* and newspaper writer in the United States, I show that a novel that has been widely read as "Cuban" was the result of the transnational print culture that Villaverde helped develop as a writer in exile. The epilogue considers the work of José Martí in relation to *filibusteros* and argues that although filibustering failed militarily, it led to the development of a Cuban print culture in exile that had great influence in the latter part of the century.

My discussion of Villaverde, Zenea, and other writers as part of the United States as well as Cuba is an attempt to remap the contours of literary history, to pull out of the nation-state's limits without negating the historical importance of the nation. *Writing to Cuba* points to the importance of understanding the dual or multiple historical and cultural contexts of writers who go into exile or migrate to the United States from other parts of the world. This study also calls on critics of U.S. literature and culture to consider the ways writers who might be categorized as ethnic or, more specifically, Latino/a, retain connections to their countries of origin or, in some cases, the countries of their ancestors. The condition of movement entails that writers respond to social and political contexts in more than one country; thus, the labels of nation and ethnicity should serve more as provisional organizational principles than as descriptive or defining categories. "No one today is purely *one* thing," writes Said. "Labels like Indian, or woman, or Muslim, or American are not more than starting-points, which if followed into actual experience for only a moment are quickly left behind."[52] What are those other things that make up a person, and how do they appear at particular moments in history? If writers are defined and define themselves in part by what they write, then what happens when their texts move beyond the starting points that might otherwise connect a person to one place or ethnic identity? To explore this question for Cuban exiles in the mid–nineteenth century, the first chapter focuses on the *filibuster(o)*.

El Filibustero

SYMBOL OF THE BATTLE FOR CUBA

In 1853, Representative Abraham Venable called on the U.S. House of Representatives to take an etymological inventory of the word "filibuster." "We have taken the liberty of altering it, and clothing it in American dress, as is our wont in such cases," Venable told his colleagues. The "dress" to which he presumably referred was a republican outfit, a reference to arguments that the filibuster embodied a noble opponent of monarchical government. But, Venable went on, a filibuster is "still a freebooter." He warned, "If the policy of any Administration is to make the United States the brigands of the world; if we are to become a race, a nation of buccaneers; if we are to adopt the policy of falling upon our weaker neighbors and appropriating their possessions, and thus fill the measure of national iniquity, I utterly denounce the policy."[1] Venable thus invoked the filibuster's etymological ancestors, the buccaneer and the freebooter.[2] In doing so, he issued a stinging critique of the expansionist impetus of the United States and, in particular, movements to filibuster and annex Cuba supported by members of President Franklin Pierce's cabinet.

Four months later, Cubans in New York began publishing *El Filibustero*, a newspaper that called for armed attacks against Spanish forces in Cuba. In its first issue, *El Filibustero* featured a bold defense of "nineteenth-century filibusterism" as a natural impulse to battle the outrages of tyrannical government. Echoing the U.S. Declaration of Independence, the newspaper argued that "all oppressed people have the right to rebel against their oppressors." By these terms, filibusters were carrying out an Enlightenment imperative to bring about equality among people and establish a just and peaceful society in Cuba. Spain was described as an "absolutist empire" that had trampled the laws of nature and "flooded the earth with blood." The newspaper argued that Cubans, lacking the necessary arms to combat the tyrants, had turned to "a powerful and free people" (the United States) as an "extreme measure to save ourselves of the eternal servitude with which the oppressor Spain threatens us."[3] By painting the filibuster as a freedom fighter, the newspaper attempted to highlight the anticolonial dimensions of the Cuba filibustering efforts and to emphasize that the island's inhabitants had a right to govern themselves.

These radically different interpretations of the word *"filibuster(o)"* and the vehemence with which each party defended its reading show that much more than semantics was at stake. Venable's charges that the United States was appropriating the territorial possessions of others and *El Filibustero*'s reference to tyrannical government indicate that battles in language were intricately connected to military events and the possibility that Cuba's governmental apparatus would change. The United States, Spain, and England as well as a rapidly growing U.S.-based Cuban exile population were engaged in a contest over national rights to territories and the role of military and political powers in the Americas. As such, "filibuster" functioned as a keyword of empire, a sign of battles for control of territory in the hemisphere, allowing for positions both favoring and opposing U.S. expansionism and Spanish colonialism.[4] "Filibuster," a term that was debated and a military enterprise, crossed national borders and prompted the publication of texts in transnational contexts in the mid–nineteenth century.

By publishing newspapers, Cuban *filibusteros* attempted to connect the material of print culture with military organizing and armed combat to gain territorial control. They sent out their articles and poems as weapons in a battle for Cuba, seeking to stand again on Cuban land and convince readers that they should fight for a new government on the island. In other words, these writers attempted to establish an ideological connection between reader (subject), Cuba (ground), and republicanism (government). In this chapter, I discuss the newspaper *El Filibustero* and show how Cuban exiles promoted the filibuster to develop a sense of the Cuban subject with a right to the island. I explicate how writers featured poetry as an important dimension of transnational writing. The filibuster helps provide an understanding of the importance of antebellum political culture to Cuban exiles, even as the transnational newspapers published by Cubans help shed light on the multilingual and multiethnic dimensions of filibustering movements.

Because the filibuster aspires to possess a territory, it is a particularly apt metaphor for framing the literary history of writers whose status in the mid–nineteenth century is one of dislocation rather than national position. The filibuster's condition—simultaneously seeking territory and experiencing the separation from that territory—is akin to the deterritorialized condition of transnational writing. In the latter part of this chapter I discuss the concept of deterritorialization in relation to Cuban exiles and their print culture. I begin by showing how in the nineteenth century, filibustering had a pronounced relationship to the publication of newspapers and books.

From Pirate to Patriot: Manifestations of the Filibuster

In "Los Filibusteros," contemporary poet Ernesto Cardenal looks back on William Walker's invasion of Nicaragua in 1855:

> O vinieron por ciento sesenta acres de tierra de Centro América
> (para venderla) y veinticinco dólares al mes,
> y pelearon por nada al mes, y seis pies cuadrados de tierra.
> O venían en busca de gloria: un nombre
> que quedara escrito en las páginas de la Historia.

> [Or they came for one hundred and sixty acres of Central
>   American land
> (to sell it) and twenty-five dollars a month,
> and they fought for nothing a month, and six square feet of land.
> Or they came in search of glory: a name
> that would remain written in the pages of History.][5]

Proclaiming himself president of Nicaragua before a Central American unified army booted him out, Walker became the best known of the filibusters in mid–nineteenth century United States. Cardenal practically quotes Walker, who issued the following proclamation as he was tossed out of the region: "Reduced to our present position by the cowardice of some, the incapacity of others, and the treachery of many, the army has yet written a page of American history which it is impossible to forget or erase."[6] A page of history would appear to be little consolation for a general being escorted away from the territory he conquered temporarily. Why, then, does Walker grant the written text such value?

Walker's *The War in Nicaragua* (1860) betrays an inordinate faith in the written word. Published to raise money for yet another filibustering expedition to Central America, Walker's "history" displays his awareness that the objects of representation are not static but rather are subject to a process of textual inscription and interpretation. Shortly after taking power in Nicaragua, Walker established a newspaper, *El Nicaragüense*, "as a means of diffusing information concerning the natural resources and advantages of Nicaragua, no less than as a chronicle of current events."[7] Articles from *El Nicaragüense* regularly made their way into the U.S. press.[8] At the same time, some of Walker's associates functioned much like present-day spin doctors, attempting to persuade the U.S. public to support their cause by publishing books and articles.

Walker shared with Cuban *filibusteros* a commitment to using newspapers and books to promote the cause of filibustering. While Walker fashioned himself as a writer of history, Cubans in exile saw themselves as participating in a historical movement and thus adopted the term "filibuster" not only as a political badge of honor but also as a description of what they were doing as writers. Cuban exiles saw filibustering as part of a historical telos leading to liberation from colonialism and democratic rule in Cuba. They believed that newspaper articles and poems would bring about this historical transformation by persuading readers that they should support the seizure of an area and accept the filibuster's new geographical, social, and/or political relocation. Putting that another way, Cubans were intent on entering debates about critical terms and political programs to usher in what they believed to be an inevitable republican future for Cuba.

Cuban *filibusteros* wrote on two fronts: the U.S. theater of public opinion and the Spanish-controlled colonial setting of Cuba. In both places, the filibuster was a vexing symbol that inspired debate and attack. In one of the most elaborate defenses of the word "filibuster," the anonymous author of *The Destiny of Nicaragua* traced the term back to the French port of Cape Finestre. From this port, the book argued, a French captain had sailed to avenge a massacre carried out by Spanish troops against a French outpost in Florida. "Sailors and those coming by sea are frequently designated by the port of their departure, and it would be natural to call this company Finibusters or Finibusterers. . . . Thus it will be seen that this term of Filibustier is not so great a reproach as some conservative old diplomatic fogies imagine."[9] In this etymological lesson, the author sought to claim an origin to the word based on an opposition to Spanish atrocities. By doing so, the author sought to associate filibustering with justice. William Walker took a different tact, disclaiming the word "filibuster" altogether from his expeditions: "That which you ignorantly call 'Filibusterism' is not the offspring of hasty passion or ill-regulated desire; it is the fruit of the sure, unerring instincts which act in accordance with laws as old as the creation. They are but drivellers who speak of establishing fixed relations between the pure white American race, as it exists in the United States, and the mixed Hispano-Indian race, as it exists in Mexico and Central America, without the employment of force."[10] Dressing his expeditions in the cloak of the racial ideology that fueled Manifest Destiny, Walker disclaimed the "ill-regulated desire" that readers might have associated with pirates.

But precisely because expeditions justified their projects by invoking notions of Anglo-Saxon superiority, some people saw filibusters as pirates. John Greenleaf Whittier's abolitionist poem "The Haschish" (1856) equated filibusters with proponents of slavery who were intoxicated with the profits of cotton, the "mad weed":

> The man of peace, about whose dreams
>   The sweet millennial angels cluster,
> Tastes the mad weed, and plots and schemes
>   A raving Cuban filibuster![11]

Whittier was able to gloss "filibuster" in a radically different manner than Cuban *filibusteros* because of a connotative ambivalence in the word. One person's republican defender of liberty was another's opportunistic land grabber. Whittier's poem, an orientalist panorama that includes whirling dervishes, situates the filibuster outside of U.S. culture and thus calls attention to one of the challenges facing Cuban exiles. Whittier's "Cuban filibuster" is part of a catalog of exoticism, most of it linked to the "Orient," its "marvels with our own competing." The poem's references to "Paradise," "Cathay," and "some Caliph's daughters" resonate with travel writings that described Cuba in orientalist terms. Julia Ward Howe, for one, compared the treatment of upper-class women in Cuba to the "seclusion of women in the East." In Havana, Howe wrote, "They of the lovely sex meanwhile undergo, with what patience they may, an Oriental imprisonment."[12] With the connection of Cuba and orientalism circulating in U.S. society, Cuban exiles faced a discursive context in which a *filibustero* might easily be seen as alien to U.S. culture.

A sense of filibustering as inappropriate and even antidemocratic is how the word made its way into the U.S. Congress. In one of the earliest known uses of the word "filibuster" in a legislative chamber, Albert Gallatin Brown of Mississippi took the floor of the U.S. House of Representatives in 1853 and accused a fellow Southern Democrat of "standing on the other side of the House filibustering, as I thought, against the United States."[13] The question under debate was whether the United States should annex Cuba. Brown wanted to see the island enter the Union as a new slave state, even if that meant wresting Cuba away from Spain in a military engagement. He was surprised that a Democrat had spoken on behalf of the "other side," the Whig position against annexation. Given the legislative setting of this exchange, it would appear that Brown accused his colleague of "filibustering" in the contemporary sense of the word, but the filibuster is possible only in the Senate, not the House. In effect, Brown used "filibustering" to accuse his colleague of taking political ground by inappropriate means and even crossing over to a less legitimate "other" side in a debate about the future territorial holdings of the United States. In other words, Brown inverted the charges of filibustering hurled at annexationists. This type of accusation that elected officials were obstructing the legislative process by resorting to stalling tactics is how "filibuster" came to refer to the Senate extended-debate clause in the 1860s.[14]

The contradictions of the word "filibuster," which simultaneously connotes opportunism and idealism, remain apparent today in the U.S. Congress.[15] The contemporary Senate filibuster, as monumentalized in Frank Capra's film *Mr. Smith Goes to Washington* (1939), emphasizes individualism and resistance to brute strength.[16] Jefferson Smith, a Boy Scout troop leader standing against a corrupt and entrenched political machine, filibusters to establish a camp for underprivileged boys. He connects his legislative speech act directly to U.S. democratic institutions by reading passages from the U.S. Constitution. The importance is that as senator sans sleaze, Smith (Jimmy Stewart) brings a wholesome dressing to a power play. In the words of the CBS radio announcer, the filibuster is "democracy's finest show, the right to talk your head off, the American privilege of free speech in its most dramatic form." He goes on, "The least man in that chamber, once he gets and holds that floor by the rules, can hold it and talk as long as he can stand on his feet."[17] The international history of the term and the military associations are erased as democracy's Boy Scout replaces soldiers of Manifest Destiny in the nation's ongoing filibustering drama. No longer a person, the "filibuster" is now a legislative maneuver and its verb form. In the process, the rules of Washington are contained within the nation, and the film erases imperial history. Nevertheless, the notion that filibustering is linked to freedom would not have been lost on Cuban *filibustero* writers who saw the United States as facilitating "freedom of speech" as well as military options for exiles who could not speak publicly against Spain in their island home.

In the nineteenth century, the battle over the meanings of *filibuster(o)* crossed nations and languages; thus, Cuban exiles were forced to respond to charges in Spanish-language newspapers that *filibusteros* were pirates. In the article "Dos Palabras sobre los Piratas" (A couple of words about the pirates), *La Verdad* argued that *filibusteros* in the United States were "men who sacrifice everything for the liberty of their motherland" and "think for themselves, publishing their ideas and opinions."[18] Pointing to Spanish military installations in Cuba, the article asked, "Who are the pirates?" The battles over the connotations of *filibustero* were particularly fierce because the word was regularly used to refer to pirates in a variety of writings, including historical romances from nineteenth-century Latin America. Eligio Ancona's *El Filibustero* (1866) and Justo Sierra O'Reilly's *El Filibustero* (1841–42) were among pirate novels that circulated in the period. Nina Gerassi-Navarro examines the contradictory uses of the pirate figure variously portrayed as "a dangerous menace, an emblem of progress, or even a symbol of independence."[19] Thus, the pirate could emerge as an anticolonial hero or a foreigner attacking Spanish America, depending on authors' political and cultural positions. The pirate shared with the filibuster an attempt to break away from the constraints of oppressive political order and restrictive social conventions. In the words of one character in Ancona's *El Filibustero*, "What happiness it is to be a pirate and speak with such liberty."[20] But where the pirate and the antebellum *filibustero* differ is that the latter fought to establish a new social and political order in a designated place.

The *filibustero* of Cuban exiles was tied to a protonational movement and thus is comparable to José Rizal's usage in his novel. Rizal (1861–96), a Filipino nationalist who fomented anticolonial insurrection in his home country, published *El Filibusterismo* (1891) as a portrait of his society in the late nineteenth century.[21] The colonial ills experienced by the characters in *El Filibusterismo*—a lack of educational independence, economic stagnation, social and racial stratification—are comparable to the conditions in Cuba that drove exiles to the United States in the 1840s and 1850s.[22] In a letter to a friend, Rizal explained his use of *"filibustero"*: "The Manila newspapers and the Spaniards use this word to describe those whom they want to render suspect of revolutionary activities. The educated Filipinos fear its scope. It does not have the meaning of *pirate*; it means rather a *dangerous patriot who will soon be on the gallows, or else a conceited fellow.*"[23] Rizal attempts to divest the word *filibustero* of its piratical baggage and does so by reterritorializing the filibuster as a patriot rather than a colonial subject; consequently, his project mirrors the use of the *filibustero* by Cubans in New York. The point was perhaps stated most clearly by Pedro Santacilia in his lessons on Cuban history: "Some men dedicated to piracy and pillaging were designated as *Filibusteros* in a historical record lacking the foresight to know that in time a day would come when that dishonorable nickname would be converted into an honorific title that characterizes the champions of democracy and defenders of liberty."[24]

Cubans did not convince people in the United States or Cuba that filibusters were anything other than U.S. soldiers of fortune seeking profit on the island. Robert May shows how the frontier culture and the militaristic spirit that followed the U.S.-Mexico War inspired young men to join filibustering expeditions. "Many Americans simply assumed that the superiority of their race and governmental institutions gave them the moral right to filibuster abroad," May writes.[25] Cuban exiles in the 1850s shared a sense of U.S. governmental institutions as superior to most others but as especially superior to Spanish rule. (Their views of race were complicated by a shift from Cuba to the United States, as I show in chapter 4.) Thus, exiles saw themselves in league with U.S. citizens seeking to filibuster Cuba but failed to persuade the public that a filibuster, whether Cuban or not, represented their claims to self-determination.

The figure that most clearly embodied the hopes and failures of Cuban writers in the antebellum period was Narciso López, the general who led the expeditions of 1850 and 1851. As I discuss in chapter 3, exiled writers believed that López was the model "man of action," a military commander who gave up his life for Cuba. That perspective clashed with those who viewed López as a dupe of annexationists. Between 1848 and 1851, López operated on U.S. soil, rallying support for filibustering expeditions to Cuba. Politically savvy if militarily reckless, López garnered support from northern expansionists, southern proslavery forces, and Cuban patriots.[26] His expeditions were manned largely by recruits from the United States. Only five Cubans were among the six hundred or so fighters, most of them veterans of the U.S.-Mexico War, who joined López for his first landing in Cárdenas in 1850.[27] López's second and final landing in Bahia Honda included forty-nine Cubans out of more than four hundred men.[28] Unable to gather military support on the island, López was captured by Spanish forces and executed publicly by garrote.

Was López an opportunist who would have annexed Cuba to the United States, or was he fighting for Cuban self-determination? From a contemporary perspective influenced by a critique of U.S. imperialist designs on Cuba, López's expeditions appear to be a nineteenth-century version of ongoing U.S. interventions in Cuba. But the relationships between López and his various supporters paint a more complicated picture. Historians have looked at his connections with veterans of the U.S.-Mexico War, politicians from the U.S. South, Manifest Destiny supporters from the North, Cuban plantation owners, and Cuban patriots.[29] Tom Chaffin, for example, argues that even if López indulged fantasies of an independent Cuba, the filibuster's public pronouncements for annexation offer more compelling evidence for his ultimate goal. "His campaign lived and died as an annexationist movement," Chaffin writes.[30] By contrast, Herminio Portell Vilá, the foremost Cuban historian of the López expeditions, argues that patriotic Cubans supported López in a bid for independence.[31] My interest here is not in framing López as primarily for annexation or independence (the two might not have been considered mutually exclusive in the antebellum context) but rather to argue that the ambivalence of López's public persona—tied to the concept of *filibustero*—motivated the production of transnational newspapers and texts. Exiled writers attempted to remake the *filibustero* as a symbol of freedom in part to seize debates over López.

The most forthright pronouncement by Cuban exiles on the relationship of filibustering and patriotism appeared in an article titled "Patriotismo Cubano, Sus Grados y Denominaciones" (Cuban patriotism, its ranks and designations). Witty and sarcastic, the article divided patriots into various types of *filibusteros*. At the top of the list was the *filibustero Lopizta*, a reference to López's ultimate sacrifice. The *filibustero Lopizta* would give up "his ranch, his life and anything else to bring liberty to the motherland."[32] The second tier of *filibusteros* were "retired," meaning they rested on past laurels but now complained of having lost money in support of filibustering. The "honorary" *filibustero* had not done anything for Cuba but still wanted to be considered a filibuster.[33] And at the bottom of the list was the *filibustero pastelero*, meaning literally a pastry maker but figuratively someone who does not get involved. The *pastelero* would speak loudly in favor of the cause but was two-faced and would not join efforts to organize filibustering expeditions.[34] By these terms, all *filibusteros* were in some way tied to gaining self-determination based on a connection between Cuba's inhabitants and the island itself. For writers, the self-abnegation of the true *filibustero* emerged in the individual decision to put aside literary careers and life in Cuba in exchange for writing as a *filibustero* in the United States.

Organ of Cuban Independence: *El Filibustero*

The transnational newspaper that most explicitly called for a military attack on Spanish forces in Cuba during the 1850s was *El Filibustero*. Juan and Francisco Bellido de Luna established *El Filibustero* with the belief that in the near future the newspaper would stop "publishing because its filibustero editors would abandon the pen and take the expeditionary rifle."[35] Exiled after publishing the revolutionary newspaper *La Voz del Pueblo Cubano* (Cuba, 1852), Juan Bellido de Luna had assisted in planning a revolt in Cuba. Originally from Matanzas, the Bellidos continued their efforts in New York with the ultimate goal of fomenting a revolutionary insurrection on the island. Just as the newspaper *El Filibustero* battled Spain through a war of words, Cuban *fili-busteros* would supposedly take to the battlefield and oust Spanish military forces. The paper was smuggled into Cuba and circulated among a growing exile population in New York and other U.S. cities with the primary goal of keeping alive the hope (and thus giving Spain the impression) that a filibustering expedition was imminent. Indeed, when the paper started publishing, preparations were under way for an attack on the island, although that one never materialized.

The United States offered a ground that allowed Cubans such as the Bellidos to conceive of themselves within two traditions that for them were interrelated: the writing of Cuban exiles and the writing of U.S. revolutionaries. In the early part of the nineteenth century, Cuban writers had marked a path by going into exile in the northeastern United States to publish materials critical of Spanish colonialism. Viewed by many as a beacon of republicanism during the Latin American wars of liberation, the United States became a site of operation for exiled writers who published Spanish-language books and periodicals. One of the most notable publishing ventures was taken on by Cuba's Félix Varela, a priest and philosopher who published *El Habanero* (Philadelphia–New York, 1824–26), which was smuggled into Cuba. The name Varela is almost inseparable from the Cuban nation: lecturing as the chair of the philosophy department at the University of San Carlos in Havana, Varela became Cuba's most illustrious intellectual and the first major figure to call for independence. "Americans are born with a love for independence," Varela wrote in *El Habanero*, positing that the people of the entire hemisphere had a natural right to control its future.[36] Highlighting a connection between nature and independence, Varela argued for an opposition between *naturales y europeos* (naturals and Europeans). The first issue of *El Habanero* called on Cubans to support an invasion of troops from South America, where forces were fighting against Spain. Liberator Simón Bolívar was contemplating that attack, and Varela argued that the plan could succeed if the invading forces showed moderation in dealing with Cuba's population.[37] Unlike his successors in the 1850s, Varela's tone was more acerbic than hopeful, and his articles raise questions about the difference between appearances and true support for changes on the island. "It is important not to lose sight that on the island of Cuba there is no *political opinion*," he wrote. "There is no opinion other than a *mercantile* one. Questions of state are resolved on the docks and in the shops."[38] Turning philosophical, Varela also considered how political efforts on behalf of Cuba came into conflict with human selfishness. *Filibustero* writers in the 1850s saw Varela as a larger-than-life figure who embodied their aspirations to promote a Cuban intellectual tradition through exile publication. The admiration was evident in a letter written by Gaspar Betancourt Cisneros, an editor at *La Verdad*, to historian and essayist José Antonio Saco, mentioning a meeting with Varela: "He came from Florida much recovered, so much that I see him but I can't believe it. I spoke to him about you and he cares for you as always."[39]

But while Varela provided an example of Cuban writing in exile, *filibusteros* also looked to the revolutionary print project of the eighteenth century. They often referred to Thomas Paine's *Common Sense* as a model of printing for revolution; Miguel T. Tolón translated that pamphlet into Spanish in 1853. In addition to Paine, Cuban writers quoted and referred to Samuel Adams and George Washington as well as French revolutionary pamphleteer the Abbe Sieyes.[40] As Michael Warner argues, the various changes that came with the U.S. revolution also brought with them "transformations *of* print, not just changes affected by a medium with is own unchanging logic."[41] In the case of the *filibusteros*, one such transformation was a transnational geographic disjunction between the production of texts and their readers. On the one hand, *filibustero* writers hoped to adopt a U.S. revolutionary model whereby the Cuban people, acting through and influenced by printed material, would determine new power relations on the island, dislodging the colonial government. On the other hand, the conditions in Cuba that prompted that revolutionary posture meant that writers had to edit and print their publications in another country, the United States. In effect, *filibusteros* were trying to reach various locations in more than one country, and the separation between a writer and readers begins to explain, as I discuss later in this chapter, the failure of their efforts to persuade a large segment of Cuba's population to support filibustering. One lesson of *El Filibustero* was that the intention of writers seeking to overthrow Cuba's government was not sufficient to close ruptures in the communications circuit that resulted from transnational conditions.

El Filibustero had an editorial office in lower Manhattan and appeared three or four times a month between April 1853 and February 1854. The front page usually featured an article focusing on major political questions, such as Spain's ongoing participation in the slave trade, which the paper opposed. The inside pages included news from Cuba, a "Chronicle of Criminal Spain" detailing abuses on the island, and, periodically, translations of articles from U.S. newspapers. Letters from Cuba kept readers up to date on the most recent events on the island. Most of the articles went unsigned, but some were attributed to "The Editors."[42] Regular contributors included F. J. de la Cruz, Fernando Rodríguez, and Juan Clemente Zenea, one of Cuba's best-known poets. Poetry was an important component of *El Filibustero*, taking up the entire back page of some issues. As I discuss later in this chapter, the poetic impulse emerged in part from the belief that readers would memorize revolutionary verses.

El Filibustero billed itself the "organ of Cuban independence," arguing that Cubans on the island should fight a revolution while proclaiming an independent voice among Cuban exiles. Although *El Filibustero* did not oppose U.S. military assistance in the fight against Spain, the newspaper took a very strong line against the U.S. purchase of Cuba, a process that would have transferred title of the land while cutting out the participation of people on the island and in exile. Arguing against the purchase of Cuba, one article invoked slavery as a metaphor, saying the island would end up in the position of a "slave that passes from the possession of a cruel master to one who is humane, benign, and generous."[43] The Franklin Pierce administration had placed on its front burner the possible purchase of Cuba, which led to the 1854 report known as the Ostend Manifesto. The manifesto, drafted in Europe by Pierce's diplomats, called for the purchase of Cuba but argued that if blacks on the island attempted a revolt, the United States "shall be justified in wresting it [Cuba] from Spain, if we possess the power."[44] *El Filibustero* supported Pierce but had a more complex position on annexation. Rather than publicly opposing annexation per se, the paper negotiated the issue by proposing that Cubans (both on and off the island) should gain control of its government and then decide whether they wanted to join the Union.

The editors of *El Filibustero* saw their textual production as integral to a protonational project: "EL FILIBUSTERO is an organ of Cuban liberty, and Cubans will exhaust all possible and honorable resources before allowing an object that symbolizes the sacred cause of its beloved motherland to perish."[45] The use of *patria* here calls attention to the ambivalence in that word, which appeared frequently in *El Filibustero* and other newspapers. It is feminine in gender yet contains an etymological connection to "father," therefore emphasizing a dual genealogical connection. To invoke *patria* was to posit a Cuba that was distinct from its colonial status. The Bellidos believed that an attack for the seizure of the *patria* "would be bloody but undoubtedly glorious"; thus, they were willing to suffer the economic hardship of putting out a newspaper.[46] One article after another took the position that a true patriot "aspires to regain independence with arms in hand."[47]

El Filibustero, which venerated López as a model Cuban patriot, called for Cubans to take the lead in combat on the island. But the newspaper did not rule out financial and military support from the United States, especially since a Democrat was in the White House. Pierce had been elected president with the support of Young America, a movement of Manifest Destiny advocates that saw Cuba as the next prize in the march of empire.[48] The crushing defeat of the antiexpansionist Whigs in 1852 was accompanied by parades in which banners featured slogans such as "The Fruits of the Late Democratic Victory— Pierce and Cuba" and "May the Queen of the Antilles Be Added to Our glorious Confederacy under the Prosperous Administration of Pierce." In the months following the election, the question of the annexation of Cuba was injected into all types of debates in the U.S. Congress.[49] When Pierce appointed to his Cabinet Jefferson Davis and Caleb Cushing, both of whom were known to be proannexation, Cuban *filibusteros* rejoiced at the possibility that the presidential administration would provide military backup for a filibustering attack on the island.[50] In July 1853, Pierce visited New York, and *El Filibustero* celebrated the great welcome given to the president as an example of "pure democracy." The paper noted that Pierce arrived aboard a steamer that flew, among other flags, the Cuban tricolor, which displayed a single star in the tradition of the Texas lone star and would one day become the flag of Cuba. The flag on Pierce's ship displayed the statement, "Cuba Must and Shall be Free."[51] *La Verdad* struck a similarly optimistic note about Pierce, with an article that said, "Let Cuba strike *now*, one ringing blow on the iron gates of her cruel prison-house and the echoes will wake up the helpful spirit of the American people, and the cordial respect of the American government to an extent and efficiency never before aroused in the behalf of Cuba."[52]

Expressing respect and admiration for principles in the U.S. Constitution, El Filibustero argued that people in Cuba should fight the island's revolution. The concept of filibusterismo promoted by the newspaper was one in which the exiled fighters would combine forces with local troops in Cuba. "Our mistake is in expecting everything from the United States, and this is a very serious mistake," said one article. "Cubans on the island believe that this people [the United States] will bestow upon them liberty and they will not have to make a move." The paper warned that the Pierce administration would help only if Cuba first declared its independence.[53] Under that vision, the paper drew a distinction between a revolution of the many and a conspiracy of the few. "Conspiracy," according to the paper, meant relying on the work of others, a critique of efforts to place expeditions of soldiers from the United States at the center of a revolutionary effort.[54] López had operated under the incorrect assumption that when he landed with U.S. filibusters, the local population would join them and rise up against Spanish forces. Thus, by 1853, El Filibustero was clear in arguing that filibusters would have to draw support from the island if they were to succeed. By calling for a native uprising, El Filibustero challenged the notion that filibustering was solely the work of U.S. soldiers roused by the fever of Manifest Destiny. This emphasis on revolution from within shows that all supporters of the Cuba filibustering expeditions did not have the same intent and did not speak in one voice. El Filibustero's attempt to connect filibustering to people in Cuba helped the paper take a position against Spain's claims that filibusters were illegitimate adventurers. Across town, the pro-Spanish newspaper La Crónica (New York, 1848–67), which I discuss in the next chapter, maintained an ongoing war of words with Cuban-run newspapers, calling filibusters "torpid and bestial pirates" who lacked the support of both the Cuban population and the U.S. government.[55]

El Filibustero's call for a native uprising and independence prior to annexation was at odds with the designs of southern U.S. planters who wanted to annex Cuba as a slave state. It also differed from the position

of Cuban elites who placed U.S. participation at the center of the move-
ment to ensure the protection of capitalist exchange. In 1854, John
Quitman, a veteran of the U.S.-Mexican War who had served military
governor of the Mexican capital, agreed to lead a filibustering attack on
Cuba. He cut a deal for financial support from the New York–based
Cuban Junta, formed in the wake of López's failure. Quitman's interests, historians argue, had more to do with sectional debates than with
Cuba. He hoped to strengthen the South with Cuba's entrance into the
Union. Quitman's plans ultimately unraveled when the Pierce administration opposed the expedition and Quitman faced internal disputes
within the Cuban Junta, some members of which opposed statehood
and slavery.[56] Had Quitman read *El Filibustero*, he might have known
that some exiles were growing increasingly critical of the notion that
U.S. fighters paid by the Cuban elite should usher the island into
separation from Spain.

In keeping with the filibusters' desire for land, *El Filibustero* displayed a protonational posture that viewed the island as the natural soil
of Cubans. In one article, the newspaper chided the "American press"
for forgetting that Cubans "have spilled their blood, have perished on
the gallows, and many today suffer from deportation, forced exile, and
the pain of imprisonment, all for their belief in liberty."[57] The newspaper also criticized the U.S. government for failing to support "Cuban
revolutionaries in their struggle for independence," instead trying to
take advantage of disaffection on the island to "acquire possession of
Cuba by negotiation." The newspaper argued that people in the United
States "are not Cubans and do not feel in their hearts the sacred love for
a country that is not their motherland." As in the paper's justification
for an internal uprising, the notion of *patria* created a genealogical
connection of body and territory based on the "pure and sublime love"
that supposedly comes from being born in a place. "We cannot demand that Americans have such sentiments because it would be asking for something that nature cannot produce."[58] The idea that nature
could produce national affiliation, as stated in *El Filibustero*, reinforced
the importance of birth in Cuba for the citizens of a new society on the
island, as opposed to the Spanish-born captain-general, the supreme
military-political authority appointed by Spain. In turn, *El Filibustero*
called on Cuba's residents to take up the banner of Cuba on the battlefield. And that call was sounded in the form of revolutionary poetry.

Cantos de Guerra: Filibustero Poetry

Poetry was common fare in nineteenth-century English-language U.S. newspapers. Editors highlighted poetry when traumatic events such as the Civil War caused emotional responses in the population. Four days after Robert E. Lee's surrender, the *New York Evening Post* said, "We have received verses in celebration of the late victories enough to fill four or five columns of our paper."[59] Similarly, the Spanish-language press from California to Florida published poetry throughout the nineteenth century, so that newspapers became a common site in which Spanish-language poets published their work. In highly political transnational newspapers, poetry often functioned in tandem with the editors' objectives. Cuban editors were likely to increase the number of poems in an issue when a filibustering expedition was about to take place or had failed to achieve its military goal. After Narciso López was killed by Spanish authorities in September 1851, *La Verdad* devoted numerous black-lined columns of tribute to the fallen soldiers of the expedition and filled some of those columns with poetry.

Several of the exiles who became active in producing newspapers had developed reputations in Cuba as poets, among them Juan Clemente Zenea, Miguel T. Tolón, and Pedro Santacilia. In Cuba, newspapers and periodicals had been the primary venue in which writers published poetry prior to releasing collections. As Larry R. Jensen notes, romanticism was a central concern of island periodicals in the 1830s.[60] In the United States, the conjunction of poetic form and newspaper publication was inscribed in Tolón's "En el Segundo Aniversario de 'La Verdad' " (The second anniversary of "La Verdad"), a poem that develops a connection between newspaper publication and military action. Invoking the "foreign sky" of New York, the speaker laments that after being in exile for two years, he has yet to see Cuba gain liberty. The second and third stanzas blast Spain for keeping Cuba a "slave" and develop a metaphor associating Cuba with a woman defiled by Spanish oppression. The poem concludes with an optimistic note proclaiming the eventual arrival of the truth (*verdad*) and freedom on the island:

> Pronto será que a nuestra patria llegues,
> "Verdad," fanal del pueblo,
> Y entre falanges bélicas cubanas,

Triunfante al fin tu alzado acento vibre
En alcázares, montes y sabanas,
Por la muerte y baldón de las hispanas.

[Soon at our Motherland you will arrive,
"Verdad," beacon of the people,
Carried by the bellicose phalanges of Cuba,
Triumphant in the end your accent will resound
In fortresses, fields, and savannahs,
And avenge the death and stain of Hispanic women.][61]

The poem elaborates a gendered relationship between the male exiled activist and women relatives in Cuba (mother, sister) as it establishes a reciprocal relationship between newspaper and poem. The newspaper carries to Cuba the poem, which, in turn, envisions fighters carrying the newspaper (the truth) as a tool and concept leading to military success.

El Filibustero, from its inception, kept up a steady stream of sonnets, dramatic lyrics, and ballads, some of which praised the dead and others of which called for war. Influenced by the romanticism of José María Heredia (1803–39), who escaped to New York after authorities in Cuba sought him for taking part in a conspiracy, Cuban poets saw the inscription of exile in their verses as a form of rebellion against Spain. They believed their poems would inspire Cubans to fight. The notion of the poem as a utilitarian document is made clear in the novel *Cecilia Valdés*, which I discuss in chapter 5, when the narrator looks back on the role of poetry in disseminating anti-Spanish sentiment in Cuba. The work of Heredia, the novel tells us, inspired youth in Havana to memorize poems and "repeat them whenever they had an opportunity to do so without fear for their personal liberty."[62] Echoing Villaverde's point, Matías Montes-Huidobro reminds us that the poems of the 1850s became part of a "patriotic catechism" passed from one hand to another.[63] Heredia was popular among Cubans in New York, where numerous editions of his poems were published in the 1850s, 1860s, and 1870s.[64] Given his anti-Spanish political posture, Heredia offered a model of the anticolonial writer that inspired Cuban exiles in the 1850s. But whereas Heredia privileged the romantic sublime, exemplified in his poems "Niagara" and "Al Huracán," the writers in *El Filibustero* were more directly military. Romanticism and writers such as

Byron influenced Cuban exiles, but the U.S. context altered their vision by opening up poetry to direct calls for war and overthrow of the colonial government and by presenting new vistas. In exile, the contemplation of a landscape could set off a tension between Cuba and New York City. In Tolón's "A Mi Hermana Teresa" (To my sister Teresa), the speaker contemplates the Hudson River from New Jersey as he looks south past Manhattan toward Cuba, dreaming of his hometown and his eventual return.[65]

The poetry published by Cubans in newspapers and books in the mid–nineteenth century ranged in style and form. In some cases, the poems looked back on popular themes from Cuba or focused most directly on a woman, either in Cuba or the United States. Not all of these works can be considered *filibustero* poetry, which I characterize a poetry of armed combat. These *filibustero* poems directly engage political topics such as filibustering, the future of Cuba, and the need for armed uprising. Such content would have been prohibited by censors in the Cuban press, so the United States offered a ground of production that made possible the incorporation of highly militaristic themes. *Filibustero* poems contain one or more of the following themes: (1) a call to arms; (2) the resurrection of a fallen fighter; (3) a recuperation of Cuban territory; (4) exile as a condition of composition. Leopoldo Turla's "Canto de Guerra" (Song of war), a short heroic poem, offered a chorus with a rhyming imperative:

> Dad el grito sonoro de guerra
> derribad el hispano león
> y trepando a la altísima sierra
> de los libres plantad el pendón.

> [Give the sonorous war cry
> overthrow the Hispanic lion
> and climbing the highest peaks
> plant the pennant of the free.][66]

Filibustero poetry commonly featured such martial language.[67] The ABAB rhyme scheme in the chorus facilitated memorization. Made up of six eight-line stanzas, Turla's war song was in effect a call for bravery in the military fight on behalf of the "beautiful Republic of Cuba."

In that spirit, Pedro Angel Castellón's "Al General Narciso López," published in *La Verdad* on 20 March 1852, resuscitates the fighting spirit of the *filibusteros* who had died in August 1851. The poem concludes with a ghostlike apparition in which a fighter returns, sword in hand, to behead a tyrant:

Ni flores, ni inscripciones, ni trofeos
Oh padre de la patria!
Se ven en tu sepulcro solitario
Que envidioso el tirano de tu gloria,
Quiere matar también en su delirio
Tu espléndida memoria:
Mas no lo alcanzará, que hacia tu tumba
Vuelve el cubano en su pesar los ojos
Buscando tus despojos.
Y ¿que importan los mármoles y bronces
Si de la gratitud al sentimiento
Tienes tu ilustre nombre en cada labio,
En cada corazón un monumento?
Descansa en paz; de tu mansión querida
Miro salir un rayo de esperanza
Que alienta mis anhelos de venganza,
Descanza en paz; la trompa de la guerra
De nuevo en Cuba sonará terrible,
La sangre hirviendo inundará tu huesa,
Animará tus restos
Y en la frente el laurel, la espada en mano,
Hollarás la cabeza del tirano.

[Not flowers, nor inscriptions, nor trophies
Oh father of the fatherland!
Can be seen on your solitary sepulcher.
How the tyrant envies your glory
Desires in his delirium to kill
Your splendid memory:
But he will not reach it, for toward your tomb
Returns the Cuban in sorrow, his eyes
Searching for your remains.
How important are marble and bronze
If you have gratitude and affection,

On each lip your illustrious name,
In each heart a monument?
Rest in peace; from your beloved mansion
I see the breaking of a ray of hope
That feeds my craving for revenge,
Rest in peace; the terrible war horn
Will sound again in Cuba,
Boiling blood will flood your burial ground,
animate your remains
With a laurel on the forehead, a sword in hand,
you will behead the tyrant.][68]

Castellón writes not only to López but also to those who remain behind after the general's death and need inspiration to continue the fight. The Lopizta fighter at the end of the poem is a metonym for Cubans on and off the island who he believes will continue the war. While the Spanish victory over López precludes survivors from granting tangible patriotic tribute (flowers, inscriptions) at the filibuster's grave, survivors can pay respect by continuing the fight. The poem presents the returning *cubano* through bodily references to eyes, lips, and hearts, all of them pointing toward a sword. In lieu of an engraved tombstone, the poem itself becomes a tribute that circulates in print culture from the United States to Cuba. In the same vein, Castellón's sonnet, "En la Muerte de Julio Chassagne" (On the death of Julio Chassagne), is written to a martyr whose sacrifice is intertwined with that of López:

Tu espíritu y su espíritu en la gloria
perpetua dicha gozan; tu renombre
unido al suyo brillará en la historia.

[Your spirit and his spirit in glory
enjoy perpetual luck; your name
united with his will shine in history.][69]

Castellón (1820–56) was able to write such militant lines by settling in the United States. The tone of his poems and his commitment to a revolutionary practice emerged from a conjunction of Cuban-based symbols and U.S. political principles. Castellón went into exile in 1850 and made his way to New Orleans, from where he sent his poems to the New York–based editorial offices of *La Verdad* and *El Filibustero*. A significant Cuban exile community established itself in New Orleans, which became a base for many of the prominent writers from the island. As Kirsten Silva Gruesz shows, New Orleans in the antebellum period was an important convergence point for intellectuals from Latin America, "a nexus of trade in goods and slaves, smuggling, piracy, capital ventures, in- and out-migration, troop movements, filibustering adventurers, and travel between the eastern United States and points southward."[70] The city was home to Spanish-language newspapers of various political stripes and the host for mass meetings in support of filibustering causes. While New York was the main publishing center for Cuban exiles in the 1850s, López's filibusters gathered in New Orleans for the Cárdenas expedition. Cuban exiles such as Villaverde moved in and out of the city at various times, and *La Verdad* even relocated its office to New Orleans for a period in 1854. Upon arrival, *La Verdad* started to feud with the *New Orleans Bee*, which had published articles calling Cuban Creoles weak and cowed and arguing that they were unable to lead a revolution in their country. The *Bee*, *La Verdad* wrote, "has deigned to drink from the beautiful flower of Cuba so as to poison its honey and deposit it in the disgusting hornet's nest that attracts supporters of tyranny."[71] *La Verdad* defended the valor of Cuban Creoles, noting that they had participated in numerous conspiracies and had consequently faced the executioner. *La Verdad* argued that Creoles had chosen not to lead a reckless revolution out of concern that Spain would release half a million slaves to destroy the island; instead, the Creoles were organizing an attack that would dethrone Spain while avoiding "destruction and ruin."

With that type of military discussion circulating in the New Orleans scene, Castellón penned radical poems calling for Cuban liberation even as he participated in U.S.-based politics. Describing the tone of his verses, José Manuel Carbonell writes, "Castellón was a blacksmith who forged detonating stanzas that smell like gunpowder recently fired for liberty and the flag."[72] Carbonell, writing a Cuban nationalist literary history, certainly has the Cuban flag in mind, but Castellón might have seen that flag as the transnationally ambiguous banner of the Order of Young Cuba, founded in the spirit of Young America, which had supported expansionism and the annexation of Cuba. Edward L. Widmer notes that during the 1850s, numerous groups took up the "young" banner—including Jung Amerika and Young Italy—even though their goals differed from those of Young America. While Widmer characterizes the filibusters in Young Cuba as "the very definition of crass capitalism," it would be difficult to pin that label on Castellón, who was not among the wealthy exiles and whose writings betray both Cuban patriotism and admiration for the U.S. Constitution.[73]

Castellón founded Young Cuba with John S. Thrasher and Angel Loño in 1853 and issued a "Declaration of the Rights of the People," which called for equal rights for all "men," free and frequent elections, free press without any restrictions, no unlawful searches, free association, the right to bear arms, separation of the three branches of government (legislative, executive, and judicial), no detention without the filing of a charge, no double trial, the right to a defense, and other stipulations that echoed the U.S. Constitution.[74] The similarities with the Constitution call to mind Castellón's annexationist leanings and provide insight into his commitment to bring that type of government to Cuba. In his poems, Castellón always retained a sentimental and political connection to Cuba. The poems regularly invoke the island's patriots and place-names. And he published under the pen name "Cuyaguateje," a river in Cuba. Readers might well have believed that Cuyaguateje was sending his poems from Cuba, not New Orleans.

One of Castellón's most notable poems, "A Cuba en la Muerte de Varela" (To Cuba on the death of Varela) exemplifies the growing sense in exile circles of a "Cuban" subject with a right to Cuban land.

> ¡Oh! No permita el cielo, dulce Cuba,
> que me sorprenda el golpe de la muerte
> lejos de tus campiñas deliciosas.

> [Oh! May heaven prevent, sweet Cuba,
> Death's blow from surprising me while
> Distant from your sweet fields.][75]

The poem invokes a desire for a circular return in death to the place of birth. That desire is the result of separation from Cuba, not just Castellón's but also that of Félix Varela, the exiled priest and philosopher whose death marked the occasion for the poem. Published originally in *El Filibustero*, the poem's production and presumed circulation moved through various locations (New Orleans, New York, Cuba) following a transnational circuit that is in tension with what the speaker seeks:

union of the writer with the Cuban earth. The territory-subject connection sought by *filibusteros* in anticipation of the future union with Cuba as a state is bifurcated by the transnational dimensions of the poem. The *filibustero* symbol as it emerges in history at this moment exemplifies the disjunction between a nation-based paradigm in which the fighter-writer-text will reunite with Cuba and the condition of exile. The concluding lines of "A Cuba en la Muerte de Varela" convey clearly the simultaneous hope and sadness of *filibustero* poetry.

Quiero volverte el ser que tú me diste
quiero el sepulcro donde está mi cuna.

[I long to return to you the being that you gave me:
I want a sepulcher in the place that holds my crib.]

Exile, a condition of separation, motivates Castellón's vision of sepulcher and crib in a liberated island. Like many in his circle, Castellón refused to return to Cuba while Spanish authorities were in power. He died, it appears, before returning.[76] Thus, he presumably withheld his body from an island that had not reached his ideal political state.

Like Castellón, Leopoldo Turla (1818–77) settled in New Orleans and lived there from 1846 until his death. Some scholars include Turla among the Cubans who sailed with Narciso López on the Cárdenas filibustering expedition, but it is difficult to confirm that contention.[77] Turla's work provides insight into the sensibilities of poems that were written so that people could memorize them and repeat them on the Cuban scene of battle. Turla's "Perseverencia" (Perseverance) exemplifies the uses of repetition to facilitate memory. Formally, the poem implies repetition; it is written in eight ten-line stanzas with an identical rhyme scheme, each stanza concluding with the line "que apoyado al timón espero el día" (for leaning on the rudder, I await daylight). The line is itself a repetition, taken from a poem by José Jacinto Milanés.[78] The perseverance of the poem's structure mirrors the message, perhaps stated most succinctly in the opening lines.

Sé firme, corazón! Sostén constante
De tu valor el indomable temple.

[Be firm, heart! Hold constant
the irrepressible boldness of your valor.]

Like his poem, Turla persevered in a life of exile full of hardship. His poverty became so notorious that exiles took up a collection for him in 1855.[79] Turla has been disparaged in Cuban literary history, as critics have called his poems "pedestrian," "weak in technique," and "uninspired." Even José Manuel Carbonell, the greatest defender of the poets in *El Laúd del Desterrado*, apologizes for Turla's poetry and points to the hardships of exile as a factor in what he considers the poet's limitations.[80] By privileging originality and aesthetic evaluation, critics miss the historical imperative of a revolutionary poetry whose primary object is not the individual creation of the poet but the furthering of a political platform. In many cases, Cuban exiles do not appear to seek originality as a primary consideration; the repetition of words and images implies that many poems were written to sustain a particular vision in exile. The rhyme schemes often imply that lines are meant to be memorized clandestinely and recited on the island. "Memory is the most secure hiding place for these stems of our doctrine," writes Tolón, who develops a metaphor of transnational writing as the planting the seeds of revolution in Cuba.[81] Facilitating memory appears to be the point of the chorus and opening lines of "Himno de Guerra Cubano" (Cuban war anthem).

> Que silben las balas
> Que truene el cañón!
> Ser libres queremos
> No más opresión!
>
> [May the bullets hiss
> May the cannon thunder!
> We long to be free
> No more oppression!][82]

Lacking artifice, these lines show that *filibustero* poetry is, first and foremost, a poetry of content within a context.

As one of the most destitute of the exiled writers and one of the most determined to continue the struggle, Turla apparently dedicated his poems to the future of Cuba, not to himself or even to literary history. Still living in New Orleans during Cuba's Ten Years' War (1868–78), Turla continued to write revolutionary poetry and gained acclaim in exile circles. Emilia Casanova de Villaverde, an activist and prodigious letter writer whom I discuss in more detail in chapter 3, calls him "one of our most illustrious poets."[83] Her terms of evaluation are based in part on commitment to the *patria* and a shared concern for the future of the island. To read Turla, then, is to enter into a realm of interpretation where two frames of reference, Cuba and exile, supersede universal themes. His poem "Oro" (Gold), for example, is an exploration of greed in which each of eighteen stanzas ends with the lines

¡Maldito el hombre que excavó la tierra
Para buscar en sus entrañas oro!

[Cursed is the man who excavated the earth
To see within its entrails gold!][84]

The poem develops Turla's commentary on greed not so much in universal terms but in relation to Spain's colonial government and conditions in Cuba. The poem has been read as an attack on wealthy Creoles who cannot commit fully to separating from Spain because of their financial interests.[85] In other words, Turla calls attention to the conflicts of interest of those who want to retain their wealth in Cuba and in exile even as they work to reform a society supported in part by racial and economic hierarchies.

As the cases of Castellón and Turla show, exile is one of the major themes as well as the material condition for the publication of *filibustero* poetry. The separation between a poem's speaker and fallen fighter emerges not only in life-and-death terms but also in the speaker's separation from the Cuban soil where the fighting has taken place. Exile frames Francisco Agüero Estrada's monody, "Poesía Dedicada a la Memoria de Mi Apreciable Amigo D. Francisco Perdomo Batista, Que Murió en la Heroíca Acción de San Carlos el 13 de Julio de 1851, al Contemplar su Retrato" (Poem dedicated to the memory of Don Francisco Perdomo Batista, who died in the heroic attack on San Carlos on 13 July 1851, upon contemplating his portrait).[86] The lengthy title is significant in that it marks both speaker and object in important ways. The occasion for the memory and poem is the "contemplation" of the filibuster's photograph, which is the scene that opens the 113-line poem. The poet describes Perdomo as "valiant," "noble," and "strong," a warrior who aspired to "death or victory" and "with martial valor and heroic fury / shook the Spanish despot." But that image of Perdomo as warrior is at odds with Agüero's memory of him as a kind and generous friend from childhood. That memory establishes a double separation, one from the dead fighter and another from the island where the two men grew up together. Agüero is bitter to find himself, he writes, on "foreign shores." Unable to reconcile memory and portrait, the speaker is alone, "far from motherland and family, / lacking friends and lovers." The conflict gains resolution when the poet imagines Perdomo's death as an affirmation of the struggle:

> No muere jamás el varón fuerte,
> que en lid noble y gloriosa halló la muerte,
> por Patria y Libertad.

> [Death never comes for the valiant man
> who in a noble and glorious struggle faced death
> for Motherland and Liberty.][87]

In death, Perdomo is free from Spanish despotism and thus reaches a state of liberty. Consequently, the poet's pain of separation gives way to a vision of a Cuba where liberty, now coded as the end of Spanish reign, will prompt hymns of victory. The future of Cuba entails the speaker's return to the island. In keeping with the goals of filibustering, the poetry imagines victory as a seizure of the island.

The militant language in these verses is a result of transnational conditions and shows why *filibustero* poetry is not only of Cuba but also of the United States. The poems can portray a vision of Cuba without Spain because they were written and published in U.S. cities. Like the poets, the poetry at times politically aligns itself with the United States. Printed in a newspaper such as *El Filibustero*, the poems work hand in hand with the political platforms proposed in prose articles. Outside of that context of publication, the poems might appear limited in scope, and thus we see an aesthetic devaluation of the political verses of *filibustero* writers. In addition, the poems' connection to a Spanish-language newspaper print culture in the United States means that these works have, until recently, remained a marginal part of U.S. literary and cultural history. But the poets have not always been marginal in Cuban literary history, so a question emerges: What happens when a canonical Cuban writer is placed in the marginalized print culture of transnational writing?

Juan Clemente Zenea: *Filibustero*

One contributor to *El Filibustero* was Juan Clemente Zenea, a figure canonized in Cuban literary history as a tragic poet executed by Spanish authorities for his participation in revolutionary movements. José Lezama Lima, whose three-volume *Antología de la Poesía Cubana* (Anthology of Cuban poetry) is a standard post-1959 nationalist poetry anthology, argues that Zenea's poetic work and his execution at the hands of Spanish soldiers turn him into Cuban poetry's "prince of blood."[88] But Zenea's death is a testament to his transnational connections; he had traveled from New York to the island for a meeting with revolutionary leader Carlos Manuel de Céspedes during the Ten Years' War when Spanish authorities incarcerated and executed Zenea. Between 1852 and his death in 1871, Zenea shuttled among the United States, Cuba, and Mexico, writing for newspapers even as he continued developing his poetic work. Born in 1832 in the town of Bayamo, in southeastern Cuba, Zenea began writing for island newspapers at the age of seventeen. At first, he contributed to a progovernment organ, *La Prensa de la Habana*, but he became increasingly disaffected. In 1852, Zenea left the island for the United States, living in New York and New Orleans. He adopted a military tone and radical attitude toward Spanish colonialism in his contributions to U.S.-based newspapers, including the abolitionist *El Mulato* (1854) and *La Revolución* (1869–71). In December 1853, a military tribunal in Cuba condemned Zenea in absentia to death "for publishing articles abroad," presumably in the *filibustero* press, that blasted Cuba's captain-general. The death order noted that Zenea had sent copies of the articles to the captain-general, "thus insulting in the person of that high authority all of the Spanish nation."[89] In New Orleans, Zenea sent a letter to the Spanish consul, saying, "Tell the captain-general of Cuba that I have written, that I write, and that I will always write against despotism."[90]

Zenea figures prominently in the pages of *El Filibustero*, publishing essays as well as the poems "El Filibustero," "Diez y Seis de Agosto de 1851 en la Habana" (Sixteenth of August 1851 in Havana), and "En el Aniversario del General López" (On the anniversary of General López), all of which are collected in *El Laúd del Desterrado*.[91] His belligerent posture toward the rulers of the island comes through in the essay "Esperanza" (Hope), published on 13 June 1853. Invoking the militarism inherent in the *filibustero*, the essay is striking in that its fluid prose intertwines an idealistic and idyllic vision of Cuba's future with calls for a violent attack. Zenea announces that Cubans in the United States are keeping alive the "beautiful hope" of returning "with arms in hand to the lovely soil where we had the luck to be born." Indeed, part of the hope is that exiled writers will embrace "our aging mothers" and return "to the bosom of our friends."[92] Reterritorialization is to take place by reconnecting with family and community through a military option: "We want to shake the palace of the despot with the noise of our arms." Spain, he writes, has held on to Cuba with a heavy hand, but Spanish "power is an edifice founded on the unstable base of tyranny; liberty has started to shake it and there is little doubt that it will be turned to ashes." By this logic, military power was tied to ideological formations. Thus, the liberation of Cuba was inextricable from the return of exiles who were developing a different conception of the government that would be established on the island when the revolutionary legions seized power. "Cuba will be a common motherland for all and in its hospitable and benevolent breast will receive the wretches that arrive at its shore, without distinctions by class, sex, or nationality. Cuba, then, will not be Spanish."[93] Here the *patria* is tied directly to the land through the image of "wretches" arriving at the island's beaches. Cuba is personified as a woman receiving these people at her breast. The land-woman connection is overt in *filibustero* writings, but it also circulates in the English-language press as Cuba is feminized as a territory to be taken by the United States. Here, Zenea's invocation of return to a woman is contingent on the support of "those who are closest to the theater in which the tragic drama of a change in government will be staged." Thus, Zenea points to the need for internal revolution that brings together the *filibustero* from the United States and the island resident.

Zenea's "Esperanza" is an overt call for combat, but in another piece he turns to more abstract imagery to convey a military posture. A prose fragment published in *El Filibustero* in 1853 invokes religious language to venerate another woman, "libertad de las Antillas," a figure of liberty "dressed in virgin white." Presumably about to arrive in Puerto Rico and Cuba, Liberty is "sister of angels" and "beauty among beauties."[94] Her antagonism to Spain is established not by references to the contemporary government in Cuba but by looking back at the conquest of the Americas, when "despotism invaded my temple." Liberty fought on the side of indigenous freedom until Spain's victory ushered in "three centuries of horror." Zenea is not alone in drawing a connection to indigenous resistance during the Spanish conquest; the trope was common among nineteenth-century Cuban Creoles, as shown in the poetry of José María Heredia and Miguel T. Tolón as well as the novel *Jicoténcal*. Zenea establishes a parallel between the worship of Liberty and the worship of "souls of the martyrs," also called "victims of the republic." At times taking on the tone of a prayer, the piece exclaims "Hosanna" to both Liberty and the fallen fighters, calling for offerings of flowers for "defenders of the motherland." The piece culminates in the union of the angelic Liberty and deterritorialized fighters who greet her:

> Bienvenida seas consoladora de los desterrados, y ojalá
> que tu destino se cumpla cuando nosotros como el patriarca
> antiguo ofrezcamos en la pira del sacrificio las vidas que sean
> necesarias para que nos cubras con tus alas. Ningún espíritu
> invisible detendrá el movimiento de nuestros brazos y el hacha
> de la revolución apartará los obstáculos que se opongan a
> nuestros pasos.

> [Welcome to you who provides comfort to exiles, and may
> your destiny be accomplished when, like the patriarch of old,
> we offer at the pyre of sacrifice the lives needed for you to cover
> us with your wings. No invisible spirit will detain the movement
> of our arms, and the blow of our revolution will remove obstacles
> that stand in our way.][95]

Here the exiles sacrifice their lives to receive Liberty, while in "Esperanza" the woman Cuba takes in the exiles.

Zenea's prose pieces in *El Filibustero* display the importance of the United States and filibustering to his growing radicalism. Most critical studies of Zenea written in Cuba do not emphasize the United States as a site for the composition and publication of his poems. In *Lo Cubano en la Poesía*, influential critic Cintio Vitier analyzes Zenea's *cubanidad*, arguing that it does not emerge in patriotism or even in poetic images of the island; rather, his Cubanness appears in his distance from the world. Vitier writes, "With him we begin to understand the *mystery of vulnerability* in our poetry and in our being."[96] The language approximates universal ontology and thus reverts to a notion of national literature in which birth on the island is what counts to make a poet Cuban. By Vitier's terms, Zenea becomes Cuban in the abstract content and aesthetics of his poetry, not in the material of the newspapers that call for Cuban separation from Spain. But if we read Zenea as a contributor to *El Filibustero*, what Vitier calls Zenea's "distance from the world" can become a literal distance from Cuba. Similarly, Lezama Lima touches on Zenea's residency in the United States but does not emphasize the overtly political content of the 1850s verses or focus on exile's effect on his writing. Instead, Lezama Lima emphasizes Zenea's ungrounded romanticism, calling him a poet of "twilight." These readings make Zenea Cuban through aesthetic and abstract readings. The flip side is Otto Olivera's emphasis on a more directly patriotic Zenea, the writer of the following lines:

> Murió López, es verdad:
> mas el tiempo se desliza
> y de su propia ceniza
> brotará la libertad.
>
> [López has died, it is true:
> but time slips away
> and from his ashes
> will spring liberty.][97]

Olivera argues that the lines are repeated throughout the century and culminate in a hymn from the war of the independence in the 1890s: "Nuestras armas darán a occidente / Y a la patria infeliz libertad" (Our arms will bring to the Occident / And to the unhappy motherland liberty).[98] Zenea's lines and the war hymn have little in common linguistically and are connected only through the belief that arms will lead to liberty. That sentiment emerged in many other poems from the 1850s in the United States, but the transnational dimensions of composition and publication are overlooked in Olivera's analysis. In effect, Cuban literary history has reterritorialized Zenea in Cuba by turning away from the question of the U.S. ground where he wrote some of his poems.

Ground, however, is at times an important element in Zenea's work, in keeping with the *filibusteros'* treatment of ground as an object of desire and temporary impossibility. Nowhere is this more evident than in the poem "Diez y Seis de Agosto de 1851 en la Habana," composed in New Orleans and published in New York in *El Filibustero*. On that date, authorities on the island executed about fifty filibusters from the United States who had been part López's final expedition. The men, fighting under William L. Crittenden, a Kentucky-born graduate of West Point and U.S. Army officer in the U.S.-Mexican War, had been captured while trying to escape from Cuba aboard four small boats. They were taken to Castle Atarés and executed on the side of a slope visible from Havana Harbor.[99] The execution became a cause célèbre against Spain in the United States, as newspapers proclaimed it a "massacre" and provided gruesome details about Havana crowds cheering the death of the filibusters. In New Orleans, riots broke out as bands sacked the Spanish consulate and burned down the offices of the Spanish-language newspaper *La Union* (formerly *La Patria*), which had published an "extra" in support of the execution.[100] Zenea's poem, echoing the U.S. mood, is packed with assaults on Spanish authorities, who are depicted as "evildoers" who revel in "strange cruelty," and the poem portrays a mob taking pleasure in the scene. At the same time, the piece pays tribute to the U.S. filibusters:

> El Aguila del Norte
> Lanzóse al aire y al abrir sus alas
> Hizo temblar el castellano solio,
> Cirnióse en "Atarés" con desconsuelo,
> Bebió la sangre, remontóse al cielo
> Y vino al "Capitolio"
> Para escuchar desde el nativo suelo
> El eco del silbido de las balas.

> [The Eagle of the North
> Took flight and upon opening its wings
> Shook the Castilian throne,
> Hovered over "Atarés" with sorrow,
> Drank the blood, rose again to the sky
> And came to the "Capitol"
> To listen to the echo of hissing bullets
> From the native soil.][101]

Filibustering is connected to a nationalist U.S. metaphor, the eagle as bravery and strength. "Capitol" can be read in reference to representative democracy, in its classical sense as a temple and more literally as the top of a hill from which a perched eagle beholds the execution. The lines create a paradox by placing the eagle of the North on its "native soil" in Havana.

The recurring and ultimately central image of the poem is that of blood—particularly spilled blood that cannot become one with the earth. The poem opens with a neoclassical stanza focusing on a shepherd standing at a spring that feeds the surrounding fields. In contrast to the pastoral opening lines, the second stanza points to a spring of blood "from the heart of the serene paladin," a reference to filibusters or, more specifically, Narciso López. The poetic shift from shepherd to historical reality becomes more pronounced as the poem rehearses scenes of "Horror! Horror!" in the particular colonial setting of Havana. The blood stains the grass purple and even splatters onto the chords of the poet's lyre. But that blood cannot enter the soil:

Y la tierra indignada
No abrió siquiera para darle entrada,
Una grieta escondida
Por donde fuese a fecundar su seno.

[And the indignant earth
Opened not to receive it,
Not even a hidden crack
Where it could fertilize its breast.][102]

The metaphor of the earth's breast harks back to "Esperanza," the article in which Cuba receives exiles at her breast. But why can't the blood seep into the earth? Is Zenea praising Crittenden and his fighters while calling for the blood of new patriots and new blood from people on the island to nourish the rise of Cuba without Spain? Or perhaps the separation of blood and earth is the bodily reality of the exiled writer.

El Filibustero Deterritorialized

Filibustero poetry culminated in the publication of *El Laúd del Desterrado* (1858), a collection that included selections by Tolón, Castellón,

Zenea, Heredia, Santacilia, Turla, and José Agustín Quintero, all of whom were exiled in the United States for months or years. Cuban critics recognize the book as a major contribution to nationalist senti-ment. In his anthology of Cuban poetry, Lezama Lima devotes a section to "the poets of *El Laúd del Desterrado.*" *El Laúd del Desterrado*, which critics read as a Cuban nationalist book, resulted from a collection of newspaper clippings printed in the United States. A reading of the newspapers still available today shows that at least half of the poems by 1850s writers in the collection were published in transnational news-papers before they appeared in the book. All of Castellón's and Zenea's poems included in the anthology appeared first in *El Filibustero*. In addition, some of the poems by Tolón, Turla, and Santacilia were pub-lished in newspapers in the early 1850s. If *El Laúd del Desterrado* con-tributes to the political construction of the Cuban nation-state, the book does so as a product of transnational writing. With New York figuring prominently in the publication of this book, *El Laúd del Dester-rado* calls attention to the tension between print culture conditions at particular points in history, in this case a transnational formation, and retroactive nationalist readings.

The steps in the circuit of production and circulation of *El Laúd del Desterrado* touch on both Cuba and the United States at various times. Not until the early twentieth century did *El Laúd del Desterrado* become integrated into a national literature, as Cuban intellectuals on the is-land supported the formation of a national literature, history, and cul-ture. But that point of retroactive reading and incorporation of histor-ical materials into documents that can help consolidate the Cuban nation-state differs from the 1850s, when transnational writing was published as part of a desire among exiles for a Cuba that was separate from the colonial parent. In the 1850s, neither transnational news-papers nor the military actions of filibusters dethroned Spain. Where does that leave a text such as *El Laúd del Desterrado*? Deterritorialized, as the book's title makes clear.

The *laúd*, a twelve-string guitar, connects the book to both Europe and Cuba. Contemporary *laúd* player Barbarito Torres explains that the instrument hailed originally from Arabia and was taken by the Moors to Spain, where the instrument's neck was elongated. "Troubadors brought the instrument here to Cuba, where it underwent its second metamorphosis," Torres says. "That resulted in the Cuban *laúd*."[103]

Just as the *laúd* follows a trajectory from one place to another to create a Cuban instrument, *El Laúd del Desterrado* results from a metamorphosis in print culture that creates a text that is Cuban but is also the product of separation from the island and integration into U.S. print culture. It is, after all, a lute (book) of separation.

Often translated as "exile," *desterrado* emphasizes a disconnection from the land, *tierra*, and takes both an adjectival and noun form implying forced removal. A lexical resemblance can be seen between *desterrado* and the theoretical concept "deterritorialized." Gilles Deleuze and Félix Guattari describe deterritorialization in reference to a body's separation from land, as in the case of the displacement as a result of exile, as well as other types of separation, including to the separation of language from the body.[104] Deterritorialization, then, describes a lifting off or a flight from forms such as family and nation and even linguistic structure, all of which fix the body, both physically and psychically. In the contemporary moment, deterritorialization is most often discussed in relation to postmodern culture and global flows of capital as well as the displacement of peoples as a result of political and social upheavals.[105] I argue that the deterritorialization of *filibusteros* and their transnational writing are historically inflected by social, political, and print culture contexts. In this case, deterritorialization provides a potential for liberation as well as a painful separation from the social structures that the *filibusteros* seek to change. In turn, Cuban exiles seek to reterritorialize themselves and their imagined government, and thus we see a political as well as personal intensity in their desire to return to Cuba.

But neither the ground of Cuba, which is the ground discussed in many of the writings, nor the ground of the United States, where the poems are published, can stake a complete claim to texts such as *El Laúd del Desterrado*. Each ground makes the other possible, and with that in mind a reader can move toward a deterritorialized perspective that allows for the weaving in and out of multiple contexts. As such, transnational writing is always deterritorialized in the sense that to stop in one country is to be separated from the other. Transnational writing moves in and out of one nation and then another, meaning that it moves beyond and within the nation. For mid-nineteenth-century *desterrados*, being out of place presented itself in the poems as sadness regarding the separation from family, friends, and the Cuban landscape.

The counterbalance and compensation for deterritorialization is reterritorialization. Both *El Laúd del Desterrado* and the Cuban exiles' transnational newspapers seek to reterritorialize language, subject, and nation on the island. In other words, the response to deterritorialization is to call for a return to a fixed existence within the island. The poems and articles call for the establishment of a state apparatus as well as a reunion with family in its specific and national dimensions. The primary concern of many poems is the referent Cuba. The language deployed to carry out this reconnection is, at its most basic, a language of fixity in a national terrain. Consequently, years after the filibustering expeditions, the language of the 1850s became integrated into a national symbolic system in conjunction with the establishment of the Cuban nation-state. *Filibusteros'* efforts to reterritorialize themselves in Cuba fed a revolutionary ethos that continued throughout the nineteenth century. In the early twentieth century, the poems of *El Laúd del Desterrado* became part of Cuba's literary history. In turn, the U.S. context was either deemphasized or effaced. In their return to Cuba, transnational writings were again deterritorialized, this time from the United States. Thus, deterritorialized texts challenge literary histories that focus on one nation and on a single dominant monolingual tradition.

In the 1850s, deterritorialization was the primary condition for textual production, which is why the *filibustero* was the most important figure to these writers. After all, the *filibustero* embodied deterritorialization. To understand that point, we can turn to a poem that captures the condition and goals of *los filibusteros*, Zenea's "El Filibustero." The poem opens with an invocation of land, "la tierra," the lush mother of the island's youth. By the end of the first stanza, the horror of slavery disturbs the calm of the land. The poet separates from the land's "breast"—again Zenea's metaphor for a grounded experience—because his heart grows somber amid the chains and the iron hand that hold the land. The masculinity implied in the gendered *filibustero* plays off against a feminized Cuba. He arrives on "other shores," where leaves are turning and falling, in contrast to the greenery of the island.

> Y desde entonces el alma
> traje de aflicciones viste
> porque es tan triste, ¡tan triste!
> ausentarse y no volver.

[And since then the soul
dons a suit of afflictions
for it is so sad, so sad!
to leave and not return.]

The poem returns to the island several times, but the speaker remains separated from it. Instead, what emerges is a tension between returns and leave takings, hopes and failures, that creates the *filibustero*. The poem implies that the *filibustero* is created in part by the deterritorialization of a castaway:

No me arrepiento de nada
porque náufrago afligido,
al verme solo, perdido,
la libertad me salvó.

[I am regretful of nothing
because as an afflicted castaway,
seeing myself alone, lost,
I was saved by liberty.]

Despite the hardships, the *filibustero* gains strength from the "sanctity" of *destierro*, which stands in contrast to the despotism of Spain. But personal liberty does not translate into the liberty of a people. At the end of the poem, the *filibustero* remains just that, a figure caught between deterritorialized reality and the hopes of reterritorializing a republican state. The poem is defiant in its association of the *filibustero* with freedom:

Porque tengo por más honra
ser libre "Filibustero"
que ser "pirata negrero"
y torpe esclavo de un rey.

[For I carry far more honor
being freedom's "Filibuster"
than the pirate of a slave ship
and a torpid slave to a king.][106]

The filibuster is not a pirate, a word that Zenea associates with Spain for its ongoing participation in the slave trade. As in many other poems by Cuban exiles during this period, "slavery" has a double connotation. Defiantly abolitionist, Zenea posits freedom in contrast to literal slavery as well as colonial subjection. At the end of the poem, the *filibustero* remains cast away, alone, outside of Cuba. While this provides insight into the ways that Cuban exiles conceived of the *filibustero*, the pessimistic conclusion does not dominate Cuban exiles' poetry. In presenting an isolated figure, "El Filibustero" contrasts with many of Miguel Tolón's poems, which end in some type of reterritorialized state, or even José María Heredia's "Himno del Desterrado," which concludes with a stanza that envisions a liberated Cuba.

To elaborate on the disconnection of the filibuster and the land, I will look at a two prose pieces written almost half a century after Zenea's poem. When he joined an 1897 expedition to Cuba, Stephen Crane recognized that the filibuster emerged only in the freedom of the ocean's open space. Crane sailed as a journalist from Jacksonville, Florida, aboard the steamer *Commodore*, which was delivering arms to Cuban rebels.[107] At this point, the word "filibuster" was still used in reference to Cuba and to expeditions attempting to oust Spanish colonialism. From his filibustering experience, Crane produced both a journalistic piece and a short story, "The Open Boat." The article, "Stephen Crane's Own Story," notes that the open ocean is crucial for filibustering.[108] It is only after the commodore has departed that "at last we began to feel like filibusters," Crane writes. Filibustering provides "not a mere trifle of danger" because the commodore could be a target for the Spanish navy. Crane is exhilarated by the exposure of this expedition. "Being an inexperienced filibuster," he writes, "the writer had undergone considerable mental excitement since the starting of the ship." When an "atrocious fog" caused the ship to ram into mud, Crane writes, "It was to all of us more than a physical calamity. We were now no longer filibusters. We were men on a ship stuck in the mud."[109] In the open space of the ocean, where the territory of nation-states is not demarcated, a writer from the United States can be a filibuster. In other words, filibustering is possible only in the space of the ocean, not the place of the mud.[110]

Crane calls attention to an important dimension of filibustering projects: when the filibuster reaches land, it enters a social or state apparatus and becomes something else. On land, a filibuster is reterritorialized. In some cases, the filibuster becomes a representative of political society or even the armed forces. Put another way, how many filibusters have become conquerors or presidents? William Walker temporarily changed his title from filibuster to president in Nicaragua, but when he was dislodged from power, he again became the *filibustero* Walker. The territory of a nation provides a ground for definition within the structure of society, and to remain outside of that definition is to remain a filibuster. Consequently, when writers such as Zenea and Villaverde enter Cuban literary history, they are framed as writers of Cuba and not as filibusters.

My use of the term *filibustero* emphasizes the failure of these military movements and of the writers' attempts to gain Cuban ground in the 1850s. The *filibustero* fighters failed because the military reality was that they were unable to seriously challenge Spanish troops. And the *filibustero* writers failed in their efforts to change enough minds in Cuba and the United States because the notion of filibustering through language was an idealistic supposition at this moment in history. The attempt to filibuster through a newspaper such as *El Filibustero* did not amount to a speech act in the way that a contemporary filibuster in the U.S. Senate accomplishes its goal through the act of speaking.

Transnational circuits were created by a separation between the place of publication (New York) and readers (Cuba and other parts of the United States). Given the technological limits at this point in history and the censorship in Cuba, ruptures emerged in the transnational circuit that prevented the full circulation of writings. In the military arena, what differentiates filibustering from a war is that the *filibustero* must appeal to a larger population for support. The belief that transnational newspapers and poems would convince enough people to take up arms was disconnected from the facts on the ground. When *El Filibustero* ceased publication on 25 February 1854, its editors explained that their belief in the power of a newspaper to bring about a revolution had crashed into a wall of failure: "Our efforts are almost in vain and our contributions altogether unnecessary under the present circumstances, for we have come to believe that the Cuban revolution should not be carried out with publications and papers, but rather with arms, gunpowder and bullets."[111] A tension between military action and written word, as I show in chapter 3, is embedded in the work of these writers. Without positing a binary opposition between the written word and military movement, the Bellidos drew an important distinction between those two approaches to prompting revolutionary change in Cuba. They came up against the reality that their newspaper is not reaching its intended audience in Cuba: "Our papers circulate very little or none at all on the island." Spanish authorities' severe restrictions on *filibustero* papers meant that smugglers encountered great risks. Someone in Cuba caught carrying *El Filibustero* would face imprisonment. In recognizing that these conditions limited their newspaper's ability to promote armed revolt, the Bellidos admitted that their idealistic pronouncements on U.S. soil did not translate to military and political realities on the island. Until full-fledged revolutionary movements broke out in the 1860s and 1890s, the reterritorializing tendencies of *filibustero* poetry remained a desire expressed in newspapers.

The newspaper *El Filibustero* eventually returned to Cuba in the form of holdings in the José Martí National Library, which has the only known run of the newspaper. It is cataloged among Cuban nineteenth-century periodicals and kept in the *Sala Cubana*, which holds the treasured publications of Cuba's lengthy nineteenth-century war against colonial oppression. As such, *El Filibustero* is reterritorialized in the nation of Cuba and remains deterritorialized from the place where it was published. The only copy of *El Filibustero* that I found in the United States is a solitary issue in the Beinecke Rare Book and Manuscript Library at Yale University. On the one hand, the absence of this newspaper in U.S. libraries, including the Library of Congress, indicates an archival lack of interest in texts published in languages other than English. Only recently, as noted in the introduction, have scholars tried to develop a history of publication in the United States by people of Latin American descent. But despite the Anglo-American emphasis in U.S. literary history, the Beinecke preserved like a treasure a single copy of a newspaper that no other U.S. library bothered to acquire and keep for its holdings. That single (supplementary) issue, in a curious way, ruptures the total and easy return of *El Filibustero* to Cuba. *El Filibustero* and *los filibusteros* remain outside the total connection to one nation. And that in-between space, the space of deterritorialization, allows for the development of the political positions taken by Cuban exiles in transnational writing even as it closes off the success of instituting that liberty on a particular soil. Perhaps only with historical hindsight can we see the irony of choosing the *filibustero*, a deterritorialized figure, as the symbol of the cause of Cubans' transnational writing.

Ultimately, *El Filibustero* (the newspaper), "El Filibustero" (the poem), and *los filibusteros* (the fighters and writers) remained outside of Cuba in the 1850s. In the case of Tolón and Zenea, they returned to die on the island. If the military filibusters had taken over Cuba, reterritorializing themselves in the most concrete of ways, they would no longer have been named as such. In victory, they would have become independence fighters, the army of liberation, founders, or some other national formation. The separation from a place (Cuba) is the important condition for the publication of transnational writings that move from the United States to the island and back but does not ensure the success of the writers' political agency. Successive military failures starting in 1850 fuel the production of transnational writing by Cuban exiles. The variety of perspectives that emerged in transnational newspapers is the focus of the next chapter.

Annexation and Independence

NEWSPAPER WARS AND TRANSNATIONAL CUBA

On 7 June 1853, poet and journalist Pedro Santacilia published a four-page, pamphlet-size paper that excoriated supporters of Spanish rule in Cuba. *El Guao* (New York, 1853), which fashioned itself a "poisonous publication," was named after a toxic Cuban tree and sought "nothing other than to flay without compassion all those reptiles who in a spirit of flattery or because of embarrassing cowardice, drag themselves before the Spanish power in Cuba, forgetting that they are men and converting themselves into miserable beasts."[1] With a fiery tone, Santacilia sought to combat colonialism through personal attacks on people who collaborated with the colonial government. The choice of a *guao* as the newspaper's symbol drew a direct connection to the earth in Cuba. But if *El Guao* represented a Cuban brand of poison, it was growing on U.S. soil.

How Santacilia came to plant his poisonous newspaper in the United States is a question he takes up in an introductory note to his poem "Mi Prisión" (My prison), published in *El Arpa del Proscripto* (The banished man's lyre), a collection that appeared in at least three editions in New York between 1856 and 1864. Santacilia was already temporarily exiled in Spain when a military commission in Cuba found a copy of "Mi Prisión" in the hands of a woman "suspected of filibusterism." Authorities, he writes, "of course, found it necessary to put on trial the subversive doctrines in the composition."[2] The poem compares the speaker's incarceration in a Havana jail to Cuba's colonial status. Santacilia was sentenced to permanent exile and made his way to the United States, where he edited newspapers, published his poetry book, and developed a series of lectures on Cuban history.[3]

Santacilia's trajectory and *El Guao* exemplify the interconnection of Cuba's literary culture, repression on the island, and the growth of newspaper publishing by Cubans in the United States. *El Guao*'s first issue, roughly five by eleven inches, betrays an optimistic view of the publication's future. It is to be published "when circumstances demand it" and to be distributed for free. It will "denounce abuses" and "combat by whatever means are at our disposal the tyrannical dispositions of Spanish power." Only one issue of *El Guao* has survived the century and a half since its publication, and the newspaper appears to have had a relatively short run.[4] Santacilia went on to edit *La Verdad* in 1856, keeping alive the vehemence he first expressed in *El Guao*.

The circle of writers tied to the filibustering cause published an astonishing variety of papers between the founding of *La Verdad* in 1848 and the U.S. Civil War, which effectively put the Cuba question on hold in the United States. The self-proclaimed voice of *patriotismo cubano*, *La Verdad* represented the widely shared conviction among Cuban exiles that the time had come to end Spanish colonialism on the island. But aside from sharing a common enemy, writers differed on a variety of crucial issues, and thus they sacrificed money, time, and energy publishing papers that debated how to bring about change on the island and how to ameliorate inequalities created by class stratification, racial divisions, and slavery. A small number of writers broke with the mainstream exile view and put forth platforms urging abolition and a revolutionary restructuring of Cuban society. A single newspaper sometimes presented differing viewpoints on an issue. These publications also kept up lively debates with English- and Spanish-language newspapers that attacked filibustering, annexation, and even the Cuban writers themselves.

In this chapter, I provide an overview of the newspapers and explain how they contributed to the transnational development of a proto-national discourse about Cuba. The newspaper was the most important venue of publication because exiles desired to circulate their writings in Cuba as well as in U.S. cities. Easily folded and smuggled, newspapers or pamphlets were less bulky than books. As the stages of composition, publication, and circulation moved from the United States to Cuba, writers deployed language of the nation as a reterritorializing strategy for negotiating exile. In other words, they sought to return to the island and establish a new government. On the one hand, these newspapers exemplify what Nicolás Kanellos characterizes as Spanish-language press in exile, "established by political refugees who took advantage of a free press to offer their compatriots (here and in their homelands) uncensored news and political commentary—even if their sheets had to be smuggled on and off ships and passed surreptitiously hand-to-hand back home."[5] But, as Kanellos points out, it is not always possible to demarcate the point of distinction between a newspaper for readers in other countries and one for a growing readership in the United States. This tension between readers in the United States and those in Cuba meant that the annexationist position of some newspapers at times clashed with the discursive development of Cuba as its own distinct country.[6] Exiles used the words "sovereignty" and "independence" to discuss Cuba's future even as other exiles promoted joining the Union. Those seemingly contradictory positions could co-exist because of an antebellum U.S. political culture that promoted the independence of U.S. states. Supporters of annexation among exiles were particularly interested in states' rights positions within U.S. revolutionary writings.

Echoes of Cuba: The Papers

The political leanings of papers were usually reflected in their names. *El Pueblo* (The people) (New York, 1855) attacked the power of the Cuban economic elite and held up the newspaper's name as "a magic and mysterious word that announces the union of all of society's classes." *El Mulato* (The mulatto) (New York, 1854), which I discuss in chapter 4, emphasized the island's mixed racial heritage and called belligerently for abolition in Cuba and the United States. *La Verdad* (New York, 1848–60), the longest running and most influential of the papers, set out to tell "the truth" about colonial rule and attempted to convince readers that annexation was the true path to prosperity for Cubans and U.S. investors. Cirilo Villaverde's *El Independiente* (The independent) (New Orleans, 1853) invoked independence in an anti-colonial sense while signaling its independence from the Cuban Junta that dominated New York exile politics and published *La Verdad*. And in a comical turn, Miguel T. Tolón named his short-lived, two-column periodical *El Papagayo* (The parrot) (New York, 1855) to emphasize that he would not be silenced but instead soar like a parrot toward a vision of "CUBA LIBRE Y REPUBLICANA [a free and republican Cuba]."[7]

A newspaper's appearance and length of publication were influenced by how much support it received from benefactors and whether it could rustle up subscribers. In some cases, wealthy donors financed newspapers, either with start-up money or ongoing funding. As a result, *La Verdad* started out as an attractive eight-column full sheet the size of a big-city daily. Publications with little money, such as *El Papagayo*, looked more like pamphlets. By 1853, the Cuban population in the United States probably numbered several hundred.[8] Before publication, a newspaper would circulate a prospectus and ask for advance payment on subscriptions. From then on, notes to readers called for new subscribers and urged those already on board to pay for their subscriptions. Some of the newspapers tried to sustain themselves by printing advertisements for tobacco stores, clothing stores, rooming houses, and other services. *El Horizonte* devoted the entire last page of four to ads that appeared in English, Spanish, French, and Italian, presumably reaching out to political refugees from the European wars of liberation who might have been interested in the newspaper's promotion of international republicanism. The longest-running newspaper, *La Verdad*, was funded by wealthy exiles, including slave-owning planters seeking to change the Cuban governmental structure. While subsidized papers appeared for years or months, the independent ones folded after putting out a dozen issues or fewer. When a newspaper stopped publishing, its writers usually continued their work at other publications or started other newspapers. In size and appearance, the papers varied. At certain points in its twelve-year run, *La Verdad* looked like a big-city daily. Other papers were roughly the size of periodicals and ran two columns on the front page. Most used sans serif block letters in their names.

Graphics were rare, but in several cases, Masonic insignia appeared on the front page, pointing to the importance of Freemasonry for Cuban exiles. *El Mulato* displayed a large all-seeing eye at the top of the left-hand column, and *El Cubano* included an equilateral triangle with rays shooting out. As Antonio Rafael de la Cova shows, many of the most prominent Cuban *filibusteros* were Freemasons, including Villaverde, Tolón, Ambrosio José Gonzales, and Narciso López. Connections among Freemasons accounted in part for the contacts that Cuban exiles developed with prominent political figures in the United States and veterans of the U.S.-Mexican War.[9] The influence of Masonic doctrine, which described tyranny as the enemy of the human race and despots as outlaws, was evident on the front page of *La Verdad*. One of the tenets of the order was that a true Mason seeks "To attain the truth, and to serve our fellows, our country, and mankind."[10] In that sense, the name *La Verdad* can also be read as a direct connection to Freemasons. On that newspaper's front page, the nameplate featured a rising sun with five triangular points, probably a reference to the Masonic five points of fellowship.[11] From the sun shot out sunbeams, which certain readers might have viewed as a reference to the failed 1823 conspiracy for Cuban independence known as Soles y Rayos de Bolívar, a movement of Freemasons who proclaimed themselves sunbeams of Bolivar.[12] In 1854 *El Filibustero* published a letter from Andrés Cassard, a Freemason who had settled in New York the previous year with his family. Responding to charges by a Cuban military tribunal of having circulated revolutionary papers on the island, Cassard pronounced himself one the most strident enemies of Spanish authorities in Cuba and even pledged to send gunpowder as well as "papers" to Cuba.[13] In the 1870s, Cassard would go on to edit a newspaper called *El Espejo Masónico* (The Masonic mirror), and in 1881 he advertised in *El Espejo* (The mirror) to sell his books of Freemasonry.

New York and New Orleans, hotbeds of filibustering that possessed Spanish-speaking populations, became crucial sites for the publication of newspapers that debated Cuba's future. The publishing scene in Cuba was closed off to people who wanted to critique social and political injustices. Everything that was published had to pass through a censor, who could deny publication without offering a reason.[14] Printers faced large fines and even expulsion from the island for printing material without going through the censor. As print culture historian Ambrosio Fornet notes, growing tension between Creoles and Spaniards meant that Spanish printers received priority in lucrative contracts for government documents and newspapers, creating a virtual monopoly for Spanish printers.[15] In the 1820s and 1830s, writers had negotiated limitations on freedom of the press by toning down their writing, publishing abroad, or, in the cases of Félix Varela, Domingo Delmonte, and José Antonio Saco, going to other countries.[16] When Richard Henry Dana visited the island in 1859, he noted the effects of censorship on the press and the population in general: "The power of banishing, without a charge made, or a trial, or even a record, but on the mere will of the Captain-General, persons whose presence he thinks, or professes to think, prejudicial to the government, whatever their condition, rank, or office, has been frequently exercised, and hangs at all hours over the head of every Cuban."[17]

Under these conditions, to publish a revolutionary newspaper in the 1850s was to risk death, as shown in the case of *La Voz del Pueblo Cubano* (The voice of the Cuban people) (Cuba, 1852), a revolutionary sheet that led to the execution of the printer Eduardo Facciolo. Printing three issues between 2,000 and 3,000 copies each, Facciolo used a movable press that he carried in a black coffinlike box from one location in Havana to another.[18] Often considered the first revolutionary paper published *on* the island, *La Voz del Pueblo Cubano* displays the links between Cuban print culture and *filibustero* writers in the United States. The main contributor to *La Voz* was Juan Bellido de Luna, who went on to edit *El Filibustero* in New York and thus carried forth revolutionary principles enunciated first in Cuba.[19] In fact, the revolutionary program put forth by *La Voz del Pueblo Cubano* called for a connection with filibusters in the United States.[20] "A multitude of Creoles have moved to the U.S., and they have armed, are arming, and will arm themselves for expeditions that will invade the island and fight for her to gain independence from the unjust metropolis."[21] In New York, *La Verdad* taunted the colonial government by saying that it would not be able to stop *La Voz* because "the people had savored the little loose sheets and would do their part to ensure that nothing would be discovered."[22] *La Verdad*'s English-language section proclaimed, "The Cubans have taken a bold and onward step in publishing and circulating at the very doors of the palace an open and high-toned declaration of war against their despots."[23] But the editors of *La Voz* were more cautious and spelled out the dangers of their project in the first issue, emphasizing that "if we are discovered as a result of an infamous betrayal, we will be killed."[24] The statement proved prophetic after an informant told Spanish authorities about Facciolo's work. Three months after the first issue of *La Voz del Pueblo Cubano* appeared, Facciolo was publicly garroted. Bellido went into exile in New York.[25] *La Verdad* responded with defiance: the colonial government "has killed one Facciolo, but hundreds have risen from each drop of his generous blood."[26]

The tragic end of *La Voz del Pueblo Cubano* clarified what many exiled writers already knew: it would be easier to publish militant tracts in the United States and smuggle them into Cuba than to publish on Cuban soil. The role of the United States as a site in the communications circuit of transnational writing cut into a connection between printed matter and local production that has been associated with the concomitant rise of print and nation.[27] Transnational newspapers differed from daily newspapers, which, as Benedict Anderson reminds us, bridge geographic separation by promoting a sense of national shared time. As Anderson argues, early newspapers in North and South America were marked by a provinciality; they were "appendages of the market," containing local commercial news as well as clarion calls of an "imagined community" of local fellow readers.[28] Anderson's argument—that in the late eighteenth and early nineteenth centuries, newspapers and novels (the convergence of capitalism and print technology) created a semblance of shared time for local imagined communities—is not particularly relevant to newspapers that negotiated readers in more than one country and thus faced not so much shared time but a time lag, both figuratively and literally at the level of circulation.[29] More to the point, these newspapers reflected the stirrings of the Cuban nation in the United States as well as depicted the ways in which Cuban support for annexation lagged behind the time of the nation in the Americas.[30] The papers focused on changing conditions in Cuba rather than timely news coverage, further deemphasizing a connection to the daily newspaper. That is not to say that Cuban writers ignored the temporal demands of journalism; when important events took place, they rushed to put out special issues or supplements. But by and large, getting the news out quickly was not as important as creating a sense of place (Cuba or Cuba as viewed from exile) and furthering a political program. Rather than promoting shared time, the newspapers created a shared place, and their focus on terrain overlapped with the filibusters' effort to take over land.

Exiled writers attempted to minimize the gulf between Cuba and the United States by invoking principles of universal rights. The union of republicanism and Cuba was most evident in José Mesa's paper, *El Eco de Cuba* (Cuba's echo), which featured the words "Libertad—Igualdad—Fraternidad [liberty—equality—fraternity]" on its masthead directly under its name.[31] Appearing concurrently with *El Pueblo* for part of its run, *El Eco de Cuba* called explicitly for a "Cuba república democrática independiente [democratic independent Cuban republic]." It envisioned a Cuba with free commerce, individual and equal rights, public schooling, and "universal brotherhood."[32] Drawing from the language of the French Revolution as well as the European revolutions of 1848, *El Eco de Cuba* deployed Enlightenment principles to assert that it would use reason as the most appropriate weapon to bring about Cuban independence from the "throne." Like *El Pueblo*, *El Eco* repeatedly referred to a revolution in Cuba rather than to a relationship with the United States that would compromise Cuban independence.

El Eco de Cuba was the culmination of Mesa's work in New York's *filibustero* print culture. For years, he had toiled to put out publications, first working for pay as an editor at *La Verdad*. He opened his own print shop, where he earned a living, and helped Tolón put out *El Papagayo* and *El Cometa*.[33] In *El Eco de Cuba*, published between June and December 1855, Mesa finally put forth his own words to call for Cuba's "separation from the metropolis and contribution to its own independent existence."[34] Mesa attempted to fund the newspaper through advertising and subscriptions. In an English-language masthead, *El Eco* described itself as "a Cuban trimonthly newspaper widely circulated in all the principal cities of the United States, Cuba, Mexico, and South America." The attempt to reach readers in so many places spoke less to the topics of interest to the newspaper, which concerned itself mostly with Cuba, than to potential advertising revenue. "We call the attention of the public," the paper said, "and particularly of those whose trade or business puts them in connection with Spanish customers, to our extremely low rates of advertising."[35] As a special incentive, the paper offered free translation of ads into Spanish.

While the commercial dimensions of *El Eco* point to the valiant attempts by the likes of Mesa to fund fledgling publications, the advertisements themselves provide insight into the lives of Cuban exiles and other Latin Americans in New York. One advertisement noted that a Cuban who had resided for many years in the United States had opened a guesthouse and now made available to all Latin Americans rooms and food that was sensitive to their palates. Another advertisement was for the "International Pharmacy" on the corner of Hudson and Reade, where Spanish was spoken along with German, French, and Italian. A clothing store advertised that one of its employees was a Cuban man who was fluent in French and Spanish. And the Lone Star tobacco store on Broadway between Eleventh and Twelfth Streets offered the finest cigars from Havana.[36] Aside from providing a window into the growth of Cuban and Latin American groups in New York, these advertisements call attention to the challenge that Mesa faced in producing his paper. While his goal was to change Cuba, the economic base in terms of advertisers and readers was in New York City.

The influence of republicanism is evident in one of the most interesting contributions to *El Eco de Cuba*: "El Guajiro Independiente," a series of "popular songs" about *guajiros*, Cuban peasants, that began in the first issue and filled a third of the front page. In the first song, "El Republicano," Andrés A. de Orihuela describes the figure as taking up arms for the *patria*:

> Mucho hemos sufrido; tanto
> fue del tirano el rigor;
> pero nos sobra valor
> guerra sin tregua, constante
> hasta que llegue el instante,
> de calmar nuestro dolor.
>
> [Much have we suffered; such
> was the tyrant's rule;
> but we have plenty of valor,
> war without truce, constant
> until we reach the moment
> when our pain will subside.][37]

By dressing a local Cuban figure in a republican outfit, Mesa promoted a sense of Cuba as separate not only from the Spanish monarchy but also from other territories yet as retaining a connection to political principles that circulated in the United States. Orihuela's "El Republicano" can be situated in a Cuban literary tradition of *criollismo*, which emphasizes the life and customs of white peasants.[38] But the poem is more republican than *criollo*. Like the militant *filibustero* poems discussed in the previous chapter, the songs that make up "El Guajiro Independiente" are full of martial and patriotic language calling for the overthrow of "despotism."

El Eco de Cuba called for equality for mankind and stressed "liberty for all as the most precious source of widespread happiness."[39] Did "all" include slaves in Cuba? Perhaps, especially if readers wanted to take the statement as such. Mesa shared with Tolón the willingness to use general language on race issues, thus allowing readers to interpret the words as either encompassing all Cubans or referring exclusively to whites. Calling for abolition would have stirred great antipathy in exile circles, so *El Eco de Cuba* ignored slavery, instead directing its most explosive language at Spain. Still, the primary concern of the paper was whites, as evident in a letter published arguing that on the island, the "disgust and discontent of the white class is universal."[40]

In New York, the nascent discussion of what it meant to be Cuban was filtered not only through republicanism but also through the influence of the city's multinational and multilingual population. A cosmopolitan and urban atmosphere came through in the pages of Tolón's *El Horizonte*, which was aimed at Spanish- and English-language readers in New York.[41] Tolón moonlighted as a teacher of languages, and his interest in language instruction comes through in the pages of his newspaper. Given the large number of Spanish speakers in the United States who were learning English, *El Horizonte* vowed to publish a column in English with grammar notes to help readers.[42] Accordingly, *El Horizonte* published an article on "Cuba, Great Britain, and the United States" that had appeared originally in the *Protective Union* of Boston. The piece blasted England for opposing the López expedition and engaged in the polemical battle over the word "filibuster" by pointing to imperialistic hypocrisy. "But England loves a bit of buccaneering herself on occasion, and is known to follow the trade with a high hand in many latitudes of the world."[43] Tolón's pedagogical concerns motivated the publication of his *Elementary Spanish Reader and Translator*, a language-learning book that remained in print in the early twentieth century.[44]

The most prolific of the exiles in the 1850s, Tolón carried on a tireless struggle to create an inclusive national community that connected exiles to the island. He was the most important and most active Cuban exile in newspaper publishing in the United States between 1849, the year he went into exile in New York, and 1857, the year he returned to Cuba and died of tuberculosis. His publication record was astonishing—he essentially worked himself to death. He founded and edited four newspapers—*El Cubano, El Papagayo, El Cometa,* and *El Horizonte*—and he edited *La Verdad* from 1848 to 1852. In cases where Tolón did not direct the editorial operation, papers would publish his speeches and even list his name as one of the subscribers. Tolón was a prolific poet, publishing regularly in the *filibustero* press and collecting his verses into a book, *Leyendas Cubanas* (New York, 1856), that comprised seven lengthy "legends" from Cuba told in verse plus twenty-seven lyric poems. Tolón also contributed more poems than any other writer to the anthology *El Laúd del Desterrado*, published the year after his death and dedicated to him.

As a journalist, Tolón used his knowledge of English, French, and Italian, among other languages, sometimes putting out multilingual issues of a newspaper. In the following selection from *El Cubano*, Tolón writes a "Remembrance of Home" in English but cannot resist allowing Cuban words to intrude into his prose: "I walked alone, unconscious of any object in my rambling, occasionally stopping to gaze with envy at the fanciful fluttering of a lovely couple of tojosas, or to breathe the perfume of garlands, expanding aguinaldos clinging to hedges of aloes, like so many gay-colored festoons of our fairy land, gently waving as the balmy breath of the evening breeze passed over them."[45] Tolón provided glosses for *aguinaldo*, "wild flowers, like lilies, which are abundant in the months of December and January," and *tojosa*, "a small wild dove of a greyish color." Aimed at English-language readers, the piece is clearly an attempt to portray the island as an idyllic paradise, thus attempting to inspire interest in Cuba.

That type of overture to English-language readers was common in *La Verdad*. Most of the paper's issues included an English-language section. "As our Trimonthly is sustained by the free will offerings and unpaid efforts of the republicans of Cuba for gratuitous circulation," *La Verdad* told its readers, "we shall be happy to mail it punctually to any one desiring to receive it who will forward his address (post paid) to Office of La Verdad, 72 Church Street, N.Y."[46] In other cases, newspapers looked to other parts of the Americas. Some of the papers claimed to have distributors in Yucatán, Mexico, while others sometimes took up the question of Puerto Rico. On 20 September 1852, *La Verdad* devoted its front page to an article about Puerto Rico in which the paper lamented its inability to focus more on that island and challenged the "press of this country" to cover Puerto Rico's plight. Arguing that exiled Cubans were sensitive to Puerto Rican conditions, *La Verdad* presented a scenario under which thousands of Cubans, finished with the struggle on their island, would make their way to Puerto

Rico to "destroy the last den of Spanish despotism in America."[47] This notion of an alliance between Cubans and Puerto Ricans became more pronounced in succeeding decades in newspapers such as *La Voz de la América* (The voice of America) (New York, 1865–67). By the late nineteenth century, Puerto Rican intellectuals joined with Cubans and other Latin Americans to support revolution against Spain and to publish books and newspapers.[48] "In clubs such as Las Dos Antillas (The Two Antilles), co-founded by the Afro–Puerto Rican bibliographer Arturo Alfonso Schomberg," Nicolás Kanellos writes, Puerto Ricans "delivered eloquent speeches that would be printed in the newspapers circulated throughout the exile communities and smuggled into Puerto Rico."[49] Because *La Verdad* circulated clandestinely in Cuba, the editors probably believed that they could smuggle the paper into Puerto Rico.

Imperium in Imperio: *La Verdad*'s Vision of Cuba

A convergence of two islands, Cuba and Manhattan, graced the front page of *La Verdad*. An impressive masthead featured the newspaper's name in large block letters over a drawing of the island menaced by storm clouds. Beneath the drawing was the phrase, "El Patriotismo Cubano Sostiene Este Periódico Para Circularlo Gratis [Cuban patriotism ensures the free distribution of this newspaper]." And immediately beneath that was the place of publication, New York. In some issues, editorial notes in English in the left-hand column touted the newspaper's English-language pages even as front-page articles in Spanish had datelines from places in Cuba.[50] Published between 1848 and 1860, *La Verdad* was smuggled aboard ships that ran regular routes from New York to Cuba, where the publication became notorious as subversive and circulated by a network of activists.

La Verdad was the longest running and best known of the papers published by Cubans in the United States in the 1850s. Edited by Gaspar Betancourt Cisneros, Miguel T. Tolón, Pedro Santacilia, and Cirilo Villaverde at different points during its lengthy run, the newspaper featured a never-ending stream of political articles and periodically showcased some of Cuba's major poets, including Plácido and Gertrudis Gómez de Avellaneda. While Cubans did most of the writing and editing, *La Verdad* was published first and foremost to promote the annexation of Cuba by the United States. The paper was distributed to English-language newspaper editors and members of Congress and was influential enough that historian Basil Rauch credits *La Verdad* "with some responsibility for the importance which the desire for Cuba began to assume in American politics after the Mexican War."[51] Because *La Verdad* published a variety of writers and spoke to readers in various contexts, I read the paper as a multivocal textual production, not a single voice.

A commitment to putting out the newspaper emerged from a meeting in Cuba that brought together U.S. journalists active in expansionist causes and members of the Club de la Havana, an association of Creole plantation owners who believed that the most effective way to protect their landholdings was to join the United States as a slave state. Held at the estate of one of Cuba's wealthiest families, the meeting brought together John L. O'Sullivan, the newspaper prophet of Manifest Destiny; Cristóbal Madan, a Cuban planter and shipowner; Moses Yale Beach, editor of the *New York Sun*; and journalist Jane McManus, who published under the pen name Cora Montgomery.[52] With $10,000 from the Cuban planters and Beach's offer to run the newspaper on the presses of the *Sun*, *La Verdad* began publishing on 9 January 1848. José Aniceto Iznaga, whose family had made a fortune from slave trading and sugar mills in Trinidad, Cuba, wrote articles and toed the annexationist line for the first few months.[53] He was joined by Gaspar Betancourt Cisneros, a wealthy intellectual from one of the richest and oldest families in Camagüey. Betancourt Cisneros became a major editorial influence at *La Verdad*.

La Verdad's bilingual attempt to reach readers reflected the paper's efforts to bring together Spanish- and English-speaking populations to effect change in Cuba. In its first issue, the paper described Spanish and English as "civilized," presumably in contrast to indigenous languages: "We have adopted the Spanish language in connection with our own, because one or the other is spoken by nearly all the civilized inhabitants of this New World, whose honor and interests are necessarily the nearest to an American heart. We also flatter ourselves that close communications with redeemed and tranquilized Mexico will induce such intimate attachments and family relations as will make her noble language a common property."[54] The belief that victory over

Mexico in the U.S.-Mexican War would "redeem" that country reflects the racial biases circulating in society at the time, for in the racial language of the mid–nineteenth century the flip side of redemption was the degeneration of hybrid and darker peoples. At the same time, the call for bilingualism and the notion that Spanish would become the "property" of the United States implies an attempt to bring together both Anglo and Hispanic languages and populations in the Americas with "civilization" as a point of union.

In presenting the union of two Americas, *La Verdad* opened the English-language section of its first issue by associating "truth" with the Americas as opposed to the corruption of Europe. A similar point was made in the first issue's lead Spanish-language article, which posited that the two Americas shared a genealogical background. The paper's anti-European posture was influenced by a tradition of exile writing that went back to the early nineteenth century, when Latin Americans published books praising U.S. revolutionary writings. *La Verdad* promoted a vision of America, in a hemispheric sense, as representing liberty from the despotism of monarchy. *La Verdad* picked up this binary division between the Americas and Europe and called for "the adoption of a general system, of a unique principle, and a political course entirely distinct from the politics of Europe."[55] The ideal of a hemispheric common ground presented in *La Verdad* was infused with a dose of Manifest Destiny ideology. In pushing its annexationist program, *La Verdad* attempted to develop a relationship of reader to territory by which Cuba would appear as a natural appendage of the United States.

The annexationist position was put most forcefully in *La Verdad* through a cognitive mapping that connected Cuba geographically to the United States. As one article said, "Will the annexation of Cuba add to our strength as a Nation? The reply is written on the map of North America, and in the last ten years of her history."[56] The sentence conjoins geographic condition with expansionist teleology. On 17 March 1849, the paper's front page featured a large map that positioned the Gulf of Mexico and Cuba at the center and did not delineate the borders of the United States. In case the map did not speak for itself, the article argued that the preceding decade of U.S. westward expansion made protection of the Gulf of Mexico a crucial part of U.S. geopolitical interests. The article noted that access to Texas ensured the shortest land route to California. In other words, Cuba was the "door to the Gulf, to the Pacific, to the mines of California and Centralia, to Oregon and the whale fisheries, with the East India trade."[57] The metaphor of the door to the gulf appeared in several variations, with Cuba sometimes as the "key" to the door, opening up naval trade and military routes: "Half a dozen steamers would bridge with their cannon the narrow straits between Yucatan and the west point of Cuba, and between Florida and Matanzas on the north, and seal hermetically to every aggressive stranger the entire coast circle of the American Mediterranean. This simple geographical fact constitutes Cuba the key of the Gulf, and it would be felt if it passed in the grasp of a strong and jealous rival."[58] The jealous rival was none other than England, which had its own interests in the Caribbean and Central America and was jockeying for control of Cuba.

In trying to remap the Americas with an imperialist eye, *La Verdad* appealed directly to commercial interests: "The central position of Cuba in the great routes of trade—opened, and to be opened, by American capital and enterprise—cannot fail to strike the most careless eye that rests on the map of North America."[59] A seven-part series of articles, "Of the Advantages Which the Annexation of Cuba Offers to America, and in Particular to the People of the United States," deployed tables with the island's imports and exports and lists of items consumed on the island to promote capitalist interest. The paper calculated that U.S. exports to Cuba suffered from an average 35 percent tariff, with some foodstuffs paying more than 200 percent on their value. "The United States could readily give Cuba an abundant supply of flour of the first quality, but the sale of this production of American industry receives a mortal blow, not only by the extraordinary protection granted to the flours of Spain, but by the exorbitant duties imposed on those of the United States."[60] Annexation would, the paper emphasized, eliminate all tariffs. Under such conditions, *La Verdad* estimated, the export of flour would rise to 2,000,000 barrels a year from 4,980 in 1846.[61] Those arguments were aimed at northern U.S. interests that stood to profit from annexation.

These appeals to U.S. commercial interests appeared alongside a growing sense of Cuba as a distinct place with its own history and culture. Given the presence of Cuban writers at *La Verdad*, a concomitant discourse emerged in which the interests of Cuban people and the terrain of the island were portrayed as separate from Spain (and, ostensibly, separate from the United States). That separation, which was part of a patriotic discourse, came to clash with the U.S. expansionist tendency of *La Verdad*. U.S. historians tend to emphasize *La Verdad*'s call for annexation while overlooking the contradictory positions of writings by Cubans.[62] A tension existed from early on, in part the result of the various social backgrounds and political leanings of the parties involved in the publishing of *La Verdad*. In its first five years, *La Verdad* was also edited by Tolón and Villaverde, writers whose interests were patriotic rather than economic. The tone of the paper was also influenced by the various correspondents from different parts of Cuba and by poetry that was more patriotic than annexationist in that it focused on the island's terrain as separate from the spheres of other powers. Like the poetry of *El Filibustero*, some poems in *La Verdad* called for revolution.

Given the different contributors and the various genres in the paper as well as its bilingual emphasis, *La Verdad* went through several evolutions. Its first issue differed dramatically in content and appearance from later issues. In the first issue, the Spanish-language section devoted half of its space to a speech by President James K. Polk, while the English-language section featured mostly a miscellany of news from Europe and Mexico. The paper started as an impressive eight-column, four-page, semimonthly paper the size of the *New York Sun*. It was printed on the *Sun*'s steam-engine press, which was so state-of-the-art that the newspaper periodically opened its doors to visitors wishing to see the operation.[63] The first two pages of *La Verdad* were entirely in Spanish, and the next two were in English. By 1849, the paper gained momentum, publishing more frequently and displaying a masthead with a drawing of Cuba on it. In succeeding years, the paper would move to other presses and set up intermittently in New Orleans. In 1853, a fire torched the offices of *La Verdad*, doing away with the fancy nameplate featuring the island of Cuba. For several months, the paper produced a journal-size two-column publication that was continuously paginated across issues. In 1855, the paper was edited by Pedro Santacilia and featured his prose pieces and poems. Throughout its changes,

La Verdad was paid for by wealthy Cubans, including planters whose primary concern was to set up a new governmental structure on the island that would liberalize trade and protect their investments, including slave plantations.[64]

In its first five years, the newspaper was filled with calls for a "free and independent Cuba," articles chronicling Spanish injustices on the island, and lengthy essays detailing the bounty that annexation of Cuba would bring to the United States. Mixing U.S. expansionism and Cuban patriotism, the paper proposed slightly different scenarios from one issue to another. The United States at times emerged as savior: "An oppressed and unhappy people desires to throw itself into the arms of this free and happy nation, who opens them as brother to receive brother."[65] Conversely, a Spanish-language piece would describe an alternate scenario that placed the population in Cuba as the actors in an independence movement: "An army of Cubans thrusting themselves with arms in hand onto the fields of the fatherland to conquer their liberty."[66] Similarly, the paper's position on who had a right to govern Cuba varied. One article could argue that "Cuba belongs to the Cubans, and they have a right higher than human convention—a right directly from the throne of Divine Justice—to govern themselves."[67] In another issue, however, the island would be described in the geographic sphere of interest of the United States: "Cuba seems placed by the finger of a kindly Providence, between the Atlantic and the Mexican seas at the crossing of all the great lines of our immense coasting trade."[68] An imperial "we" and "our" in many articles implied that the island was already incorporated into a U.S. national voice.

But the paper's Spanish-language poems by no means presented the island as a part of the United States. More often, the poems employed various forms to present the beauty of Cuba and the writer's patriotism. In Santacilia's "A Una Nube" (To a cloud), published on 15 October 1855, the speaker addresses the "vaporous daughter of ether" in eight stanzas of eight lines with an ABBCDEEF rhyme scheme and concludes by asking the cloud to take a message to his adored *patria*. The piece ends with a postscript specifying that the poem had been composed while Santacilia was imprisoned in Havana.[69] The description of a cloud going to Cuba, presumably from the exile position of the writer and reader, is actually a vision within Cuba itself. While such a poem did not directly oppose *La Verdad*'s annexationist program, the work did offer an alternative perspective on what should be privileged—liberty in Cuba as opposed to U.S. economic and geopolitical goals.

Cracks in the annexationist program were evident beginning in the newspaper's earliest years. A front-page article on 1 May 1849 argued that the "government of the American Union has harmed efforts to liberate the people of Cuba."[70] This was a reference to a historical event that would become infamous in succeeding decades among exiled Cubans. In 1824, proposals had floated in Colombia and Mexico to organize a joint expedition of troops to oust Spanish forces from Cuba and Puerto Rico. Among those who considered taking part in this plan was Simón Bolívar, who wrote to the vice president of Colombia, "The Government should let Spain know that if in a specific space of time Colombia is not recognized and peace made, our troops will go immediately to Havana and Puerto Rico."[71] The United States opposed the plan and made its position clear at a congress of Latin American nations in Panama. The U.S. sought to prevent a Haiti-like independent state in Cuba while leaving open the possibility of annexing the island to the Union.[72] By the mid–nineteenth century, Cubans were increasingly aware that U.S. involvement in the matter was a foil for their goal of a separation from Spain. "If only [the United States] had never been invited to the Panama congress," said the article. The underlying assumption was that the United States was a separate power from Cuba, thus contradicting *La Verdad*'s efforts to redraw geopolitical borders in the Americas. Later in the century, the Panama congress would become part of the revisionist narratives of U.S. imperialism in Latin America developed by Villaverde and Martí.

Critiques of U.S. intervention in the hemisphere were rare in *La Verdad*; thus, the newspaper's subtle inscription of a Cuban political and social space outside of the United States differs from the ways other nineteenth-century Spanish-language periodicals distinguished U.S. populations from the U.S. government. In the case of *Nuevomexicano* newspapers, articles overtly opposed efforts by Anglo Americans to displace and dominate local populations.[73] With the U.S.-Mexican War as an important historical context for the production of newspapers in the Southwest, attacks on Anglo-American culture were not uncommon. Mary Pat Brady, for one, shows how the newspaper *Las Dos Repúblicas* (The two republics) in Arizona responded to insulting portrayals by arguing in favor of the superiority of Mexican culture and against the failures and social degradation of U.S. imperial capitalism.[74] By contrast, the writers at *La Verdad* did not see themselves in opposition to the U.S. government or its political tradition but conceived of Cuba as distinct from the United States. In seeking to create a space for Cuba that was separate from Spain, Cuban exiles at *La Verdad* variously argued for a politically ambiguous "liberated Cuba" or a notion of statehood by which the island would retain its culture and language.

Some writers argued that as a state in the Union, Cuba would retain great autonomy. In 1849, Betancourt Cisneros published a pamphlet that deployed the concept of *imperium in imperio* to conceptualize a future for Cuba as a U.S. state that simultaneously would have sovereignty: Cuba "will be that which it cannot avoid being viz:—a sovereign state; as sovereign as any other State in the world;—as sovereign as any one of the thirty composing the Union;—as sovereign as all of these united, and like them, AN EMPIRE within AN EMPIRE. This is what Cuba will be by annexation into the Union."[75] The slippage from state in the union to nation-state ("as sovereign as all of these united") is not so much a rhetorical sleight of hand as indicative of how Betancourt Cisneros and the *La Verdad* circle viewed states' rights in the antebellum United States. Like states in the Union, Betancourt Cisneros argued, Cuba would draw up its own constitution, organize a militia, and establish courts while adhering to U.S. laws. Betancourt Cisneros argued that the "constitution of each individual State harmonizes with that of the Federal Constitution"; thus, "it becomes easy to comprehend the contemporary duality and unity of American sovereignty."[76]

The notion that power existed in state and nation (duality) could be traced back to the eighteenth century, when the building blocks of U.S. independence were placed in part on the notion of *imperium in imperio*. As Forrest McDonald shows, *imperium in imperio* as deployed in the founding documents of the United States pulled sovereignty away from a singular monarch and divided it between the federal government and the states. The phrase *imperium in imperio* "was used commonly when the United States was founded and can be translated as 'supreme power within supreme power, sovereignty within sovereignty, the division of sovereignty within a single jurisdiction.'"[77] McDonald writes, "Congress had sovereignty, the supreme lawmaking power, in regard to the matters entrusted to it. The states had sovereignty in regard to matters entrusted to them; and the people reserved sovereignty in still other matters, refusing to entrust it to government at any level."[78] Cubans at La Verdad were schooled in the founding documents of the U.S. Revolution, including the Declaration of Independence and the Constitution, so it is not surprising that Betancourt Cisneros would deploy *imperium in imperio* before the U.S. Civil War.

Betancourt Cisneros's work at La Verdad serves as a reminder of the types of negotiations with U.S. political culture that exiles undertook as they developed a national consciousness. Educated in the United States in the 1820s, Betancourt Cisneros returned to Cuba and published literary essays on the island under "El Lugareño," a pen name that emphasized the local *lugar* (place).[79] Appearing between 1838 and 1840, Betancourt Cisneros's essays critiqued the local society of his native town, Camagüey, while celebrating local customs. But if his pen name tied him to a Cuban place, his new city was New York. Betancourt Cisneros was wealthy and well connected, so doors opened for him in U.S. political circles. He was one of three Cubans who met with President Polk in 1848 to advocate annexation of their island home.[80] It is difficult to decipher the extent of Betancourt Cisneros's writing for La Verdad because many articles were published without bylines, but he was certainly active as an editor for years and wrote lengthy pieces arguing that annexation would bring great benefits to Cuba as well as to the United States.[81]

In supporting annexation, Betancourt Cisneros answered the concerns of exiles, and particularly the landholding elite, about Cuba's ability to defend itself should Spain be ousted. Betancourt Cisneros was probably familiar with article IV, section 4 of the U.S. Constitution, which guarantees the states protection against invasion. In turn, Betancourt Cisneros invoked the metaphor of the "temple of Liberty" as a model of the future that would please slaveholders and *filibustero* separatists. Presenting Cuba as a pillar that both held up and received protection from a larger edifice, Betancourt Cisneros wrote, "How inspiring the thought that this our column will be protected and supported by thirty or more columns which will shield it from Spain, and England, Europe, negro-traders, or abolitionists—in a word from enemies within and without."[82] A notion of "protection" was based in part on the acceptance of slavery; thus, annexation simultaneously became a reason to oppose a type of social change (abolition) that could threaten the interests of rich Cubans funding *La Verdad* and the southern U.S. planters whose support those islanders coveted.

Betancourt Cisneros's argument placed him directly at odds with José Antonio Saco, an influential Cuban intellectual who wrote that the beneficiary of annexation would be the United States. Saco, as the next chapter discusses in more detail, blasted the *filibusteros* and went so far as to argue that under annexation Cuba would become a victim of "American rapacity" and that the island's "traditions, its nationality, and even the last vestige of its language" would perish "in the claws" of the United States.[83] It would be hasty to characterize Saco's antiexpansionism as anticolonialism or a broader antiimperialism of the type that Martí would develop, for Saco's denunciation of the United States was accompanied by arguments for continuing Spanish colonial rule in Cuba. Betancourt Cisneros and other writers for *La Verdad* responded to Saco with numerous articles and pamphlets, even as Betancourt Cisneros continued to exchange with Saco affectionate letters addressed to "Saquete Mio" (My Little Saco) and signed, "Siempre tu Narizotas" (Always yours, Huge Nose).[84] Betancourt Cisneros responded to the charge that Cuba would lose its nationality with the argument that a government does not construct nationality: "The fact is we have not been able to comprehend what nationality it is of which Saco speaks—whether it is the one belonging to government, or the one appertaining to nature or race. The first Cuba does not possess, unless the condition of *enslaved colony* of Spain is the glorious nationality worthy of being inscribed on armorial bearings. . . . But if it is the nationality of race he means, we do not understand how one born a Cuban, and wishing to preserve his character as such, would lose it, whatever the government may be."[85] Thus, Betancourt Cisneros argued against governmental sanction and race as determinants of nationality. By his definition, someone born in Cuba would be Cuban, but Betancourt Cisneros was talking only about whites. He envisioned a scenario in which whites from the United States would emigrate to the island and give birth to Cubans, thus increasing the island's white population.

Another enthusiastic supporter of annexation at *La Verdad* during the paper's early years was journalist Jane McManus Storm Cazneau

(1807–78), who wrote as Cora Montgomery.[86] One of the most avid supporters of filibustering in the English-language press, Montgomery was in charge of the English-language pages at *La Verdad* for several years. Her name was displayed prominently at the top of the left-hand column of the front page in a small headline that read, "La Verdad / Por Cora Montgomery / Luz y Paz [The truth / By Cora Montgomery / Light and peace]". Until 1852, when Cirilo Villaverde's name appeared on the front page alongside Montgomery's, she was listed as the sole editor, even though Cubans handled the Spanish-language writing. Letters to *La Verdad* from Cuba usually opened with the address, "Mi Lady." In addition to working at *La Verdad*, Montgomery sent dispatches from Cuba to New York newspapers and published a book about Mexico, *Eagle Pass; or, Life on the Border* (1852). Driven by enthusiasm for expansionist causes, Montgomery made her way to Santo Domingo and Nicaragua, the latter in an attempt to stir up support for William Walker's filibustering expedition after she departed from *La Verdad*'s editorial offices.[87]

The relationship between Montgomery and Cuban writers was strained at times. Villaverde, for one, criticized her for neglecting the English-language section.[88] Still, Montgomery could turn eloquent at the picture of two-way traffic between Cuba and the United States: "Relieved from the iron net of domestic repression, under which Cuba now suffocates, and fairly launched into free traffic with the Northern States, her citizens would send their children here by hundreds, for education, and come themselves by thousands, to enjoy the bracing air of a higher latitude, while in return thousands from the North would hasten there in winter, to enjoy her perpetual spring and ceaseless round of fruits and flowers, which are the fairest and brightest in Cuba when our fields are buried under chilling robes of frost and snow."[89] The reference to tourism was in keeping with the 1850s enthusiasm for travel to Cuba. In fact, Montgomery had first tried to drum up support for annexation through a series of "Tropical Sketches" in the *New York Sun*, pieces that strongly criticized Spain's administration of the island.[90] The difference between the cold North and tropical Caribbean in this passage informed other travel writing about Cuba.

La Verdad resorted to the tropes circulating in the period, framing Cuba as the "Queen of the Antilles" or the "pearl of the American Islands." Montgomery described Cuba as a "priceless jewel that clasps into one magnificent, unbroken chain, the vast circle of our Pacific, Gulf, and Atlantic Trade."[91] The need to challenge a masculine European rival for a feminized territory was shared both by the U.S. expansionist group and by the Cuban exiles. *La Verdad* also invoked the metaphor of the Garden of Eden that circulated in the mid–nineteenth century. In the following passage, the mythical garden came together with economic imperatives: "It must be borne in mind, that a vast amount of rich coffee and sugar land lies wasted and untouched on that island, which would bloom into a garden, under the genial breath of liberal institutions."[92] The passage is reminiscent of Richard Henry Dana's call in *Two Years before the Mast* to bring California under U.S. control: "In the hands of an enterprising people, what a country this might be!"[93] But the difference between Montgomery's "institutions" and Dana's "people" is crucial, for Cuban writers at *La Verdad* saw the needed change not in ethnic terms but in relation to government: U.S. (slaveholding) democracy in exchange for the "perdition" of Spanish colonialism. As this implies, the attacks leveled by *La Verdad* and other papers against Spain overlapped with anti-Spanish sentiments in the United States that could be traced back to Europe and a tradition of anti-Catholicism among Protestants in the Americas.

Spanish Tyrants: The Black Legend in Exile

In 1699, Boston saw the appearance of a curious little pamphlet titled *La Fe del Christiano* (The Christian's faith). This sixteen-page Spanish-language tract included selected quotations from the Bible and statements such as "The Pope of Rome is the Antichrist."[94] Its author was "C. Mathero." Cotton Mather's goals in publishing this pamphlet were stated in the full title: *La Fe del Christiano: En Veyntequatro Articulos de la Institucion de Christo. Embiada a los Españoles, Para que Abran Sus Ojos, y Para Que Se Conviertan de las Tinieblas a la Luz, y de la Potestad de Satanas a Dios: Para Que Reciban por la Fe Que Es en Jesu Christo, Remission de Peccados, y Suerte entre los Sanctificados* (The Christian's faith: In twenty-four articles from Christ's establishment, sent to the Spaniards, that they will open their eyes, and that they will convert from darkness to light, and from the dominion of Satan to God: that they will receive from Faith in Jesus Christ forgiveness for sins and luck among the blessed). As Stanley Williams notes, Mather and Samuel Sewall committed themselves to learning the Spanish language to "bomb" the Caribbean and Mexico with Bibles and other writings that would bring Spanish America out of "darkness."[95] That intellectual commitment, Williams points out, was driven by a deep hatred of Spain's "Catholic tyrannies," economic rivalry, hostility toward English colonies, and legends about the cruelty and craftiness of Spanish conquerors.[96] Mather's pamphlet not only illustrates the long history of anti-Catholicism in North American culture but also highlights the discursive history preceding the Cuban-U.S. expansionist alliance to produce newspapers and pamphlets that blasted Spain for its misdeeds in the Americas. The United States was as propitious a place as any for Cuban exiles to find an audience for their attacks on the "Spanish tyrant."

Perhaps not inadvertently, Cuban exiles engaged in a type of propaganda war against Spain that resonated with the centuries-long dissemination of the "Black Legend" that portrayed Spaniards as fanatically cruel and greedy in their conquest of the Americas. The Legend went back to sixteenth-century Europe, when Spain's enemies made ample use of Bartolomé de Las Casas's *Brevísima Relación de la Destrucción de las Indias* (Brief account of the destruction of the Indies), an inflammatory summation of Spain's treatment of indigenous people. While Las Casas attempted to intervene in debates in Spain about the rights of indigenous people, others picked up his writing to call into question the legitimacy of the Spanish empire. First published in Seville in 1552, the *Relación* appeared five years later in French and Flemish and then was translated throughout Europe into English, German, and Latin.[97] The Black Legend was revived in succeeding centuries, and in the nineteenth-century United States, some of the stereotypes were transferred to Mexicans during the U.S.-Mexican War.[98] As scholars note, the Black Legend in the United States was deployed to create stereotypes and portray people of Latin American descent as evil.[99] As late as 1898, a translation of Las Casas's *Relación* was published in the United States to build opposition to Spain during the Spanish-Cuban-American War.[100] These types of depictions often gave rise to a binary division between Anglo-American and Spanish/Latin American attitudes and predispositions. The Black Legend fed the belief in Anglo-American superiority to other peoples in the Americas that was part of the ideology of Manifest Destiny.[101] Given racial perspectives circulating at the time, the language associated with the Black Legend (cruelty, laziness) was easily transferred to assumptions about the character and race of all Spaniards and Latin Americans.

But Cuban writers did not see themselves as one with Spain or its functionaries in Cuba. All too aware of the social distinctions and political favors granted to Cuba's *peninsulares* (Spaniards on the island), Creoles such as the editors at *La Verdad* were eager to attack Spain. In other words, the exiles did not see the Black Legend as characteristic of Latin America but rather as characteristic of Spain's colonial rulers, who benefited not only from their racial privilege but also from having been born in Spain, a status that granted them access to certain economic benefits. In turn, Cuban writers invoked Las Casas, whose name, wrote Pedro Santacilia, "we will pronounce always with veneration."[102] In his lessons on history, which Santacilia delivered publicly in Manhattan and then published in *La Verdad* and as a book, Santacilia described Cortés, Pizarro, and other conquistadors as having the hearts of hyenas. "They were all alike," Santacilia wrote. "They were all equally cruel, all equally bloody."[103]

In some cases, writers connected the treatment of Cubans on the island to the killing of indigenous populations during the conquest. Miguel T. Tolón's poem, "Al Pan de Matanzas" (To the Pan of Matanzas), published in *La Verdad* on 4 June 1851 and later anthologized in *El Laúd del Desterrado*, envisions the poet scaling the heights of the Pan, a hill in Tolón's native city of Matanzas, and calling out to the surrounding people:

> Sois hombres, y si noble y generoso
> Tenéis un corazón americano
> Y corre indiana sangre en vuestras venas,
> ¡Ved la Patria infeliz! . . .
>   ¡Gime en cadenas
> Esclava vil del opresor hispano!

> [You are men, and if noble and generous
> You have an American heart
> And Indian blood runs through your veins,
> Behold the wretched Motherland! . . .
>   It grieves in chains,
> A debased slave of the Spanish oppressor!][104]

By connecting "Indian blood" genealogically to Cubans, Tolón invoked the flip side of the Black Legend and resorted to a popular trope of Cuban romanticism: the association of the nineteenth-century fight against colonialism with the heroic efforts of indigenous people in previous centuries. Among Cuban writers, José María Heredia, Plácido, and Gertrudis Gómez de Avellaneda had invoked indigenous figures from the conquest to signify resistance to oppression. In an interesting allusion to the indigenous, poet José Jacinto Milanés drew a lineage between the "barbarous" conquest of indigenous people and the status of black slaves in Cuba.[105] Milanés's direct statement about enslaved blacks differed from the more common association between indigenous people and white Creoles.

The association of Spaniards with the Black Legend continued among Cuban exiles long into the nineteenth century, as exemplified in Francisco Sellén's dramatic poem, *Hatuey* (1891). Like Varela in *Jicoténcal*, Sellén presented a heroic indigenous figure killed by Spanish conquerors and, in turn, gave voice to sentiments that echoed the position of many exiled Cubans: "And while the Spaniard rules the isle of Cuba / Hate will be my calling, vengeance my virtue."[106] In *El Laúd del Desterrado*, the poem that most forcefully presents a degraded and decadent Spain is Pedro Santacilia's "A España" (To Spain). Angry and accusatory, the speaker of the poem attempts to situate Spain in a historical trajectory, screaming out that although it had previously "filled the Universe with glory," Spain had been revealed as a malignant nation. Invoking the killing of Moctezuma, Guatimozín, Atahualpa, and other indigenous leaders, the poem holds them aloft as the victims of Spain's presumed iniquity. As such, the poem presents a succinct and lyrical version of the historical vision offered by Santacilia in his *Lecciones Orales*. "A España" rehearses an experience of individual ideological unmasking and establishes a parallel between the poem and a revisionary history that is at the center of Santacilia's work in exile. The poem opens with the speaker remembering how as a young child he heard of the strength, grandiosity, and magnanimity of Spain and, in turn, dreamed of seeing its "fecund soil." But time and maturity eliminated the "prism of deception," and the speaker encountered disenchantment. "¡Palpé la realidad! [I felt reality)," the speaker tells us, comparing his new vision of Spain to the ruins of Rome. The poem concludes with the following inversion of the initial dream of visiting Spain:

Por eso con amargo desencanto
Vi tus ciudades, y estudié tus pueblos,
Y en vez de admiración, sentí en el alma
Un sentimiento, España, de desprecio.

[And thus with bitter disenchantment
I looked upon your cities and towns,
And instead of admiration, I felt in my soul
A sensation, Spain, of contempt.][107]

The goal in this unmasking is no less than to call for revolution. In 1855, Santacilia wrote that salvation from the "despot's insolent whip" had to come from inside the island. Echoing his poem, Santacilia wrote, "It is time to cast aside forever the mendacious illusion of the past."[108]

Supporters of Spain in the United States responded strongly to the attacks from Cuban exiles. Not long after *La Verdad* began publishing in New York, the city saw the appearance of *La Crónica* (The chronicle) (New York, 1848–67), a pro-Spain paper that attacked annexation, filibusters, and Narciso López. *La Crónica*'s contemptuous tone prompted a flurry of exchanges. Reported in both English- and Spanish-language publications to be an organ funded by Spain, *La Crónica* critiqued U.S. expansionism and glorified Spain. When López's May 1850 expedition failed, *La Crónica* opened its account quoting a Havana newspaper that proclaimed, "Viva la Reina!—Primera victoria sobre los piratas [Long live the queen!—First victory over the pirates]."[109] Positioning itself as a paper for and of people of Spanish descent, with a circulation that spread to Cuba, Puerto Rico, and Mexico, *La Crónica* reported news from throughout Latin America and kept a watch on U.S. congressional events of importance to the region. On its masthead, *La Crónica* featured the phrase, "España y los pueblos hispanoamericanos [Spain and Hispanoamerican peoples]," thus positing a unity between Spain and Latin American countries. The promotion of unity among "Hispanoamericanos" privileged the mother country in its vision of a Spanish American subject.

The battle between *La Verdad* and *La Crónica* clarifies how newspaper print culture and the attendant battles over territory promoted the development of identities, either of a Hispanic subject with a connection to Latin America and Spain or of a Cuban national subject. *La Crónica*'s pro-Spain position was clearly entangled with the geopolitical battle for control of the hemisphere. In a sarcastic tone, the paper attacked "young adventurers" and "greedy politicians" from the United States as well as newspapers that it saw as appealing to a U.S. national greed for new territories. Calling into question the Cuban exile fili-bustering project because of its links to the United States, *La Crónica* wrote, "Certain Cubans who are disaffected or speculators, and who for the most part reside in this country and are good patriots only after leaving their own [country], have united with certain American specu-lators and European refugees to establish what they call a provisional government, and to hire contractors and enlist troops and officials in the name of the people or the imaginary republic of Cuba."[110] The passage simultaneously is skeptical about exiles' claim to represent the Cuban people and about the claim that Cuba can be its own republic. Instead, *La Crónica* sought to bring legitimacy to Spanish colonialism. Accordingly, the newspaper's notion of "Hispanoamericano" stemmed from the belief that "no nation in the world has peopled with its sons, governed with its laws and defended with its blood such magnificent provinces as Cuba, Puerto Rico, and the Philippines."[111] Cuba and the other territories were framed as provinces of Spain. The economic context for the pro-Spanish position becomes clear when *La Crónica* calls for a regular shipping line between Spain and "tropical America" to compete against "the United States, which has taken possession of the principal arteries of navigation in the New World."[112]

Another paper that promoted Hispanoamerican unity in contrast to the Cuban support of filibustering was *La Patria* (Our country) (1846–51), published in New Orleans. Calling itself the "Organo de la pobla-ción española de los Estados Unidos [Organ of the Spanish population of the United States]," (*La Patria* opposed the U.S. war on Mexico and U.S. expansionist designs on Cuba.[113] The level of hostility between Cuban exiles and *La Patria* is evident in an exchange from May 1850. *La Patria* had published an article ridiculing Miguel T. Tolón's wife, Emilia Teurbe Tolón, by announcing that the "marchioness de Toulon" had arrived in New York to join her husband and calling into question news reports that she had been forced into exile by authorities in Cuba. *La Patria* accused newspapers of inventing the expulsion of Emilia Teurbe Tolón to rally readers against the island's government. Miguel T. Tolón responded by publishing a copy of the order of exile and attacking Spain for its "ridiculous" actions in expelling someone who had done nothing except exchange letters with her husband. Tolón also clarified that he and his wife had no use for monarchial titles from an "enthroned tyranny."[114]

The political platforms supported by *La Verdad*, *La Crónica*, and *La Patria* show the tortured alliances that emerged in the mid–nineteenth century. Cubans trying to dethrone Spanish colonialism lined up behind U.S. expansionism, while proponents of *Hispanoamericanismo* opposed to U.S. expansionism embraced the colonial rule of a decaying monarchial empire. Were writers able to pull out of the ideological weight of dominant discourses such as the Black Legend and Manifest Destiny to come up with new political programs? As the 1850s progressed, the annexationist program of *La Verdad* lost support among Cuban exiles. By 1854, newspapers published by Cubans were challenging one another.

Voices of Independence: Paper Wars

Eventually, annexation became the platform preferred by wealthy exiles but not by liberal patriotic writers who had originally signed on to that program out of what they viewed as a historical necessity.[115] Writers began by inserting subtle critiques of the United States and annexation. *El Filibustero*, for example, published in both English and Spanish the following lines from Lord Byron's poem "The Isles of Greece":

Trust not for freedom to the Franks—
They have a king who buys and sells;
In native swords and native ranks
The only hope of freedom dwells.

The insinuation would have been clear to readers: "Franks" could be read as a reference to Spain as well as to the United States, with "buys and sells" a critique of U.S. efforts to purchase Cuba from Spain.[116] The point was that Cuba would have to rely on its native fighters to gain "freedom," an apparent substitution for the word "courage," which appears in other versions of the poem.

Distancing themselves from the annexationist exiles in New York, newspapers increasingly used the word "independence." That was the case for Villaverde and his newspaper, *El Independiente*. After editing *La*

Verdad for several months in 1852, Villaverde broke with the New York group that funded the paper and went to New Orleans to establish *El Independiente*. Coedited by Manuel Antonio Mariño, *El Independiente* sought to be the free voice "not of a party, but of an entire people." In their prospectus, Villaverde and Mariño noted several reasons for establishing their own publication. First and foremost, they argued that *La Verdad* was subjected to the "inspection and censorship" of the Cuban Junta in New York. They viewed Miguel T. Tolón's *El Cubano* as putting forth positions that were almost identical to those of the junta. Consequently, Villaverde and Mariño set out to intervene with a unique voice, seeking to draw readers from the "immense number of immigrants not just from Cuba but from all the republics of South America who reside in these states for a more or less lengthy period" and from nonimmigrants conversant with Spanish.[117] One major point of departure from *La Verdad* was the call for armed revolution in Cuba as opposed to "conspiracy," which connoted both U.S.-based filibustering efforts and annexationist plotting. That call to arms reflected Villaverde's growing radicalization in the wake of López's death. But as I discuss in more detail in chapter 5, it also marked a point in the development of Villaverde's critical position toward the United States.

To understand Villaverde's call for independence, we need to consider the evolution of the Cuban exile leadership and its relationship to López's filibustering expeditions. Annexation had been supported first by the Cuban Council of New York, a group founded in 1847 that brought together Cuban planters and critics of colonialism.[118] The planters, who controlled the purse strings at *La Verdad*, had a vexed relationship with López, for whom Villaverde had served as secretary. Some planters envisioned a scenario in which someone other than López would lead filibustering expeditions, so López released a statement in 1849 announcing the establishment of another group, the Junta Promovedora de los Intereses Políticos de Cuba, which proclaimed López the head of efforts to liberate Cuba.[119] After López's death, exiles held elections for representatives to a Cuban Junta that sought to represent exiles as well as Cubans on the island. In one contentious meeting, exiles debated whether fellow Cubans living in the United States but outside of New York City should be allowed to vote by mail on matters before the junta. Villaverde spoke strongly in favor of mail-in ballots, but the proposal was voted down. Villaverde and others then stormed out of the meeting.[120] This incident exemplified Villaverde's efforts to build a coalition with a broader base and thus dilute the power of the New York leadership. Villaverde presumably left or was pushed out of his role as editor of *La Verdad* because he believed too much power was concentrated in the New York junta and instead wanted to call for a revolution that would bring independence to Cuba.

El Independiente appeared as a four-page paper with an editorial office at 85 St. Peter Street in New Orleans. The first three pages were in Spanish, while the fourth was in English, with a separate English-language masthead reading "The Independent." *El Independiente* was alarmed by plans for the purchase of Cuba from Spain, either by Washington or by wealthy exiles, and overtly lamented the possibility that the people of Cuba would not have a voice in their future. The worst-case scenario, the newspaper argued, would be to turn the Cuba question over to diplomats and statesmen who would ferry notes back and forth from one capital to another.[121] In the English section, the paper made clear its position: "We believe that Cuba can yet gain her independence by force of arms, the only resource left to downtrodden people, the only one which, through a process of purification, can adequately prepare them to pass from illimited despotism to absolute freedom by purging them of many evils which otherwise would lurk in the body politic, and the only one which, by enabling them to count the cost, will lead them properly to value and to keep intact the sacred boon of liberty."[122] By these terms, revolution would provide a pedagogical function, instructing citizens on how to sacrifice themselves for participation in a republic.

With its concern about the people of Cuba, *El Independiente* explicitly called for an alternative version of the "truth" offered by *La Verdad*. By putting the idea of "truth" under surveillance, Villaverde and Mariño disrupted the opposition between a Cuba-based censored press and New York–based *La Verdad* and thus called for a variety of perspectives within the exile theater of operations. Liberal in its vision of a new society, *El Independiente* argued that a newspaper should inform its readers without loyalty to a particular party. The "simple and naked" truth, according to Villaverde and Mariño, was that a revolution was necessary but difficult. Never one to back down from a polemical stance, Villaverde called for "the truth" about members of the junta, charging that they were planning to take control of "public destiny of the country." But exerting such independence had its price, and *El Independiente* appears to have had a relatively short run.[123]

Between 1854 and 1856, newspapers broke openly with annexation and its tacit acceptance of slavery in a post-Spanish Cuba. The harshest criticism was splattered all over the pages of a newspaper that issued a biting class-based critique of the New York Cuban Junta. *El Pueblo* began appearing on 19 June 1855 and called for new leadership from "men of the people without aristocratic and oligarchic tendencies and who do not aspire to monopolize glory and are not avid about riches."[124] Contrasting the "aristocracy" and "monopoly" with "the people," *El Pueblo* charged that the Cuban Junta had mismanaged the revolution. The event most directly tied to the publication of *El Pueblo* was the aborted mission of John Quitman, who had been enlisted by the New York junta to lead a filibustering expedition that included exiled Cubans waiting to take up arms. The editor of *El Pueblo*, Francisco Agüero Estrada, emphasized that he had been ready for the battlefield. Agüero argued that impoverished exiles had suffered from hunger in the United States "waiting for the day they could march on Cuba with arms in hand."[125] But their hope had evaporated, he charged, because the Cuban Junta had not completed its mission. For Agüero Estrada, who went into exile after taking part in a revolt in Cuba, the junta had failed because it attempted to control Quitman's expedition rather than promoting an island-based, far-reaching revolutionary effort that might challenge the interests of the landed elite.

El Pueblo called attention not only to class differences in the exile community but also to changes in New York's Cuban population. As the 1850s wore on, more and more impoverished exiles arrived in the city. They became wary of a leadership that saw the United States as the savior of the Cuban cause. In an explosive article, "Errores de la Revolución Cubana" (Errors of the Cuban revolution), *El Pueblo* shot down annexation as a viable option, arguing that only by putting on blinders to the U.S. political arena could Cubans have believed that the U.S. government would follow through on annexation. In a trenchant analysis, the newspaper emphasized sectional differences between the North and South, arguing that it was unlikely that the two would come together to act decisively on Cuba. *El Pueblo* went on: "We have never believed that the United States is where we should work for the liberty of our motherland: this was not the best place to establish a base of support for our revolutionary program. In regard to annexation, we have never been persuaded that this evil is necessary."[126] The point was clear: the revolution should be organized and fought in Cuba. If anyone had the ethos for such a claim, it was Agüero Estrada, who had attempted such a fight before exile and in the process lost his brother, Joaquin, whom exiles in New York considered a martyr. Three years after the publication of *El Pueblo*, even *La Verdad* became more critical of the United States. In a reversal of its pro-U.S. position, *La Verdad* blasted the country for trying to take "ownership" of the Americas. The paper published a front-page article arguing that Cubans should accept that the liberation of the island as "our matter, exclusively ours, and the resolution should be ours."[127]

El Pueblo went one step further. Agüero Estrada called for blacks to be included in the revolutionary program: "One of the capital errors of those who have so far directed our revolution has been to attempt to exclude a large class of the Cuban people."[128] He accused López of cutting out blacks to gain the support of the U.S. South and called racial exclusion "antirevolutionary." "Justice is equality," Agüero wrote, "and equality is the basis of democratic institutions."[129] Agüero Estrada subsequently took his antislavery views across town to the pages of *El Mulato*, as I discuss in chapter 4. These pronouncements point to the evolution in the political thought of exiled Cubans, as Gerald Poyo notes.[130] But more to the point here, such statements show the extent to which writers were willing to challenge the party line of the Cuban Junta in their newspapers. Agüero Estrada was taking on the exile establishment, and the result was the quick end of *El Pueblo*. From the start, the paper's financial footing was shaky. The opening issue stated that a wealthy Cuban had agreed to fund the circulation of the first issue but that the paper needed other sources of money or subscriptions to keep going. "If patriots do not come to its help, the paper will die," a note to readers said.[131] And die it did after four issues.

The short life of *El Pueblo* showed the extent to which the transnational print culture of these newspapers was at the mercy of subscribers. *El Independiente* sent out its first three issues for free, hoping to drum up subscribers. "Should you plan to subscribe, we will take the liberty of informing you that the subscription most convenient to us is the quarterly one," Villaverde wrote to readers in English.[132] The basic economics of paying for printing had as much effect on these newspapers as did the political conditions that gave rise to filibustering and annexation. The economics of publishing affected other Spanish-language publications in the 1800s. A. Gabriel Meléndez argues in his study of the periodical press in New Mexico that during the middle decades of the century, printing and publishing "were activities characterized by scarcity and disjuncture."[133] Despite the short run of papers such as *El Independiente* and *El Pueblo*, these publications broke new ground by putting annexation in check and bringing forth the issue of class as a dominant concern for the revolution to come in Cuba. In some ways, *El Pueblo*'s radical position resulted from republican language coming back to claim its due. How many times could newspapers throw around words like "equality" and "independence" before someone would attempt to uphold the *filibusteros'* ideals?

Packages of Truth: Breaks in Circulation

More than a decade would pass before the patriotic sentiments expressed by the *filibusteros* developed into a full-fledged revolutionary movement that challenged Spanish forces. In the 1850s, writers were unable to bridge the disjunction between their conceptions of Cuba's future and conditions on the island. In effect, writers created a community in exile and published texts that expressed patriotic sentiments, but these efforts did not amount to changes on the island. This disjunction is evident in the introduction to the poetry anthology *El Laúd del Desterrado*, published in New York. "In this collection we do not include any names that are not well known in the republic of Cuban letters," José Elías Hernández wrote.[134] The book called attention to the reality that writers of the republic were unable to claim their place in Cuba, instead existing within a U.S.-Cuban discursive space. Cuba remained just that, a republic of letters fashioned in part through a U.S.-based print culture, but that status did not translate in the 1850s to a nation-state.

One reason for *filibusteros'* failure to rally significant support for their cause was that transnational writing was based on a division in readership between Cuba and the United States. While U.S. revolutionary writers such as Paine, whom the *filibusteros* admired, had worked within a certain geographic context, an ocean divided Cuban exiles from their readers. As such, circulation was a problem. Steamers that traveled regularly from U.S. cities to Havana transported issues and news reports from one country to another. Smuggled newspapers took on the function of clandestine letters, with papers sometimes printing communications addressed to people on the island. "We gratefully accept your offer to be a correspondent," one note in *El Cometa* said, addressing "Atayala de Atarés," the pen name of someone in Cuba.[135] (Atarés was a reference to the castle where filibusters had been executed in 1851.) Spanish authorities in Cuba banned *La Verdad* early in its run. The newspaper had to be smuggled from the United States into Cuba aboard ships, including some vessels subsidized by the U.S. government as part of the United States Mail Steamship Company. Spanish authorities searched ships regularly to see if they contained bundles of the newspaper, which smugglers referred to as "packages of truth." As an indication of the newspaper's influence, authorities in Cuba arrested a U.S. ship captain and charged him with treason for smuggling *La Verdad*, creating an international incident that drew the attention of Secretary of State James Buchanan.[136] In part because of the repression of Spanish authorities, newspapers published in exile became notorious and helped foster a sense both in U.S. cities and on the island that filibustering expeditions were about to strike a blow.

It is difficult to gauge how widely *La Verdad* and other newspapers circulated in Cuba. The quick rise and fall of so many papers shows the financial difficulties faced by *pobres desterrados* (poor exiles). The hopes of New York–based writers apparently were at odds with the facts on the ground. Tolón summed up the beliefs of the staff at *La Verdad* in a column commemorating the newspaper's fourth anniversary:

> *La Verdad* difundía en el pueblo las doctrinas liberales;
> preparaba a las masas para el momento de la acción; y al mismo
> tiempo, dando a conocer al mundo entero los horrores de nuestra
> situación política, despertaba en Europa, en América, y particular-
> mente en los Estados Unidos las más vivas simpatías a favor de
> la causa de nuestra Libertad.

> [*La Verdad* spread liberal doctrines among the [Cuban] people,
> preparing the masses for the call to action; at the same time, we
> informed the world of the horrors of our political situation and
> awakened in Europe and in America, and particularly in the
> United States, vibrant sympathy for the cause of our Liberty.][137]

Tolón probably based his analysis on notes from readers on the island, such as one who wrote to the paper, "I have received the latest issues of *La Verdad*, which have been read and reread by interested parties and sent out to public and general circulation."[138] But this intention of circulating papers and drumming up support for filibustering and/or annexation did not materialize on the scale needed for a successful overthrow of Spanish authorities.

By 1855, it became increasingly apparent that *filibustero* writers were failing in their efforts to persuade readers in Cuba to rise up against the government. "Events prove that the inhabitants [of Cuba] as of today have not wanted revolution," said one article in *El Pueblo*. "Those of us who desire it should not delude ourselves: this is one truth."[139] *El Pueblo* stated outright what writers had feared all along: that a published text could not do the work of a soldier. That is one reason why even as *La Verdad* and *El Filibustero* promoted the idea that newspapers constituted a crucial component of efforts to oust Spain from Cuba, writers also grew to venerate the *filibustero* as a military man. In the next chapter, I examine writers' anxieties about the relationship between publication and military action and how they connected revolution to the promotion of a masculine Cuban subject.

Men of Action

REVOLUTIONARY MASCULINITY AND WOMEN WRITERS

In a poem delivered before a gathering of Cuban exiles at 600 Broadway in New York on 1 September 1853, Fernando Rodríguez, an intermittent contributor to transnational newspapers and proprietor of a commercial exchange house, invoked the blood of *filibusteros* as a seed for future military attacks:

> ¡Oh! ¡No importa por Dios! Que los tiranos
> Hagan rodar al suelo una cabeza,
> Si la sangre que corre fertiliza
> El terreno sagrado
> Donde la libertad, hondas raíces / tiene.

> [Oh, by God! It is not important that tyrants
> Roll a head on the ground
> If the blood that runs fertilizes
> The sacred soil
> Where liberty has deep roots.][1]

Rodríguez was commemorating the second anniversary of the execution of Narciso López, the general who had led the Cuba filibustering expeditions of 1850 and 1851. The ceremony, which included speeches by Juan Clemente Zenea and Miguel T. Tolón, was not only solemn but also lavish. An ostentatious display at the back of the hall featured an urn engraved with López's name in golden letters. Above it hung the U.S. flag and the tricolor banner that would go on to become the flag of Cuba. No one would have believed, the newspaper *El Filibustero* reported, that it was a gathering of impoverished exiles.[2]

Rodríguez's poem sheds light on how exiles came to emphasize a connection between militarism and masculinity in the years following López's death. Rodríguez opens by invoking the "Venerated shadows /

Of the heroes of Cuba"—both López's troops and the men from the United States who had fought by his side. More militant than lyrical, the poem asks the heroes to forgive the poet's impotence and his impudence in disturbing their rest. He draws a distinction between exiles on a "foreign shore" and the "valiant and generous citizens" killed with López. Referring to López as the "Illustrious father / Of Cuba's future liberty," Rodríguez turns the dead general into a model revolutionary and founding patriarch of an island that would be liberated in the future.

Most of the participants in the newspaper culture that emerged in the 1850s were men. A gendered sense of the revolutionary fighter was evident in Cirilo Villaverde's invoking of "el hombre de acción [the man of action]" to describe soldiers and activists committed to changing Cuba's governmental structure. Writers associated the new man of Cuba with masculinity and militarism in part to compensate for anxieties about the writers' efficacy to bring about change. As I show in this chapter, writers agonized over the difference between pen and sword and settled on the figure of López to craft a vision of the Cuban revolutionary fighter. This influenced the way writers responded to women and to Cuba, which was figured in poetry and prose as feminine and passive (sometimes defiled by the Spanish tyrant). What was lacking in the papers was the active woman writer. *Filibustero* newspapers published texts by Cuba's women writers only rarely, despite the acclaim enjoyed by Gertrudis Gómez de Avellaneda, Luisa and Julia Pérez, Mercedes Valdés Mendoza, and others. Not until later in the nineteenth century did women became important writers in the theater of U.S.-Cuban letters. I conclude the chapter by discussing the work of one such woman, Emilia Casanova de Villaverde, who was inspired by the *filibustero* López on his first expedition and later became one of the leading voices of Cuban independence in exile. But I begin by discussing why among men in the 1850s, military organizing commanded more respect than writing.

Anxious Compatriots: Letters and/as Arms

Throughout the nineteenth century, Latin American revolutionaries, among them José Martí, Simón Bolívar, and Argentinean president and novelist Domingo F. Sarmiento, grappled with a perceived opposition between intellectual work and military action. Martí, for one, wrote of the "abhorrence that I hold for words that are not accompanied by acts" and ultimately gave his life on the battlefield.[3] Writer-revolutionaries would surely have been aware of the distinction made by Don Quixote in his discussion of "arms and letters": "Now to attain eminence in the learned professions costs a man time, nights of study, hunger, nakedness, headaches, indigestion, and other such things, some of which I have mentioned already. But to reach the point of being a good soldier requires all that it requires to be a student, but to so much greater a degree that there is no comparison; for the soldier is in peril of losing his life at every step."[4] Cervantes's passage establishes a hierarchy in which arms demand more than letters, the difference being the threat of death. Some Cuban exiles might have agreed with Cervantes as they considered the execution of López. But in 1852, they also had before them the case of Eduardo Facciolo, who was executed for printing a revolutionary paper in Cuba. *La Verdad* used the language of martyrdom to describe Facciolo's sacrifice: "the martyr's death with serenity and calm on the infamous gallows has sealed the truth and justice of the political principles that he held in life."[5]

Julio Ramos argues that Martí's envy for those on the battlefield leads to "the constitution of a new kind of intellectual as subject," a poet-soldier who insists that literature is part of social practice, even in the face of a growing late-nineteenth-century belief in the aesthetic as autonomous from the political. Through this conception of the poet as soldier, Martí elaborates the meaning of justice behind war's violence.[6] Like much in Martí's work, a thread runs back to writers from the 1850s whose poems offer not only in their content but also in their appearance an example of how the (literary) pen can mediate military attack. In Miguel T. Tolón's "La Pluma y la Espada: Fantasía" (Pen and sword: A fantasy), a poetic dialogue recounts a contest between a pen sitting on an inkwell and a sword hanging on a nearby wall. With the speaker on the edge of sleep and entering into a romantic state of dreamlike contemplation of the beautiful soil of Cuba, the pen lobs the first salvo by claiming to prepare the military struggle. The sword replies,

¿Qué valieran tus consejos?
Tus rasgos, ¿qué aprovecharan
si en el campo no brillaran
de mi acero los reflejos?

[What value would your counsel possess?
Your strokes, what would they accomplish
if on the field, the reflection
of my steel did not shine?][7]

The poem draws a distinction between "here" (the United States) and "there" (Cuba), with the pen working in the former and the sword acting in the latter. The *aquí* (pen) and *allá* (sword) will resurface in the prologue to the 1882 *Cecilia Valdés o La Loma del Angel*, when Villaverde claims that during the Ten Years' War, writers in the United States worked simultaneously with fighters in Cuba: "Here they deployed pen and word at least with as much vehemence as they did there the rifle and machete."[8] In response to the battle of pen and sword, Tolón echoes the Cervantine tendency to privilege arms when the speaker proclaims,

La Espada por el viento remecida
Chocó en el muro, y desperté a su son:
Por el viento también voló impelida
Levemente la Pluma hasta un rincón.
    Juzgué claro el augurio y verdadero:
Dejé rodar la péñola olvidada,
Y exclamé, descolgando el limpio acero:
"Te dejo, Pluma, por ceñirte Espada."

[The Sword, rocked by the wind,
Knocked into the wall, and I awoke to its sound:
Thrown by the wind, the Pen also flew
Landing lightly in a corner.
    I judged the augury clear and true:
I let the forgotten pen roll,
And exclaimed, taking down the clean steel:
"I leave you, Pen, to gird you, Sword."]

Thus, a poem that begins with a state of romantic contemplation ends with the speaker on his feet, no longer alone but claiming the sword as a companion. The irony is that Tolón, like most of the *filibustero* writers, never took to the battlefield. Instead, he contributed his interpretative faculty, for it is only in reading the wind's metaphorical "augury" in favor of arms that the soldier-reader can take up the cause.

Tolón's emphasis on arms was in keeping with one of the writers he greatly admired, Tom Paine. "By referring the matter from argument to arms, a new era for politics is struck; a new method of thinking hath arisen," Paine wrote in *Common Sense* to justify the North American colonies' war against England.[9] Paine's pamphlet opens with words that Tolón picks up in his writing. "Volumes have been written on the subject of the struggle between England and America," Paine wrote, adding that those debates have been ineffectual. "Arms, as the last resource, decide the contest; the appeal was the choice of the king, and the continent hath accepted the challenge."[10] *Filibustero* writers learned a similar lesson after López's death, which led exiled activist writers to conclude that only arms would bring about changes in Cuba.

In the wake of López's execution, Cirilo Villaverde issued an explicit argument for the primacy of military act over word. A man of action should be ready for the battlefield, Villaverde argued, with "action" signifying military attack and the organization of such. In a series of articles in *La Verdad*, Villaverde explained that armed attack was the man of action's primary (pre)occupation. Writers should not reach for personal literary greatness, Villaverde argued, but should deploy their texts only in support of and in conjunction with the taking up of arms.[11] As such, he developed a sense of the revolutionary intellectual whose work is embedded in armed struggle—an idea with which, as I discuss in chapter 5, Villaverde struggled throughout his life in the United States.

Villaverde's invoking of "man" to motivate action was in keeping with nineteenth-century intellectual efforts to venerate men committed to the Cuban nation. In her insightful study of Cuban biography as nation formation, Agnes Lugo-Ortiz shows how a notion of *el hombre útil*, which can be translated as "useful" as well as "able," emerged in texts by Cubans from Antonio Bachiller y Morales's *Galería de Hombres Útiles* (Gallery of able men) to Martí's writings in the newspaper *Patria*. Unlike Villaverde's man of action, *el hombre útil* is not necessarily tied to military attack but is an image that allows for the imitation of a national subject who can work for Cuba in a variety of ways, including the economic improvement of the country, and thus pay a debt to the motherland, the nation to be.[12] In the case of the man of action, the debt owed to the nation is no less than the man's life. Writers negotiated such a commitment by conceiving of themselves as having sacrificed their lives, metaphorically speaking, by going into exile and publishing transnational newspapers.

Villaverde's argument about the man of action emerged in a series of articles that lambasted essayist and historian José Antonio Saco. In keeping with the multiethnic context of New York, where the articles were written and published, Villaverde opens his analysis by discussing the work of Irish leader Daniel O'Connell (1775–1846), a renowned orator who argued forcefully in the British Parliament for Irish home rule and led a series of demonstrations for Catholic emancipation. Villaverde's choice of O'Connell to open an article about Cuban affairs calls to mind the large number of immigrants from Ireland arriving in New York in the wake of the potato famine of the 1840s. Known as the "great migration," the arrival of the Irish transformed the city's politics and neighborhoods.[13] Villaverde likely drew a parallel between Ireland's colonial status and Cuba's situation; thus, he asserted that O'Connell's efforts failed to liberate Ireland because of a lack of military power, a point echoed by some recent historical evaluations of O'Connell.[14] According to Villaverde, O'Connell relied extensively on "words" by seeking to bring about change through public speaking rather than a military option. Villaverde chastised "el gran O'Connell" for not having found "a more effective approach than public mass meetings and long interminable speeches." The charge was issued in a beautiful turn of Spanglish: "medio más expedito ni eficaz que el de los públicos mass meetings y los largos, interminables speeches."[15]

By turning to O'Connell, Villaverde distinguished between the use of language for political purposes and other physical acts necessary to throw off oppressive regimes. In other words, O'Connell failed in his political aims because he was a "man of the word" and not "a man of action." The opposition between "word" and "action" unraveled in Villaverde's articles, as we will see shortly, but he used the difference between the two to critique what he viewed as intellectual arrogance, the use of words and nothing else in attempting to bring about political change. For a writer/activist to rely exclusively on language, according to Villaverde, amounted to "literary vanity." Villaverde said he did not want to offend the memory of O'Connell but found it necessary to point out that the "illustrious" Irish leader's patriotism was tainted by literary vanity.

That kind of opposition was common in *filibustero* circles. Ambrosio

José Gonzales, who was wounded in the filibustering expedition of 1850, described himself in a letter as "a man of action and not of words."[16] Gonzales, who moved in the *filibusteros'* inner circles, probably had read the Villaverde articles on Saco. A lifelong soldier, Gonzales went on to become a colonel in the Confederate forces and lived his later life as a dedicated veteran of two lost causes. Educated in the United States and fluent in English, Gonzales was the author of a notable proannexation pamphlet, *Manifesto on Cuban Affairs Addressed to the People of the United States* (1853), which he issued after López's death as a call for ongoing U.S. support of a Cuban revolution "replanted upon its native soil."[17] While most of the tract retraces recent events leading to the López expeditions, Gonzales provides a glimpse into his anxieties as a "man of action." Discussing why he had not joined López on the fatal final expedition, Gonzales explains that he was still recuperating from injuries and from exhaustion after having continued to rally support for López. "I found it necessary to recruit my health," he wrote, explaining further, "I was unequal to the duties of an active summer campaign."[18] According to Gonzales's account, López had encouraged Gonzales to rest and follow up with an attack force of 1,500 to 2,000 men. Gonzales quotes López in Spanish only: " 'Cúrese V. con esmero,' said he, in his last letter to me; 'para que vaya a apoyar a su amigo de corazón' [Take good care of yourself so you can go and support your genuine friend]." Absent at López's final hour, Gonzales found himself fielding criticism about his dedication to military action: "I have thus entered into details somewhat personal to me, from the necessity of answering the malignant insinuations of some of the friends of Spain in this country, who wondered, and perhaps regretted, that I and other Cubans were not included in the massacre of August and September 1st."[19] The "massacre" is a reference to the execution of the filibusters and López. Gonzales finds it necessary to validate his honor by claiming to be "the first Cuban who has ever bled in battle in the assertion of his country's rights," an exaggeration unless "battle" is read as a synonym for "filibustering."[20]

The issue of military commitment cannot be divorced from masculine self-definition either in the Gonzales pamphlet or in the Villaverde articles about the man of action. Masculinity is an important dimension of Villaverde's attack on Saco, and I will review that exchange to provide a new perspective on a polemic that has prompted previous evaluation in Cuban historical studies. Villaverde denounced Saco because the latter had published pamphlets opposing Cuba's annexation by the United States. One of Cuba's most prominent intellectual voices in the period, Saco challenged filibustering out of a belief that annexation would strengthen the United States as an expansionist power and lead to the elimination of Cuban nationality as Anglo-American populations took residence in Cuba. Coming from Saco, whose ethos as a writer and thinker stemmed in part from his battles against the Spanish colonial government, this argument was devastating. In 1832, Saco had published an article in the Cuban magazine *Revista Bimestre Cubana* in which he called for an end to the slave trade and urged landowners to compare the cost and benefits of wage labor to slave labor by running the two side by side on their plantations. Proposing a system of tenant farming, Saco wrote, "Would it be possible to distribute all or part of the land of the sugar plantation among free men, who, committing themselves to growing cane, would be given a specific portion of the sugar produced?"[21] Although Saco did not call for abolition, the article infuriated some members of Cuba's elite, who convinced the newly arrived governor, Captain-General Miguel Tacón, to expatriate Saco. The case came to represent the colonial repression of writers and Tacón's heavy-handed rule.

Putting forth positions against U.S. expansionism, Saco's antiannexation writings attacked the U.S. "march of territorial expansion" from the purchase of Florida and Louisiana to the "infamous" seizure of Texas. Saco used the word "iniquity" to describe the U.S. attack on Mexico and the subsequent war. Given this trajectory, Saco argued, U.S. support of filibustering expeditions to Cuba was another example of "the criminal ambition of a runaway democracy." Saco's argument went straight to the questionable alliances of Cuban annexationists: "Two principal motives compel a part of the American public to support the acquisition of Cuba: a desire for expansion, and the interests of slavery."[22] For Saco, annexation would serve the U.S. South, which sought to strengthen its influence in the Union with the entrance of Cuba as a slaveholding state.

Filibustero writers, some of whom were Saco's friends, responded with various counterpunches.[23] For seven issues in *La Verdad*, Villaverde was unrelenting in his attacks, calling Saco in effect a hypocrite, an apostate, and a sophist—"a man completely lost for Cuba." Villaverde invoked the language of military attack to belittle Saco as a man of too many words, "a man of the pen and not of action."[24] The exchange has become notorious, as Doris Sommer notes, among critics in Cuba who have positioned Saco as the more politically mature and astute of the two men.[25] Villaverde's annexationist position and tacit approval of slavery in a post-Spain Cuba embarrasses some critics and even leads to a sense that Saco got the better of Villaverde. Such evaluations accept the wrestling-match aspect of the debate (inherent in Villaverde's language) without considering fully the doses of testosterone circulating in this debate. Read against the recent death of López, Villaverde's argument in part concerns the definition of masculine strength at this period in Cuban and U.S. histories. For Villaverde, arms make more of a man than words; thus, he venerates the *hombre* who dies on the battlefield.[26] Villaverde's use of "vanity" feminizes Saco, and by invoking the personal lives of Saco and López, Villaverde brings to the forefront the full sense of masculine competition.

Saco had met López's wife, María de los Dolores de Frías, in Cuba, and many people in exile circles believed that Saco had fallen in love with her. Invoking that curious triangle, Villaverde argued that Saco's jealousy of López and "wounded pride" prompted Saco to oppose the López expeditions. In other words, Villaverde proposed that Saco hated the cause because its leader was López.[27] If we consider the romantic dimensions of the debate, it is necessary to note that Saco would go on to marry the widowed Frías in 1856. But regardless of the merits of his accusations, Villaverde distinguished between revolutionary men and Saco, who had chosen to settle in Europe and work with Spain to bring about reform in Cuba. Arguing against annexation, Saco called on Spain to institute liberal and democratic policies on the island "to ensure without armies or squadrons a tranquil and endurable possession of the queen of the Antilles."[28] Such pronouncements played right into New York's newspaper wars. Villaverde was livid that Saco fed the presses of *La Verdad*'s crosstown nemesis, *La Crónica*, which reprinted Saco's pamphlet against annexation. *La Crónica* praised Saco for presenting "incontrovertible evidence that a rupture of the bonds that unite Cuba with its ancient metropolis, no matter how that is accomplished, would lead immediately and undoubtedly to the total ruin of that precious antille."[29]

Villaverde's equation of masculinity with military attack is in keeping with currents in U.S. society in the years after the U.S.-Mexican War; the notion that a man could define himself in and through military adventure fueled filibustering expeditions. As Robert May shows, young men of various classes were attracted to filibustering forays into Cuba, Nicaragua, and Mexico, sometimes as a romantic alternative to service in the U.S. Army.[30] In addition, *filibustero* writers saw themselves working in the tradition of 1848 republican revolutionaries in Europe. When Hungary's revolutionary fighter Louis Kossuth arrived in New York, Cubans met with him and delivered a laudatory statement: "Honor us, illustrious Kossuth, honor us in accepting the testimony of admiration, friendship, and benevolence which we have the honor of offering in the name of all Cuban patriots."[31] Thus, twin militaristic strains—one from U.S. culture and the other from Europe—fed a growing sense among *filibustero* writers that war and the work of men of action would be needed to end colonialism in Cuba. For writers, the fighter who came to embody this goal was López.

General Martyr: The López Poems

"To the Poets and Prose Writers of Cuba," said a small, boldface headline in *La Verdad*. "Having received various excellent compositions both in verse and prose dedicated to the memory of General Narciso López, martyr of Cuba's Liberty, we have decided to bring them to light in a book that will be titled *Corona Fúnebre* [Funeral wreath], in honor of the hero whose apotheosis is not far behind us."[32] The paper asked for more submissions to a forthcoming collection of tributes to the recently deceased leader. If the book was ever published, it does not appear to have survived the passing of time.[33] But poems that monumentalized López as a founder of Cuban liberty appeared in *La Verdad* and other papers. Poetic tributes included Juan Clemente Zenea's "Diez y Seis de Agosto de 1851 en la Habana" and "En el Aniversario del General López," Miguel Tolón's "En la Muerte de Narciso López," and Leopoldo Turla's "A Narciso López," all four of which were published originally in *El Filibustero* and *La Verdad* and then collected in *El Laúd del Desterrado*.[34] *La Verdad* even reprinted "Adieu, Dear Cuba," an English-language piece from *Gleason's Pictorial Drawing Room Companion*:

Rouse, rouse thee, Cuba!
  Fairest land of earth;
Shake off thy shackles, sweetest Isle
  Of my adopted birth![35]

Other poems were not directly about López but were about and written to soldiers who fought at his side; one poem even addressed López's executioner.[36] All of these works positioned López as a model for a future revolution.

I call these verses the López poems. They are militaristic, bloody, and angry, and they share a defiant call for sending more troops to Cuba after López's death. Varying in form from sonnets to elegies of more than a hundred lines, the López poems envision a future when the *filibustero*'s death will feed symbolically the establishment of a liberated Cuba. As if in dialogue, the poems repeat words, metaphors, and images. They can be read as reflecting and informing the language circulating in exile communities. In many cases, the poems place López in a historical continuum that includes George Washington, Simón Bolívar, and William Tell. As a hero of the future nation, López supposedly ushers Euro-American republicanism into the island. In that sense, the poems deploy a universal sense of liberty, even as they ground López's sacrifice in Cuba, *patria*, and *cubana tierra*. López's magnanimous spirit, his commitment to Cuba, is juxtaposed to Spanish colonial rulers, who are characterized as "tyrant," "despot," and "executioner." Some lines describe the battles that López fought and the execution itself, an event shrouded in darkness. In one of the more memorable images, Zenea portrays Spanish soldiers stealing trinkets from the bodies of filibusters killed by a firing squad:

Allí se disputaron los malvados
El robo vil sobre el cadáver frío,
Y entre tantos horrores
Repartieron después desordenados
Las reliquias de amores,
Que con sarcasmo impío
Sirvieron de juguete a los soldados.

[There evil men quarreled over
The spoils, robbing frigid corpses,

> And amid such horror
> They distributed in disarray
> Mementos of love,
> Which served as toys for the
> Impious sarcasm of soldiers.][37]

These somber scenes stand in contrast to the "light" of Cuba and the "sun" and "sky" that signal a brighter future. López's redemption is achieved through the anticipation of an ultimate victory against colonialism and the general's eventual ascendance into historical immortality.

The poems paint López as a martyr of Cuba who has set the standard for future patriots. If Villaverde's man of action commits himself to military attack and/or the organizing of expeditions, then the martyr of Cuba takes it one step further and gives his life to the cause. The López poems provide literary support, verses that can be recited, for a conception of a revolutionary fighter that is tied to the people of Cuba. As one piece in *El Filibustero* asserts, López was the "genius of the revolution" because he took action out of his own free will at a time when conditions for a filibustering attack were not propitious.[38]

Castellón calls López the "Nuevo Jesús de los modernos tiempos [New Jesus of modern times]." The Christ imagery reemerges in several pieces, and it takes an allegorical turn in Turla's "A Narciso López," a sixteen-stanza poem that opens with the line "¿Quién más grande que tú? [Who is greater than you?]" and proceeds with a series of descriptions that could be read in relation to Christ or the filibustering general. No "magnanimous heart" could compare with the "noble abnegation" of the dead general, whose forehead was punctured by "thorns." In case the reader misses the point, the sixth stanza states it overtly by calling López "Emulo de Jesús," with the word *émulo* implying both emulation and rivalry. The issue here is no less than a giving up of the body for the redemption of other people.

But in the second part of the poem, Jesus imagery is replaced with apocalyptic prognostications of Spain's downfall. It becomes clear that a poem written to López is also written for *cubanos* who will follow the martyred general. The lines "nobles cubanos / Apresten ya las vengadoras manos [noble Cubans / Prepare to lend hands of vengeance]" are a threat that more filibustering expeditions will be forthcoming.

Indeed, the López poems feed enthusiasm for expeditions that are planned after the general's death, including the one discussed in chapter 1 that was aborted in 1854. Envisioning a victory, Turla proposes that the "fatal soil" of López's death will become sacred and that a statue will be erected in memory of López. In the end, the Cuban people honor his sacrifice: "Y a ti tan solo ¡oh mártir! deberemos / El don precioso de tan alta gloria [And to you only, dear martyr, we will owe / The precious gift of so much glory]."[39] The body of Christ is transformed into the body of a warrior that will be celebrated in a colossal statue "placed on a giant pedestal." The brow punctured by thorns is replaced by the "frown on your grim forehead," presumably the look in battle. Death is exchanged for the collective identity of the nation, "an entire people" who rally around López's statue.

Most of the López poems conveniently bypass the language of annexation (the United States is rarely mentioned) and focus instead on a connection between López and Cuban soil. "Sólo para ti, Cuba, vivía [Only for you, Cuba, he lived]" is the second line in Tolón's "En la Muerte de Narciso López." When the United States does appear, it is as part of a grand project leading to Cuba. Lorenzo Allo's "A la Memoria del General López" (To the memory of General López), a biographical documentary poem that traces López's travels through the United States, acknowledges that the general turned to a "generous people" for help:

> Hora del Potomac al Hudson corres,
> Y a la Mobila y Savanah recorres,
> Y ya al Misisipi tornas ufano.
> Pocos tus hombres, pero esforzados;
> Y una nave no más, toda tu flota.
> ¡Hurra! gritan al verte tus soldados
> Y ya las ondas el *Pampero* azota.
>
> [Now you run from the Potomac to the Hudson,
> And Mobile and Savannah you traverse
> And make the Mississippi proud.
> Few your men, but with great strength;
> And your entire flotilla one vessel, no more.
> Hurrah! Scream your soldiers upon seeing you
> And the *Pampero* whips the waves.][40]

In keeping with a documentary poetic style, Allo attempts to be faithful to events. The *Pampero* was the steamship that sailed out of New Orleans with López's fighters on their fatal expedition. Filibuster Louis Schlesinger wrote that when López boarded the steamer, he was "greeted with wild hurrahs both from the officers and men already collected on board, and from the thousands of Citizens who were assembled to witness the departure."[41] Allo recognizes López's place in the United States but omits mention of López's relationships with southern U.S. planters or northern supporters of Manifest Destiny. Instead, López is the "powerful genius" who operates on U.S. soil to change Cuba's history.

As the López poems show, exiled writers in the 1850s adored López with a patriotic intensity that complicates the association of López with annexation and U.S. expansionism. In contrast to contemporary historians who have painted López as an annexationist, the López poems invoke words and phrases—*patria, liberación, independencia de Cuba*—that connote liberal patriotism in Cuba. Tolón wrote after López's death, "I loved you the way one loves the father of the *patria*. When we were ejected from Cuba at the same time and you honored me with your trust, I dedicated from the depths of my heart my entire being forever and always to you as the emanation of the holy case of my patria."[42] Tolón's use of the word "father" points to a masculine connection between López and future fighters.

Many of the López poems display an acute interest in the dead general's body, spinning a symbolic association between body parts and the concepts of strength, determination, and liberation. Thus, Allo wrote,

> La santa libertad era tu guía;
> Tu heroico corazón ella inflamaba;
> Tu brazo ella animaba;
> Y ella también tu vencedora frente
> Con el laurel de la victoria ornaba.

> [Holy liberty was your guide;
> She elated your heroic heart;
> She animated your arm;
> And she also your triumphant forehead
> Crowned with the laurel of victory.][43]

The feminine "liberty" fuels the body, which rises to victory through action on the battlefield. Similarly, Zenea's "En el Aniversario del General López" portrays the general in battle with a "cheerful countenance" and "serene heart":

Reverdecieron en tu frente entonces
ricos laureles de gloriosos días,
y al estampido atronador del bronce
otro laurel te conquistaste en Frías.

[On your forehead again blossomed
rich laurels of glorious days,
and to the deafening report of bronze
you conquered another laurel in Frías.][44]

"Frías" is a reference to the Cafetal de Frías, a plantation in Cuba where López's filibusters staged their final successful battle by fighting off a Spanish force of nine hundred soldiers. (It was also owned by López's wife's family.)[45] Zenea emphasizes the forehead in his allusion to the laurels of military victory, as if the mark of success is engraved on the *filibustero*'s body.

The numerous uses of *frente*, which can be translated as forehead and brow, are in keeping with a phrenological interest in López. In June 1849, López had visited a phrenologist in New York and received a detailed description of his attributes. The report, reprinted bilingually in *El Eco de Cuba* in 1856, associates López with a host of attributes that can be read as masculine in their context: "Few men can endure more hardship and fatigue than you can. . . . You are very firm and persevering in what you undertake, and it is no use to attempt to drive you, for threats and scolding would only excite your firmness."[46] According to this reading, López was brave, in control, and certain. The phrenological report connected López's military leadership to gender when it noted that López would "sacrifice much to protect and defend woman." The report went one step further, noting that López was "a ladies man—gallant, polite, easy and affable."[47] With López presented as not only a martyr but also a good-looking one at that, it was not surprising that his image inspired more than one run of lithographs in the years after his death.[48]

The focus on López's body and ostensibly masculine attributes also circulated in U.S. culture at large. As historians have shown, the U.S. press was fascinated with López and became particularly critical of Spain when he was executed following the daring August 1851 attack.[49] English-language papers characterized López as "swarthy," and some popular writings brought forth facial descriptions that marked López as racially "dark." In her novel about the López expeditions, *The Free Flag of Cuba; or, The Martyrdom of Lopez* (1854), Lucy Holcombe Pickens described the general as "dark, with the passionate splendor of southern clime; his face, although open and generous, had an air of sturdy resolve and perseverance. His eyes flashed with patriotic enthusiasm."[50] The passage contrasts with the preceding paragraph, which presents U.S. General John A. Quitman, whose face "was calm, almost stern, with clear searching eyes of patriotism's 'true blue.'" The blue eyes, possibly conjuring blue blood, play against the sense of López as "dark," a description that makes its way even into the writings of present-day historians. If anything, these descriptions show the relative perspective of writers, for in Cuba López would have been considered white.

The association of López with darkness and passion further plays into nineteenth-century racist U.S. characterizations of Cubans as incapable of self-government. In his popular travel book, *To Cuba and Back*, Richard Henry Dana Jr. argued that Cubans' "Spanish blood, and their utter want of experience in the discharge of any public duties" made it unlikely that they would "work out successfully the problem of self-government."[51] In assessing the López expedition, Dana separated the general from the U.S. filibusters: "Their little force of a few hundred broken-down men and lads, deceived and deserted, fought a body of eight times their number, and kept them at bay, causing great slaughter."[52] The fighters from the United States were presumably "deceived and deserted" by López, who exaggerated the amount of support he would receive from fighters on the island. Noting twice that the Spaniards took large casualties, Dana feeds into a conception of the U.S. fighter as a fierce soldier who can inflict damage on "the whole power of the government" on the island.

That distinction between López and the U.S. military men is central to Holcombe's *The Free Flag of Cuba*. This novel sets a romantic plot in the historical context of the López expeditions. An aristocratic southern woman begs her filibustering beau not to go on the expedition, but he insists on supporting López and the liberation of Cuba. As scholars note, *Free Flag* inscribes a set of conventional gender roles for wealthy southern white women and frames the filibuster's quest in terms of masculine duty.[53] But where is López positioned in this portrait? On the one hand, the novel shares with the López poems an attempt to vindicate López's memory, describing the general as "a patriot, pure in heart and honest in purpose, a noble champion for Cuba's liberty and humanity's rights."[54] But on the other hand, the novel develops a perspective that U.S. soldiers are superior to López. The character Ralph Dudley, who joins the filibustering expedition, believes that López will have trouble instituting order among his filibusters. " 'What we most want,' continued Dudley, not heeding the want of sympathy in his listener, 'is an American commander.' "[55] López ultimately is an impractical idealist whose feelings for Cuba do not lead to realistic military planning. *The Free Flag of Cuba* concludes with a benevolent interventionist position that calls for U.S. filibusters to assist Cubans in gaining their freedom: "If our own immediate government be not extended, it behooves us as freemen to recognize the extension of its free institutions and liberal spirit."[56] What is cut out is the local connection of people on the island to their own liberation.

By contrast, Cuban exiles developed a notion of the revolutionary fighter with a familial connection to Cuba, not through birthright but through nurture on the island. Born in the region of South America that would become Venezuela, López became "Cuban" through service (willingness to die for Cuba). The *United States Magazine and Democratic Review* described Cuba as López's country "by adoption and marriage."[57] The word "adoption" was used in other cases, as in the poem "Adieu, Dear Cuba," quoted earlier, which describes the island as the place of his "adopted birth." Adoption, of course, is a metaphor of family, and it is through family that López reterritorializes himself in Cuba after the dislocation brought on by his service to Spain. Lorenzo Allo's poem, published in *La Verdad* under the pseudonym "El Peregrino," brings forth an intergenerational connection for López:

En Cuba hallaste padre, hallaste hermanos:
Cuba siempre formó tu regocijo,
En ella te adoraron los cubanos,
Y el ser a Cuba le debió tu hijo.

[In Cuba you found a father, you found brothers:
Cuba always brought you joy,
In her you were adored by Cubans
And your son his existence owed to Cuba.][58]

López and the island exchange a commitment. He takes on family (Cuba); Cuba gives him a son, who owes a debt to the island. The family-nation combination, one of the most reactionary forms of reterritorialization, begins to explain the fascination with names in the López poems.

In a future when the revolutionary fighter will enjoy the honor of Cuba, onomastic privilege will be given to those who sacrifice themselves. For writers from a society where family names and Spanish titles are highly influential, death on the battlefield prompts the writing of a new list of the island's illustrious names. As Rodríguez says in his poem,

El virtuoso siempre vive
En los recuerdos del hombre,
Y en cada siglo, revive
Porque en los cielos escribe
La virtud su hermoso nombre.

[He who is virtuous survives forever
In the memories of men,
And he revives in every century
For in the heavens virtue
Writes his beautiful name.][59]

Rodríguez lists the names, starting with López and proceeding with Joaquin Agüero, Isidro Armenteros, and Eduardo Facciolo, along with more than a dozen filibusters who died fighting with López. Thus, in keeping with other poems, privileged names are those belonging to men who gave their lives for the nation to be. The covenant here is one in which Cuba, personified in the form of the people, promises to incorporate the fighters into its future history after the fighters give themselves up to the island.

In a curious turn away from the masculine-centered notion of the names of Cuba's future liberators, Miguel T. Tolón concluded one of his speeches by proposing that women would join the ranks of the honored on the "day of glory for the patria." Tolón envisioned a moment when a sculptor would carve women's names on a tombstone erected in memory of heroes who fought for liberty. The sculptor would have to engrave, Tolón predicted, the many names of "las Mujeres de Cuba Independiente!"[60] To understand Tolón's call for the inclusion of women in the revolution, we need to consider how Cuban exiles and Tolón himself viewed women and women writers.

Adoring the Motherland: Cuba's Women Poets

In one of the rare instances when Cuban women writers were published in the *filibustero* press, two sonnets by Gertrudis Gómez de Avellaneda appeared in *La Verdad* on 20 March 1852. The first was the well-known "Al Partir" (On leaving), which can be read as a record of her departure from Havana for Europe in 1836:

> ¡Perla del mar! ¡Estrella de Occidente!
> ¡Hermosa Cuba! Tu brillante cielo
> la noche cubre con su opaco velo,
> como cubre el dolor mi triste frente.

> [Pearl of the Sea! Star of the Occident!
> Beautiful Cuba! Your refulgent sky
> Night covers with its murky veil,
> Like sorrow covers my saddened visage.]

Gómez de Avellaneda's poem, which situates the speaker in the uncertain and deterritorialized space of the ocean, has much in common with *filibustero* poetry, particularly in its emphasis on the pain of departure from the home island. The final lines of "Al Partir," in which a steamer "cuts the waves, and flies silently," resonate with José María Heredia's "Himno del Desterrado" (Hymn of exile), in which the vessel leaves behind "shining foam" as it departs from Cuba. Gómez de Avellaneda, like *filibustero* writers, had come into her own poetically after reading Heredia and Byron. Editors at *La Verdad* would have responded to Gómez's sense of being in flight, as enunciated in her pseudonym, "La Peregrina," a reference to a migratory bird but more generally to one who wanders in unknown lands. (Her friend, Lorenzo Allo, who wrote under "El Peregrino," may have submitted or suggested the poems to the newspaper, then edited by Tolón.)[61]

The second selection was the more overtly political "A Washington," a celebration of the U.S. president that establishes him as an "American" giant whose deeds are "admired by the world and envied by Rome."[62] The poem presents Washington as a revolutionary hero who broke the chains of English colonialism and challenged Europe to look to the Americas for the great men of the age. *Filibusteros* surely would have concurred with the sense in "A Washington" that the American hemisphere was a battlefield for liberty, a point echoed in Gómez's novel of the Spanish conquest, *Guatimozín, Último Emperador de México* (1846).[63] But she stopped far short of writing the type of incendiary revolutionary verses that I have associated with *filibustero* poetry. Despite issuing a stinging critique of slavery in her novel *Sab*, which was banned in Cuba, Gómez de Avellaneda did not break with Spain, and her literary stature allowed her to move within the upper-class circles of Madrid as well as Havana.[64] When she returned to Cuba in 1859 after twenty-three years in Europe, Gómez de Avellaneda traveled with the island's new colonial governor, Captain-General Francisco Serrano, and his wife, company that would have been anathema to the *filibusteros*. As such, *La Verdad* effectively wielded one part of Gómez de Avellaneda's work to support its anticolonial positions.

The publication of those poems is unusual. Quite simply, women writers were almost absent from these publications. With the exception of Cora Montgomery at *La Verdad*, men almost exclusively put out and wrote for these transnational newspapers. Periodically, a letter from a woman in Cuba would be published, and in later decades, writers such as Sofía Estévez appeared in U.S.-based revolutionary publications.[65] But at least in the 1850s, the *filibustero* press was by and large run by men. This was in part the result of the exclusionary male-centered culture that led to the development of the revolutionary man of action, but in addition, conventions in Cuba made it unlikely that women would travel to the United States on their own. While Creole male writers from Heredia to Martí were willing to rupture family ties by leaving the island to carry out political-literary work, Cuba's major women poets did not make a break for the United States. It would have been unusual for an upper-class woman to move on her own. Two of Cuba's best-known women poets, the sisters Luisa Pérez de Zambrana and Julia Pérez y Montes de Oca, remained in Cuba. In the case of the

Pérezes, it took their father's death for the family to relocate within Cuba from a rural home to the city of Santiago. Luisa Pérez later moved to Havana when she married professor and literary critic Ramón Zambrana. Similarly, women who went into exile in the United States did so with relatives. In 1854, Emilia Casanova moved with her family from Cuba to Philadelphia, where she met Cirilo Villaverde. The following year the two married and settled in the New York area. As I discuss in more detail later in this chapter, Casanova went on to become a prominent activist and writer in the New York exile community.

Being outside of the U.S. publishing scene in the 1840s and 1850s, Cuba's best-known women writers did not adopt the militant attitude of calling overtly for an end to colonial rule, and they could not have done so on the island because of censorship. Nevertheless, they expressed sentimental attachment to the land around them and celebrated the island's flora and fauna to create a nascent sense of the *patria* that deepened local attachments to Cuba. Luisa Pérez de Zambrana wrote poems that presented a deep connection to her family and nature on the island, marshaling metaphors to create a distinct relationship between the self and Cuba. Pérez de Zambrana's poems betray anticolonial sentiments, but because none of her works directly challenge the island's governors, the political content of her verses has sometimes been deemphasized. Max Henríquez Ureña argues that Pérez de Zambrana never aspired to become a "social poet," which would have been out of character with her "dreamy temperament." But he acknowledges that "from her earliest poetic prattle she took an ideological position against all oppression and tyranny, be it of the rich who exploits the poor, or of the strong who annihilates the weak."[66] The issue is not so much "social" content, because Pérez de Zambrana's celebration of nature in Cuba can be read as a social commentary. Rather, the difference between Pérez de Zambrana and *filibustero* writers is that she does not call for revolutionary action. A brief glance at her biography will help illuminate important differences between the work of men in exile and women on the island and how the contexts in which they worked led to different poetic approaches to figuring Cuba as its own distinct territory.[67]

Pérez de Zambrana's writing evolved as she experienced personal traumas and historical cataclysms, including the death of all her five children and the various wars that led to Cuba's independence. Today, she is best known for family elegies, which she wrote as various relatives died. "La Vuelta al Bosque Después de la Muerte de Mi Esposo" (Return to the woods after the death of my husband), for example, is a masterful meditation on the subjectivity of perspective in nature. Pérez was born into a family that owned a small farm in mountainous eastern Cuba. After publishing verses in Santiago de Cuba's newspapers in the early 1850s, Pérez put out her first collection of fifty-one poems in 1856. Those verses invoked the rivers, flowers, birds, and plants of the area where she had grown up. Aside from bringing Pérez literary success, the poems caught the attention of Zambrana, who married her in 1858. The couple moved to Havana, where Pérez de Zambrana visited *tertulias* (literary salons) and came into contact with intellectuals who sought liberal reform or considered more radical changes for the island.[68]

Pérez's early poems from the 1850s provide a lucid view of her bucolic experience in Cuba's eastern section. "El Lirio" (The lily), for example, opens with the lines "Una mañana deliciosa y pura / de esas que brillan en mi patria amada [A delicious and pure morning / such as those that shine on my beloved motherland]" and proceeds to describe a romantic delirium experienced upon contemplation of a lily "the color of pearl." Her poems are songs to tropical nature, but they connect the description of flowers, sunlight, and greenery directly to Cuba. In most cases, Pérez inserts a line or even a frame of reference that establishes a familial or spatial connection Cuba. "Nights under the Moon" (Noches de Luna), for example, concludes by invoking the *patria* as the reason for experiencing a communal vision of the moon.

Pérez de Zambrana's early poetry differs from work of *filibusteros* in that it celebrates Cuba without attacking the state apparatus. This difference becomes most evident in a comparison of two poems, both titled "A Cuba," one by Pérez published in Cuba in 1853, and another by Miguel T. Tolón published in *La Verdad* in 1852. Pérez de Zambrana's eighteen-stanza poem focuses on the speaker's love for the land around her, opening with an invocation of the patria:

> Patria adorada, Cuba encantadora,
> rosa que vuelves a mostrar brillante
> tus sonrosados pétalos que dora
> un sol de fuego y de esplendor radiante.

[Adored motherland, enchanting Cuba,
a rose that returns to display your brilliance
in pink petals that are gilded by
the fire and radiant splendor of the sun.]

"A Cuba" is a festival of nature's delights, filled with tremulous creeks and soft perfumes. If beauty is universal, these poems imply, it takes on a particular hue in Cuba. The speaker asks herself, "¡Por qué mi pecho conmovido siente / al verte, Cuba, sensaciones gratas! [Why does my heart, aroused, / feel pleasant sensations on seeing you, Cuba!]." In response, she turns to a metaphor of motherhood in which the island offers a maternal seat and "crib to my innocent infancy." The familial and genealogical connection posited here attaches a Cuban-born subject to land in a way that would have appealed to *filibustero* writers seeking a similar connection. But for Cubans in New York, the connection to a local family in Cuba was complicated by exile; consequently, their revolutionary verses were a response to that break in the family.

Tolón's "A Cuba" views the island's territory from the exiled perspective of New York City:

Ay Cuba! dulce Cuba! Patria mía,
De mis padres hogar, de mi amor nido;—
Que encierras cuanto me es lo más querido
De todo ¡ay triste! ¡lo que yo tenía!
Cielo de amor, de luz, de poesía;
Eden del Dios del Inca bendecido,—
¿Será que para siempre te he perdido,
Y en ti al menos morir no pueda un día?
Oh! si nublada la esperanza toda
en mi horizonte viese . . . mi verdugo
Antes fuera, por Dios, mi propia mano;
Mas no, que pronto la potencia goda
Vencida ha de caer, y, roto el yugo,
Patria, hogar, Libertad tendrá el Cubano!
N. York, Enero—1852.

[Oh Cuba! Sweet Cuba! My motherland,
Home to my parents, nest to my love—
You hold that which I cherish

And all, so sad, that I possessed!
Sky full of love, of light, of poetry;
Eden so blessed by the Incas' God
Will it be that I have lost you forever,
if I cannot die within you some day?
Oh, if every hope were overcast,
on the horizon I would see . . . my executioner.
But I would rather it be, by God, my own hand;
But no, the Gothic power will soon
Fall in defeat, the yoke of tyranny cracked,
Cubans will have motherland, home, and liberty.
New York, January—1852.][69]

The metaphors that dominate Tolón's vision of "Cuba" are physical markers of Cuban place. The island is simultaneously his parents' "home" and his own "nest." Cuba offers not just a refuge but also "light of day," a point further emphasized by calling the island "Eden . . . blessed by the Incas' God," a reference to the sun. This light marks a contrast to the overcast skies that cover his hope, the skies of New York in January, the place and time specified at the end of the poem as the site from which the perspective emerges. The distinction between the island and New York emphasizes the poet's deterritorialized state, which then becomes one of the conditions of composition. Contemplating the impossibility of that return, the speaker considers suicide. Only the hope of seeing Spanish power defeated pulls him away from that possibility. One could say that Tolón aspires to the type of experience described in Pérez de Zambrana's poem, a communion with Cuba as mother and land. Unable to do that, Tolón takes on a tone of desperation.

Angel Huete argues that Pérez de Zambrana has much in common with Zenea.[70] These two poets share a tendency toward abstract visions at times, and critics thus argue that both Pérez de Zambrana and Zenea are part of a resistance to the excesses of the vigorous and exclamatory romanticism that appealed to Tolón, instead opting for more melodious tones and relating the outside world to the interior sense of self.[71] That point is well taken for some of Zenea's work, but as I discussed in chapter 1, Zenea was also a polemicist *filibustero* who sometimes chose the pamphlet alongside the poem. What Pérez de Zambrana ultimately shares not only with Zenea but also with many of the *filibustero* writers is an obsession with nature and land. For her, however, the important connection was land-country-family, whereas the *filibusteros* threw revolution into that mix.

With women active in Cuban poetry circles, why did *filibusteros* not include more of female writers' pieces in transnational newspapers? Without a definitive answer, it is important to note that the newspapers were largely homosocial. The Creole emphasis on the revolutionary man of action relegated women (and blacks) to the periphery. As late as 1875, José Martí gave us a vision of what Pérez might have faced during her lifetime as a Cuban woman writer. In a short critical piece, he opened with the following description: "Luisa Pérez is a pure child, sensible to all pain and accustomed to being delicate and generous. Her dark hair falls in curls around her temples; in her dark eyes is the inexorable force of delicate passion and of tenderness."[72] In the brief chronology of the piece, Pérez is first a sensuous woman and only later a writer. The focus on a woman poet's body continues when Martí compares Pérez to Gómez de Avellaneda, of whom he says that everything about her "implied a potent and manly spirit; her body tall and robust, just as her poetry was rough and energetic."[73] Martí establishes a correspondence between body and poetry without offering a significant reading of either woman's poems.

Some Cuban exiles took a romantically condescending attitude toward women in Cuba and the United States. Kirsten Silva Gruesz notes that the poems of *El Laúd del Desterrado* often addressed women, developing a convention that Gruesz describes as "a carpe diem seduction poem directed toward a beautiful, virtuous, but ignorant Anglo-American girl that explains [the poet's] higher loyalty to Cuba and her freedom."[74] Another loyalty expressed by writers was to women in Cuba, often figured as mothers, sisters, or lovers; in these cases, women and country function simultaneously as objects of desire. Tolón's "A Mi Madre" (To my mother), written in 1851, captures the internal conflict of an exile pulled by his mother's call to return to Cuba after having committed himself to remaining in the United States until the island is free of colonial rule. The poem opens with the mother calling her son to return to her arms:

Muévante las ansias mías,
mi gemir y mi llorar
y consuelo venme a dar,
hijo, en mis últimos días.

[Moved by my anxiety,
my howling, my weeping,
may you return to console me,
son, in my final days.]

The speaker responds, emphasizing his sadness and "agony":

Que no puedo, que no quiero,
porque, entre deber y amor,
me enseñaste que el honor
ha de ser siempre primero.

[I am unable and unwilling
because, between duty and love,
you taught me that honor
should always be first.]

More than any of his peers, Tolón carried on a literary affair with his beloved Cuba. While women sometimes were passive objects for his poetic vision, Tolón also offered a different perspective on the role that women could play in the revolution.

Where Is *la Filibustera*?: Miguel T. Tolón's Vision of Community

On 28 October 1851, a poem appeared on the front page of *La Verdad*, calling on women to mourn the death of Narciso López:

¡Venid las cubanas! ¡Con llanto reguemos
La huesa de López que está en soledad!
Venid, mis hermanas! ¡Venid, y cantemos
El réquiem del Mártir de la Libertad!

[Come Cuban women! Let us water with tears
The hole where López is buried in solitude!
Come, my sisters! Come, let us sing
A requiem for the Martyr of Liberty!][75]

Written in the voice of a woman, "Cantar de las Matanzeras en la Muerte del General Narciso López, Mártir de la Libertad de Cuba" (Song of Matanza's women on the death of General Narciso López, martyr of Cuba's liberty) was signed by "Lola." Positioned strategically on the front page of the newspaper, the poem could have been read as a missive from a Cuban woman who had sent her verses from the port city of Matanzas through *La Verdad*'s transnational publication circuit. In actuality, the poem's author was the Matanzero Tolón, who published under a slew of pseudonyms during his years in exile.

"Cantar de las Matanzeras" represented Tolón's view that Cuban women should play an important role in the revolution as supporters of Cuban fighters, a position he would elucidate in future years. Although the poem is a requiem that emphasizes "tears," the concluding stanza is a call to action:

> ¡Hermanas! Solo un grito
> escale nuestro labio;—
> ¡Muerte al poder maldito!
> ¡Venganza a tanto agravio!
>   Vosotros los Cubanos,
> no más infamia,—alzad
> y armando vuestras manos
>   ¡O muerte, o Libertad!

> [Sisters! May one cry
> reach our lips;
> Death to the evil power!
> Vengeance for so much wrong!
>   And you, Cuban men,
> no more infamy—rise
> and with arms in your hands,
>   Death or liberty!]

First speaking to women about the need to keep alive the filibustering project, the stanza then addresses men directly; thus, the pseudonymous Lola sets an example for women to urge their relatives and friends into battle.

By writing as Lola, Tolón functioned as a ventriloquist who put revolutionary fervor into a woman's mouth. In doing so, he broke ranks with some other exiles who ignored women in newspaper articles or political programs. Tolón's writing was influenced by gender hierarchies that circulated in Cuba and the United States, and his ventriloquism is highly problematic. But, at the same time, Tolón departs from his contemporaries by focusing on women and proposing that they take a radical posture in relation to the revolution. Tolón believed that if Cuba were to oust its Spanish colonial rulers, women needed to be full participants in the revolution. In 1855, Tolón delivered a lecture in Manhattan in which he called on women to hand guns to their relatives:

> Habrá fuego y habrá sangre: habrá lágrimas y habrá luto; familias sin padre; hogares sin familia;—pero habrá también almas de héroes en cuerpos de mujeres: habrá en Cuba Lucrecias como en Roma, Carlotas como en Francia, Martas Washington como en los Estados Unidos, Policarpas como en Colombia;—habrá mil esposas como la de Joaquin de Agüero, que al estrecharlo entre sus brazos, en la hora de partir para el combate, no le llora, sino le sonríe; no lo detiene con sus lágrimas, sino lo anima con sus miradas de entusiasmo: no le pide que se quede, sino que vuelva,—como decían las Espartanas,—o vencedor o muerto, por su patria y por su honor!

> [There will be fire and there will be blood; there will be tears and there will be mourning; families without fathers; homes without families—but there also will be heroes in the bodies of women: In Cuba there will be Lucretias as in Rome, Carlottas as in France, Martha Washingtons as in the United States, Policarpas as in Colombia—there will be a thousand wives like that of Joaquin de Agüero, who taking him in her arms at the hour of departure for combat, does not cry but rather smiles; does not detain him with her tears but rather encourages him with her enthusiastic glances; does not ask him to remain but rather to return—as Spartan women used to say—either triumphant or dead for the motherland and its honor!][76]

The passage places Cuba in a telos of republican liberation and portrays women as giving priority to the *patria* over their families. Among his allusions is Policarpa la Salvarietta, a Colombian patriot who was executed by Spanish forces for her work raising the spirits of independence fighters. Almost speaking prophetically of the battles that would engulf Cuba both during the Ten Years' War and the war for independence in the 1890s, Tolón tells women they will have to contend with bloodshed and that it is best if they prepare to act rather than respond passively. The vision of homes without families creates an image of a war-ravaged living space that has lost its inhabitants. The model relationship of woman to man is established through the case of Joaquin Agüero, a lawyer and landowner in Cuba who had been executed in 1851 for trying to lead an uprising. Agüero's widow, Ana Josefa Agüero, who went into exile in the United States with her two children after the death of her husband, is praised for encouraging her husband's mission. Tolón would have readers view Ana Agüero as the model Cuban woman, willing to choose correctly between "the tyranny of Spain and the rights of Cuba."

Later in the speech, Tolón went further. In addition to putting radical words into the mouths of women, he also put guns in their hands. Cuba will also have, he argues, its Joan of Arc and its Amazons, who will "exchange silks and jewels for military harness." The association of women with the military masculinity of the revolutionary man of action is yet another gender-bending move by Tolón. Just as he is willing to become Lola, the women of Cuba can become López-like warriors. Tolón's interest in women and revolution is in keeping with the life and work of a writer who planted seeds for the development of a transnational Cuban nation.

As a public intellectual, Tolón worked to build an exile community that would develop a revolutionary commitment. In 1853, he founded the Ateneo Democrático Cubano (Cuban Democratic Athenaeum) in Manhattan, arguing that this center was in keeping with the indispensable need for armed combat against Spain. Housed in assembly rooms at 600 Broadway, the ateneo sought to develop an intellectual foundation that would feed the struggle on the battlefield. In his inaugural speech, Tolón took up the questions of arms and letters: "To say let us study does not mean let us avoid the fight. Letters are not opposed to arms; instead, they provide assistance. The educated mind does not impede the valiant hand; on the contrary, the mind provides the vigor of reason and upright conscience to direct it."[77] Tolón and others, including Pedro Santacilia and Lorenzo Allo, delivered lectures at the ateneo focusing on topics such as political economy and the U.S. Constitution. It was there that Tolón delivered the oration quoted earlier on the role of Cuban women in the revolutionary struggle.

Not leaving anyone behind, Tolón saw on the horizon a future moment when women and slaves would become full participants in Cuban society. As a supporter of López and filibustering, Tolón did not regularly focus on the issue of slavery. But in 1854, he collaborated with the abolitionist publication *El Mulato*, which I discuss in the next chapter. Tolón gave the editors of the newspaper a copy of a speech he had delivered to an international group of exiles gathered to celebrate the founding of the French republic. Calling for universal emancipation from monarchical rule, Tolón's speech, delivered and printed in French, contained the following line: "The day approaches when the words 'oppression' and 'slavery' will be forever erased with the debris of monarchy." The editors of *El Mulato*, widely condemned in the Cuban exile community for going public with their views, referred to Tolón in print as "our distinguished friend."[78]

Tolón's efforts to build a broad-based program explain his cross-gendered use of pseudonyms. Many of the writers for the *filibustero* press used pseudonyms. Juan Bellido de Luna, whose last name means literally "of the moon," published under the name "Astro de la Noche" (Star of night). Villaverde was "El Ambulante del Oeste" (Wanderer from the West), a reference to his birthplace in Cuba's western section. Zenea crossed genders in his pseudonyms, publishing under the names "Una Habanera" and "Azucena" (white lily) as well as under his initial, "Z."[79] Among his fellow exiles, Tolón took pen names to an extreme, sometimes writing under "Una Cubana" and the anagram "Tello Rubio Montegú." Even when his own byline appeared, Miguel María Teurbe Tolón y de la Guardia usually truncated the paternal "Teurbe" into an initial and cut out his mother's last name, Guardia, thus writing as Miguel T. Tolón. That name was not a capricious choice but an effort to connect himself to Toulon, France, and thus ally himself with republican movements tied to the founding of the French republic of 1848. "My name reveals well that the blood of the Gauls runs in my veins," he said in French. "Some of my ancestors saw the light of day under the beautiful sky of Provence; but I, I was born on one of the islands of the seas of America, unfortunately oppressed until today."[80]

Because Tolón and other writers published some articles under their

own names, it does not appear that writers used the pseudonyms to protect themselves from colonial authorities. Rather, as A. Gabriel Meléndez argues in reference to New Mexico's nineteenth-century periodical
press, the use of pseudonyms is a practice that can be connected to
romantic and neoclassical writers who sought to mask their identity.
"The pseudonym offered the possibility of controlling authorial dis-
closure, an advantage to any author wishing to deflect responsibility
and engage in scathing verbal attacks on politicians and rival *periodi-
queros*," Meléndez writes.[81] The use of pseudonyms among Cuban
exiles prompted several results. First, the practice created a semblance
of a multiplicity of voices circulating in the transnational circuit. A lack
of bylines and the use of pseudonyms meant that the same writer could
produce various pieces in a single issue of a newspaper. Pseudonyms
also erased the location of writers in exile. In the case of "Cantar de
las Matanzeras," the name Lola gives the appearance that women in
Matanzas are responding to filibustering and are in contact with U.S.-
based writers. A second effect is that pseudonyms replace the individual writer with someone who is writing on behalf of a community and
in support of a political project, in keeping with what Gilles Deleuze
and Félix Guattari describe as a "minor literature." Rather than feed the
reputation of a man of letters (Tolón), a pseudonym offers a communal
utterance (Cuban women). In other words, "Cantar de las Matanzeras"
gave readers of *La Verdad* a sense that people on the island were actively
writing poems praising *filibusteros* even though support for López's
fatal expedition just two months prior to the poem's appearance had
been minimal.

The name Lola further staked a claim to the island by connecting the
exiled Tolón to the heroine of his novel *Lola Guara*, the first part of
which Tolón had published in Matanzas in 1846, before going into
exile. Set on a coffee plantation, the novel describes the sixteen-year-old
Lola as a "true Creole in body and soul." As such, she can be read as
Tolón's romantic kindred spirit: "An expression of poetic melancholy
that reigned on her countenance would have awakened the interest of
the most prosaic soul."[82] While Tolón in the 1850s imagined Creole
women in a revolution, not until the late 1860s did a woman emerge
publicly in New York as a leader in the Cuban independence movement. More than a decade after Tolón's death, Emilia Casanova de
Villaverde went on to use the pseudonym Lolita.

Woman of Action: Emilia Casanova de Villaverde

At the age of twenty-one, Emilia Casanova was a declared supporter of Cuban independence and an avid reader of transnational newspapers published by exiles in New York but banned in her hometown of Cárdenas, a port west of Havana. "Whenever she acquired one of them, she would read it enthusiastically, comment on it and pass it on to her friends, with the goal of giving the greatest possible circulation to the news and new ideas," Cirilo Villaverde wrote in a thirty-six-page biographical sketch of his wife.[83] The link between newspaper and political commitment would have made Casanova the model reader envisioned by *filibustero* writers. Influenced by Narciso López, Casanova became one of the most passionate activists in exile during the Ten Years' War (1868–78). Rather than turn to newspapers, as her husband did, she offered the revolution another form of transnational writing: letters. A collection of her correspondence published in the nineteenth century includes more than eighty letters and other documents that she authored.[84] Raising money for arms even as she wrote her letters, Casanova performed the tasks that her husband had associated with the "man of action."

Born in 1832 to a slave-owning family, Casanova's political awakening at a young age was tied to an episode that has fed Cuban nationalist histories.[85] On 19 May 1850, during Narciso López's most successful filibustering incursion into Cuba, his troops landed in Cárdenas and flew the banner that would become the Cuban flag. The way the story goes, Casanova opened the shutter of her window, and her eyes met "with unspeakable sweetness the new flag of the Cuban nation, made out of rich silk by Creole women in New Orleans."[86] According to Villaverde's biographical account, *Apuntes Biográficos de Emilia Casanova de Villaverde* (1874), "From that memorable date, Emilia committed herself to the cause of liberty and independence for her motherland. All of her preferences, her thoughts, even her pleasures focused on that seminal idea, which came to be the religion of her soul, gave her new energy, conferred on her a new character and ushered her into a new life."[87] Casanova confirmed the influence of the López raid on her life, writing that the beauty of the flag and the strength of the man carrying it prompted her to swear that her life would be devoted to the "sacred and noble" goal of bringing liberty and independence to Cuba

(C 147). In 1854, Casanova moved with her family from Cuba to Philadelphia, where she met Villaverde. The following year the two married and settled in the New York area, where they lived for most of the rest of their lives. Together they would become the first couple of revolutionary Cuba in exile.

In the late 1860s and early 1870s, Casanova worked tirelessly to gather military, monetary, and political support for rebels fighting in Cuba. Ana Cairo argues that Casanova is a "figure who symbolizes women's support for the founding of the Cuban nation."[88] That support was coming via the Bronx. In her daily routine, Casanova would have breakfast at seven in the morning, travel nine miles from her home in Mott Haven into Manhattan via train and car, then carry out revolutionary work, sometimes going from house to house trying to inspire exiles to support her various projects. In the evenings she would spend time with her children. And throughout the day, she would attend to what she called "a protracted correspondence" with international political leaders, Cuban exiles, and generals on the battlefield (C 107–8). As secretary for a women's revolutionary group, la Liga de las Hijas de Cuba (The League of the Daughters of Cuba), Casanova helped to organize a concert to raise money for arms. She also took up a collection for poor exiles, and she sold raffle tickets to outfit military expeditions, which were still sometimes referred to as filibustering. Her work was threatening enough that Cuba's pro-Spanish press mocked her in satirical columns and caricatures. In Cárdenas, a group even burned her in effigy.[89]

Fluent in English, Casanova made her way to Washington on more than one occasion to meet with President Ulysses S. Grant and members of Congress, urging them to recognize Cuban revolutionaries. Her ability to cross from one language to another is clear in an 1871 letter to the editor of the Daily Telegraph: "We Cubans, allow me to state once more, having failed to obtain from Spain every sort of concession, even the autonomy England has readily granted you long ago, are fighting for dear liberty for ourselves and for thousands of poor African slaves, as well as for entire independence" (C 158). Comparing Spain to England, Casanova drew a revolutionary parallel and attempted to capitalize on antislavery sentiment in post–Civil War New York.

The extent of Casanova's military commitment became public in 1870 when she began raising money for an expedition of women who hoped personally to deliver arms to the battlefield in Cuba. "You should not laugh," she wrote to General Federico Cavada. "The revolution in Cuba has prompted a moral revolution in us, Cuban women, and I believe myself capable of that duty and much more" (*C* 99). In the days following that statement, Casanova wrote letters to numerous exiled women asking for help in collecting money for the women's expedition. "Here we have collected a good amount, and promises of more," she wrote, for an "enterprise not yet undertaken by those of our sex" (*C* 101). Although it appears that the women never boarded this expedition, Casanova's letters show that she raised money to arm and pay the passage for dozens of men, who traveled to Cuba and joined the revolution. Writing to General Barnabé Varona in 1873, Casanova stated that she had been able to "arm and equip completely not only the 26 men I offered for your guard, but also four more that came to me at the last minute" (*C* 203). Casanova situated these activities in a historical continuum; she saw Cuban revolutionary movements as progressing from a period of education to a period of action, with the former starting in 1818 and the latter inaugurated at the outbreak of the Ten Years' War (*C* 169). That teleological perspective also influenced Villaverde and Santacilia.

Casanova's writing offers a forceful response to the type of distinction between arms and letters that had disturbed *filibustero* writers, including her husband, in the 1850s. The letters took up military questions directly or indirectly and thus sought to affect the battlefield in Cuba. As such, the letters can be read as a form of transnational revolutionary praxis; they often request money or political support or even encourage generals to proceed in battle. Casanova wrote to revolutionary Giuseppe Garibaldi; Cuban independence fighter General Máximo Gómez; Cuba's Captain-General, Domingo Dulce; poet Leopoldo Turla; novelist Victor Hugo; and Chilean historian and journalist Benjamin Vicuña Mackenna. Casanova also kept up a regular correspondence with Cuban women in exile, including Filomena Callejas, Caridad Callejas, and Teresa de Galvez. In some cases, Casanova wrote to ask for money for arms, thus acting to bridge the perceptual gulf between pen and battlefield.[90]

Casanova walked a fine line between pathetic appeals and the lofty rhetoric of nation. She invoked personal connections and even appealed to vanity to prompt a response. In her letter to Garibaldi, Casanova explained that she had been "reading the European press to see if I could find a single word in support of the Cubans from the heroic Garibaldi, who has never turned away his sword or the support and influence of his great name to a people who have struggled for their liberty" (C 59).[91] Referring to Garibaldi in the third person, Casanova played to his vanity and seized the opportunity to instruct him on the particulars of the Cuban situation:

> Pero después de algunas reflexiones me he convencido que la causa del silencio de Garibaldi, es porque no conoce la cuestión cubana ni sabe el alcance de sus aspiraciones políticas. Nosotros principiamos la revolución dando libertad a nuestros esclavos, armándolos e incorporándolos en las filas patrióticas, y por esto poco, comprenderá Vd. Que nuestro propósito es de libertad universal . . . y a estas horas, apesar de los grandes inconvenientes con que hemos tropezado, ya los patriotas dominan las dos terceras partes de la isla.

> [After some reflection, I have concluded that Garibaldi is silent because he is not familiar with the Cuban situation, nor is he aware of the extent of our political aspirations. We began the revolution by liberating our slaves, arming them and including them in the patriotic columns, and you should take this minor point to understand that our goal is universal liberty . . . and at this time, despite the challenges that we have encountered, the patriots dominate two-thirds of the island.] (C 59)

In response, Garibaldi wrote a three-sentence letter less than a month later saying he had supported the Cuban people "since the start of your glorious revolution" (qtd. C 60).

Casanova's work complicates gender roles in exile. She did not hesitate to argue with General Manuel Quesada when he attempted to derail her plan to raise money from women to give him a sword. Pleading modesty, Quesada argued that such a gift would aggravate a growing perceived division between him and revolutionary General Tomás Jordan. Casanova, however, was a staunch supporter of Quesada, whom she viewed as a true representative of the people of Cuba, unlike Jordan. She responded, "In this matter, general, I am nothing but the intermediary through which a large number of your fellow citizens in New York desire to offer public testimony of the gratitude and admiration that they experience upon thinking of the services that you have offered to the motherland" (C 69–70).[92] The spectacle of a group of Cuban women handing a sword to Quesada in a public ceremony in New York's Irving Hall on 29 July 1869 certainly raised some eyebrows. The newspaper El Demócrata foregrounded the importance of gender in the ceremony: "Before a relatively large gathering, we witnessed an act entirely new for us who are not accustomed to seeing the fair sex figure in any way in public events of social importance."[93]

Bucking conventions, Casanova eagerly engaged in polemics against Spanish authorities and leaders in exile. She allied herself with the more radical wing of the revolution, calling early on for full abolition, democratic representation for the island's lower classes, and total independence. Her letters contain a string of critiques of a junta in New York at the center of exile revolutionary politics. The junta was dominated by landowners who had declared themselves in support of the rebels but were intent on protecting landowners' interests on the island and thus more willing to negotiate with Spain than were the rebels on the battlefield. Whenever necessary, Casanova attacked the junta and anyone else who she believed was compromising with Spanish authorities. Nowhere was this more evident than in her vituperative denunciation of Juan Clemente Zenea, the poet who had written for filibustero papers in the 1850s and continued to work in exile circles until his death in 1871. The Zenea case has been notorious in Cuba's literary-political history. He was executed at the hands of Spanish authorities even as Casanova and other exiles accused him of being a traitor to their cause. Zenea traveled from New York to Cuba as a representative of the New York junta with safe-conduct papers issued by the Spanish legation in Washington, D.C. His mission was to propose a peace plan to the rebels that would have given Cuba autonomy and its own constitution but not total independence from Spain. That plan did not appeal to rebels intent on continuing military operations, and they turned over Zenea to Spanish authorities, who did not recognize Zenea's safe conduct.[94] Detained, Zenea wrote his last cycle of poems, Diario de un Mártir (Diary of a martyr), just prior to his execution. It is unlikely that Zenea ever acted in support of Spain, a power that he abhorred and attacked in his writings.[95]

Casanova, however, was ruthless in her efforts to build a case against Zenea. As secretary of la Liga de las Hijas de Cuba, she wrote the resolution adopted by the group describing Zenea's mission to Cuba as "traitorous to the highest degree." In turn, the *liga* called on all Cubans to "condemn the name of the traitor to perpetual infamy and total execration" (*C* 123). From Casanova's perspective, Zenea had been intent on deceiving the revolutionary president, Carlos Manuel de Céspedes, into accepting the New York junta's autonomy proposal and discrediting the radical wing of the exiles, which continued to support a military solution. Consequently, Zenea, if successful in halting efforts "to liberate the motherland through the force of arms," would "reduce us all to the necessity of negotiating with Spain," Casanova wrote in the league's resolution, which was published in several Spanish-language newspapers (*C* 123). It becomes apparent, then, that Casanova's disdain for Zenea was the result of a hard-line military posture that saw victory on the battlefield as the only solution to the Cuban impasse. If Casanova's attacks on a poet-martyr who had devoted so much of his life to Cuba's liberation appear distasteful, her reason for them—military necessity—can be read retroactively as politically astute. With the failure of the rebels in the Ten Years' War, Cuba plunged back under Spanish domination. Another revolutionary movement and another group of exiles would be needed to reach the goal sought by Casanova.

Casanova helps us unmask the masculinist assumption of the man of action culture that circulated in the 1850s. She also exemplifies the growth of Cuban exiles as a political group committed to liberation for all of Cuba's people. In her letters, Casanova was passionate about abolishing slavery, a position surely influenced by having lived in the United States through the Civil War. Villaverde wrote that the Civil War "agitated" Casanova because she witnessed how social ills could lead to the type of war that would later overtake Cuba.[96] An antislavery ethics motivated Casanova's posture as a woman of action. She was not the first Cuban exile to go public with this position. In 1854, a group had published a newspaper that took issue with the tacit approval of slavery in the annexationist and filibustering program. The appearance of *El Mulato* in New York, as the next chapter shows, placed slavery and race at the center of debates among Cuban exiles.

EL FILIBUSTERO.

ORGANO DE LA INDEPENDENCIA DE CUBA.

OFICIO: 252 BROADWAY.

EDITORES.

Francisco B. de Luna.
Juan B. de Luna (Redactor.)

AVISO

Se publica los dias 5, 15 y 25 — la suscricion vale 1 $ por 4 meses, adelantado.

NUMERO II   NUEVA—YORK ENERO 15 DE 1854   EPOCA 2ª

Todo artículo ó comunicado que se inserte con firma ó seudónimo no pertenece á la redaccion.

Suplicamos á nuestros suscritores de los Estados Unidos se sirvan remitirnos por el correo, en Billetes de Banco, el importe de la suscricion del cuatrimestre que principió el 5, del corriente.

Los sobres bajo los que se remitan los billetes, vendrán con la direccion á esta Oficina— 252 Broadway —room number 14 —third floor.

ORDENANZA
PARA LA INTRODUCION DE COLONOS EN CUBA.

Sin que hayamos podido dijerir el material que contienen los sesenta y siete artículos de que se compone la "Ordenanza que establece y manda observar" á los colonos y contratistas importadores el Capitan General de la Isla de Cuba, Marqués de la Pezuela, vamos á trazar algunas observaciones que nos ha ejerido su cansada lectura; aunque las haremos muy sucintamente, pues de otra manera no bastarian las estrechas columnas de nuestro periódico á hacer un completo análisis de esa obra estupenda del Gobierno colonial.

Antes de entrar en pormenores quisieramos preguntar á las personas que han leido como nosotros el valor y la calma de leer la citada Ordenanza: ¿Si creen de buena fé que el Gobierno español desea la introducion de colonos españoles, indios y asiáticos en la Isla de Cuba?

Nosotros creemos plenamente que no. Hemos leido con detenimiento todos los sesenta y siete artículos, los cuales hay treinta y dos que se oponen al proyecto de colonizacion. Es imposible que ninguna persona que sepa raciocinar, concilie medios mas torpes, mas bárbaros y mas contradictorios para establecer un sistema que se tiene la desvergüenza de patrocinar, manifestando los mejores deseos de contribuir al aumento de brazos, de que carece la Isla. ¿En que pais civilizado de la tierra se llaman hombres libres de otros pueblos para hacerlos esclavos bajo el pretesto de una colonizacion? ¿Como y por qué toleran con tanto desden semejantes atentados contra la humanidad, esas grandes naciones respetadas por su ilustracion y filantropia? Nos asombramos de ver que España cometa tantas atrocidades impunemente á la faz del mundo. Aun mas, nos sorprende que el Gobierno colonial establezca en Cuba la introduction de colonos españoles en la condicion de esclavos en que se tiene á los negros, asiáticos y yucatecos, sujetos á la voluntad de un amo investido por el mismo Gobierno con la facultad de castigarlos cuando incurrieren en una falta, empleando el cepo, el grillete, la prision

y la suspension de salario y aun si no bastasen estos castigos crueles, podrán recurrir á otros mayores, como el de la escalera y los azotes, segun espresan los artículos 57, 61, y 62 del Capítulo 3º de la Ordenanza. ¿Podrá creerse que haya hombres libres á quienes se les lea esta ordenanza militar, que abandonen voluntariamente su pais natal para ir á colonizar la Isla de Cuba? Muy necio seria ó mas bien un idiota que admitiese tan ventajosa proposicion: y muy cándido seria quien creyese que los colonos que vayan á Cuba bajo ese sistema no son hombres arrancados de su pais por la violencia, el robo y la seduccion, por mas que el Gobierno pretenda hacer creer que "los colonos han de enterarse bien de las obligaciones que contraen" ántes de venir á la Isla.

Bien mezclada de desprecio nos causa comparar el reglamento de colonizacion del Marqués de la Pezuela que él ha titulado muy propiamente Ordenanza, con el sistema que para el mismo objeto se observa en los Estados Unidos.

A la vez que en la mayor parte del tiempo de la introduccion de colonos al término fijo de dos años; que se designan los puertos por donde deben ser introducidos; el secso, la clase, el color, la edad; "la sujecion estricta á la disciplina de las fincas" (militarmente hablando), las penas, los castigos &c. todo con el fin de poner obstáculos á la inmigracion de hombres blancos: en los Estados Unidos estan abiertos todos sus puertos constante y eternamente para recibir brazos estranjeros que gozan del privilegio de ciudadanos libres desde el momento que pisan las playas de este venturoso pais, sin leerse ordenanzas, ni preguntarles quienes son, ni de donde vienen. Son emigrados blancos de todos los paises, de todas relijiones, de todas edades, hombres, mujeres, ancianos, jóvenes y niños; artistas, navegantes y labradores que vienen en pos del trabajo, del pan y de la libertad. A cualquiera de ellos que se le leyese una ordenanza como la del Marqués de la Pezuela para obligarlo por fuerza á someterse á tan bárbaras disposiciones, la rechazaria con indignacion, y con la firmeza de un hombre libre que no sacrifica su dignidad apesar de su pobreza.

Si no comprendiesemos que el gobierno colonial de Cuba no quiere la colonizacion blanca, sino la de razas abyectas y degradadas como la de negros, asiáticos y yucatecos, nos tomariamos el trabajo en beneficio de nuestra patria de remitirle libre de costos, un Reglamento de colonizacion semejante al que se observa en estos estados, el cual no se compondria de esenta y siete artículos opuestos los unos á los otros, sino que bastaban con una docena tan solamente, capaces de inundar la Isla de trabajadores blancos en el prefijado término de "dos años." Pero ni el gobierno quiere colonos blancos, ni quiere reglamentos que se ase-

mejen á nada á los de aquí, ni que los colonos sean hombres libres; lo que él quiere son negros de Africa que dan tres ó mas por cabeza, que sean esclavos, estúpidos y bárbaros; porque con únicamente los que se dejan seducir por su ignorancia y se someten al cepo al grillo, al azote y á la escalera; ro bre todo, el gobierno español no quiere reglamentos sino Ordenanzas. Cuba está en estado de sitio, y los colonos que á ella se traigan deben someterse á las ordenanzas escepcionales que rijen en el pais.

Respecto á la sabiduria con que están dictados y redactados los artículos de la Ordenanza, no puede negarse que el Marqués de la Pezuela, la segunda lumbrera de España, el alumno de Lista y el condiscípulo de Larra, posee un talento lancero de primer órden. Algunos periódicos han aventurado tanto el juicio sobre el talento de este ilustrado Señor, que lo han hecho hasta la poesía; y efectivamente que la ordenanza revela sus dotes en este divino arte, Hay en ella estrofas bellísimas y una fluencia y dulzura de lenguaje, que rivaliza con la de los mejores cantores ó cuerpos de guardias y fortalezas.

En la quinta estrofa ó Artículo 5.º encontramos una bella idea. Tratando de la importacion de colonos, dice: que "no podrá embarcarse mas de cuatro personas por tonelada, inclusa la tripulacion." Esto solo se le ocurre á una imaginacion tan privilejiada como la de Pezuela. Como que el plazo es corto, de dos años, sin duda es esta la causa porque se han de aprovechar los colonos y los contratistas de que en un buque se embarquen mas individuos de los que pueda contener; de manera, que una fragata de 600 toneladas podrá conducir á Cuba 2385 colonos y 15 hombres de tripulacion, que hacen un total de 2400 personas; número exorbitante y asombroso de pasajeros que no quieran transportar los vapores de la línea de George Law de 3.000 toneladas, á ménos que se adopte con los colonos el sistema de transportarlos en latasy barriles como las sardinas de Nántesy los arenques; pues de otro modo no creemos posible el transporte de tan crecido número de personas con víveres y equipajes.

Se nos ocurre un cálculo brillante y de muy buen éxito para la colonizacion, partiendo de los principios sentados por la Ordenanza. Este cálculo puede traer grandes ganancias á la empresaria vapores ó trasportes que como los de la línea de Law, midan un número crecido de toneladas. Por ejemplo: impongamos que los vapores Georgiay Ohio que miden cada uno 3.000 toneladas se contratasen para traer colonos de España á Cuba. Haciendo cada vapor veinte viajes en los dos años y conduciendo en cada viaje 12.000 colonos calculados á cuatro por tonelada, tendriamos que al vencimiento del término prefijado trasportarian estos dos vapores solamente, 480.000 colonos españoles que aumentarian la

poblacion blanca, en alto grado, y se borrarán de la historia el pronóstico de que "Cuba será Española ó Africana;" porque con tal avenida de españoles nodadamos que seria el número y no lo segundo, mucho mas cuando vendrían en clase de colonos, ministros y empleados cesantes que trasladarian la Corte de Madrid á la ciudad de la Habana, unico puerto por donde permite la Ordenanza de Pezuela el desembarque de colonos.

Las leyes de Inglaterra y los Estados Unidos no permiten el trasporte de pasajeros en buques á mas de uno por cada cuatro toneladas; ni de la humano que escedan á mas. Pero cupo á Pezuela este nuevo descubrimiento de trasportar hombres como si fuesen sardinas.

El Artículo 15.º escesera al colono de todo derecho de hombre libre: prohibe el matrimonio de ellos si no fuese conveniente al patrono ó dueño de la finca; lo que equivale á poner á estos hombres bajo el capricho y la arbitrariedad de un Señor absoluto cualquiera. Este Artículo se contradice torpemente con el Artículo 18.º en que se concede los mismos derechos que á los estranjeros domiciliados, y nosotros no sabemos que á estos estranjeros se les trate como á los negros esclavos ó á los colonos en los casos que espresan los Artículos 41.º y 57.º de la Ordenanza.

En resúmen vamos que es una tarea muy dilatada enumerar una por una el cúmulo de contradicciones que se encuentran en todos los artículos de la Ordenanza, que muy léjos de patrocinar la colonizacion blanca y españoles asiáticos y yucatecos solo tiende á impedirla; para que el pueblo de Cuba se convenza que no bastan los esfuerzos y protectorado del Gobierno paternal á reemplazar los brazos negros con los colonos blancos y cobrizos; sino que al cabo, satisfecho de la nulidad de los colonos rechazos por parte del Gobierno se abandone el plan de Colonizacion para volver al sistema de africanizacion, que es el único que presenta ventajas evidentes y lucrativas al Gobierno de S. M.

Los Capitanes Generales de Cuba conocen perfectamente el arte mágico para ser buenos prestidijitadores y llenar su bolsa.

ERRATA.

Despues de haberse distribuido á los suscritores la edicion del número anterior correspondiente al número 5 del presente Enero, notamos que el mes de la fecha no se varió por un olvido involuntario. Aunque muchos de nuestros lectores habrán notado el error, llamamos la atencion de aquellos que tienen la curiosidad de reunir coleccion del "Filibustero" para que teniendo presente este aviso no trastornen el órden numérico de los ejemplares, guiandose por la fecha "Diciembre" en vez de ser Enero. ¡Quiera el cielo que no llegue-

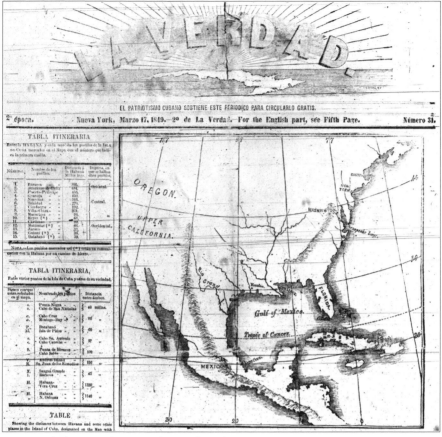

La Verdad, 17 March 1849. Library of Congress.

Masthead from *El Independiente*, 20 February 1853. Duke University Rare Book, Manuscript, and Special Collections Library.

Miguel T. Tolón. The New York Public Library.

EL MULATO.

AÑO 1.° · Periódico político, literario y de costumbres. · NUM. 7.°

Nueva-York, Abril 1.° de 1854.

EDITOR, Carlos de Colins.
No. 46 Chariton street, cuartopiso.

Los tiempos no retrogradan, las ideas avanzan, los principios mejoran y se rectifican, las doctrinas fundadas en una buena razon, adquieren proselitos y el progreso anuncia que las futuras jeneraciones recojeran los frutos de los grandes afanes de la presente. Allí donde se encuentre el verdadero mérito, debe reconocersele, ensalzarsele; el talento no se compra, ni la riqueza produjo los injénios esclarecidos. Leed la historia, recorred las épocas mas remotas, y os habreis desengañado que la fortuna halagó por lo comun á las medianías, colmó de favores, con jeneralidad, á la ignorancia. Durante la espinosa carrera de la vida, fórmanse grandes capitales, ó como fruto de una degradante economia, en que se desconocen ó rechazan todos los goces sociales, ó por medios casuales, ó con el sacrificio de una gran porcion de individuos, ó á merced de la astucia, la violencia ó el engaño.

Los grandes esfuerzos de nuestros padres hacen trasmitir á sus familias caudales cuya legal adquisicion se halla envuelta en la noche de los mismos tiempos, y sus poseedores, con vano orgullo, hablan de vinculadas riquezas, ultrajando á aquellos á quienes el pasado no atormenta y el presente les colma de verdadera gloria. Viene luego el egoismo despótico, con máscara hipócrita, á tomar aquel aire de autoridad que rechaza el patriotismo y la verdadera virtud, y los devotos de tan oscura escuela quieren rejir los destinos del mundo que los contempla y desprecia. Derrotados en sus planes, confundidos en sus propios principios, fulminan en su cólera impotente, mil anatemas contra la pobreza, la injurian como si fuese un delito, la abaten como si estuviese a nuestro arbitrio nacer ricos... ¡Miserables! asi ocultais insolentes vuestros vicios y defectos, vuestra impotencia y malignidad: nada debe esperarse de esos espíritus despóticos que aspiran á subyugar el pensamiento, destruir el progreso de la sociedad y apoderarse de los destinos de los pueblos.

Hablais de pobreza y no reconoceis vuestra triste ignorancia; quereis conservar destinos que exijen mérito, talento, virtudes y, como título, alegais que los demas son pobres: con nombres que nada significan, aspirais á realizar sublimes, nobles pensamientos: ¡qué error!! Echais en cara á vuestros semejantes una condicion que honra, que no deja tras de si melancólicos recuerdos, ni una huella de horror y de sangre: abogais por la esclavitud, porque no sois dignos de conceder á la LIBERTAD todos sus atributos.

Cuando vuestras intenciones y doctrinas son combatidas con las que os cuentan con otras armas que el egoismo, el orgullo y la ambicion de honores y destinos.—Los hombres se adquieren con los esfuerzos del entendimiento, con los buenos escritos que el público juzga y ensalza, la opinion es debida á las sanas doctrinas, á la noble abnegacion de los goces sociales, al deseo de mejorar la condicion humana, al interés de crear beneficios y garantías en favor de la libertad universal, y la riqueza, en fin, en su camino, deja recuerdos que la posteridad repite con horrible desconsuelo.

Hablan de nuestros escritos, los condenan sin que no los entienden, ó aquellos que conociendo su espíritu ven desaparecer los goces que se encuentran disfrutando en una estension ilimitada: espíritus asustadizos juzgan desplomarse el mundo en la menor alteracion de sus comodidades y placeres, y éstos son los que se titulan Padres del Pueblo, Directores de la Revolucion, Libertadores de la oprimida Cuba. ¡Qué inconsecuencia! No son esos impugnadores gratuitos los que rebajan nuestro crédito, ni pueden alcanzar que se desprecien nuestros escritos: emitan sus ideas con nobleza, dignidad, decoro: entren en el campo de la discusion sin orgullo y altanería, presenten sus principios con claridad, fijen sus doctrinas y verémos cuan pronto la opinion nos hará justicia, y la pobreza realzará nuestro mérito. Entre tanto, pobres fueron Virgilio, Homero, Ciceron, Descartes, Newton y otros muchos colocados en esa escala, á quienes no podrán alcanzar los tiros del venenoso artículo inserto en el NEW-YORK ENQUIRER del 23 del pasado marzo, ó los nuevos que escriba la envidia, el egoismo, ó salgan de plumas oscuras, mercenarias, enemigas de

todo progreso. Razones, razones, Sres. impugnadores, son las que deben oponerse á las nuestras, sin echar mano del arma ruin de la personalidades.

ESTUDIOS FILOSÓFICOS.[†]

ARTÍCULO III.°

| La "ley y el principio" son únicos en lo moral como en lo físico. | Abolicion de la ignorancia y de la miseria. |

DOCTRINA SOCIALISTA.
DE
JESUS-CRISTO.[‡‡]

No es mi ánimo discutir en este lugar la cuestion de la divinidad de Cristo; lo admitiré tal como la iglesia lo presenta, como Dios: 1.° para no herir las creencias relijiosas de los devotos; 2.° para darle mas fuerza y veracidad á la doctrina socialista de que me ocupo, fundándola, como la fundó Cristo, en el Cristianismo.

Si no queremos ver en Cristo mas que un hombre de un jénio colosal, el mas grande de todos los hombres por su amor y su rendimiento al Pueblo, hácia la Humanidad, asi como por la sublimidad de su palabra y de su filosofia, de todos modos debemos reconocerle como el ser por escelencia, como el ser superior á los demas que se adoran sobre la tierra como Dios, ¿no estaremos entónces forzados á escuchar y seguir sus opiniones y preceptos?

Si por otra parte, como quieren muchos, es el mismo Dios, ¿qué nos queda que hacer, sino escuchar, concebir y practicar su Doctrina?

Cristo no se presentó al mundo, como Moises, jefe de un reducido pueblo del cual arrebata del Ejipto para dictarle leyes especiales: se presentó como un libertador, que en medio del imperio de las lejiones romanas, emprende la árdua y benemérita tarea de salvar, no tan solo á los Judios, sino á la humanidad entera; de cortar de raiz la opresion, la esclavitud y la miseria; destronar á Júpiter y á sus Paganos Dioses; destruir sus templos y altares, establecer sobre la tierra la Fraternidad, la Igualdad y la Libertad....¡Que empresa tan colosal, si este hombre no es mas que un operario, un proletario de nacimiento!...¡Qué espectáculo!

Mayor será nuestra admiracion y el espectáculo mas grandioso, si este hombre, si este Reformador, si este Libertador es un Dios, el hijo de Dios, enviado por Dios, despues de haber resuelto entregar á su hijo bajo la forma humana

[†] Véanse los números 4.° y 6.

[‡‡] Para dar á conocer la verdadera doctrina social de Cristo, me he valido del Evanjelio y de la obra del comunista Cabet, titulada: "Le vrai Christianisme suivant Jesus-Christ." Paris, 1846-

Advertisement for *Cecilia Valdés*, *El Espejo*, April 1883. The New York Public Library.

El Mulato

RACE, LAND, AND LABOR IN THE AMERICAS

In 1854, a handful of exiles broke ranks with their compatriots and published an abolitionist newspaper that unabashedly set out "to attack slavery in whatever form it takes, out of a belief that it is baneful and incompatible with legitimate and true liberty."[1] The editors of *El Mulato* (New York) challenged exile leaders' decision to avoid the issue of slavery in Cuba out of fear that to call for abolition would brand their cause as extremist. In the United States, Cubans had turned to members of Congress from slaveholding southern states to back their filibustering cause. That type of compromise was unacceptable, argued Lorenzo Allo, who proclaimed in *El Mulato*, "For these thirty years I have been accustomed to hear that it is not yet the proper time to discuss slavery. How is the time designated? For me, it is always time to impugn whatever is evil, whatever is immoral, whatever outrages humanity, and whatever may inflict on Cuba great injuries."[2]

Belligerent and independent, *El Mulato* was the most radical of the transnational newspapers published by Cubans in the 1850s. The editors billed it as a "periódico político, literario y de costumbres [newspaper of politics, literature, and customs]" and published thirteen issues between February and May 1854.[3] In addition to placing abolition at the forefront of debates, the newspaper described itself as "socialist" and argued against the excessive U.S. influence on the "cause of the Cuban revolution." The newspaper called on Cubans to recognize the African racial and cultural influence on the island. To this end, *El Mulato* published a serialized abolitionist novella, *El Negro Mártir*, and touted the importance to Cuban literary culture of poet Gabriel de la Concepción Valdez, better known as Plácido, who had been executed by Spanish authorities in 1844 for supposedly helping to plan an uprising. The newspaper's name was itself an implicit nod to Plácido as an alternative to the filibustero Narciso López, whose death, as I discussed in the preceding chapter, had inspired exile writers to compose poems. Comparing López and Plácido, *El Mulato* foregrounded the question of race in looking back at those who had fallen: "If white patriots cry for General López and his unfortunate comrades, colored patriots cannot ever forget the memory of the sublime poet Plácido."[4] A brilliant poet, Plácido became a cause célèbre not only for some of the island's exiles but also for African American writers and abolitionists in the United States. As scholars of U.S. literature have noted in recent years, the debate over race and slavery crossed national borders in the nineteenth century, and U.S. writers as varied as Herman Melville and Martin Delany turned to the Caribbean, and particularly Cuba, to articulate the full hemispheric dimensions of slavery during the antebellum period.[5] Keeping that transnational perspective, the editors of *El Mulato* challenged slavery in the United States as they developed their liberation project.

El Mulato faced swift condemnation from Creole exiles. Not long after the editors circulated a prospectus, a large group of Cubans gathered for a contentious meeting to denounce the publication.[6] Why the effort to silence *El Mulato* in a community that valued the right of freedom of the press? For one, the newspaper unmasked how the racial ideology of filibustering and annexation rested on an ambivalence between a claim to Cuba based on Creole (and thus unstated white) right to land and a simultaneous refusal to discuss race and the influence of Africa and slaves on the island's society. *El Mulato* broke the silence on which Creole exiles relied to promote their program. As Ada Ferrer notes, "In Cuba, the conception of a raceless national community—very much dominant to this day—emerged in the period of independence struggles of the late nineteenth century and amidst multiracial mobilizations that sustained three full-fledged rebellions against Spain in the thirty years between 1868 and 1898."[7] Thus, independence fighters such as José Martí and General Antonio Maceo promoted the development of a Cuban citizen, not a racialized person, as the subject of the nation. (This attempt to erase racial difference has also been an important dimension of the post-1959 revolutionary Cuban nation.)[8] But whereas Martí proclaimed "There are no races" as a critique of nineteenth-century theories of essentialism, proannexation exiles in the 1850s papered over the importance of race to make their project more palatable to a U.S. public facing its own national anxieties about the sectional balance of power and the future of slavery.

In this chapter, I argue that contrary to the dominant position of exiles, slavery and race were a central concern in exiles' transnational writings and in U.S. debates about filibustering and the question of Cuba's future. Scholars such as Reginald Horsman and Thomas Hietala show how the ideology of Manifest Destiny became inextricable from theories of Anglo-Saxon superiority and efforts to preserve slavery.[9] In the case of the filibustering expeditions to Cuba and Nicaragua, racial ideology fed implicit or explicit support of slavery. But the belief that the Anglo-Saxon race had a natural right to take over the hemisphere directly confronted Cuban Creole claims to a local and cultural right to control the island. Certain Creoles attempted to paper over the distinction between Anglo-Saxon racial claims and Creole cultural claims by avoiding race and slavery altogether. *El Mulato* challenged that effort to create a Cuban revolutionary project that went unmarked in its racial affiliations. I begin, then, with an overview of *El Mulato*'s transnational critique.

Independence and Abolition: *El Mulato*

The editors of *El Mulato* were eager to turn a critical eye on the nation that had taken them in as exiles. In an English-language article, a headline posed a question, "Ought a Free Republic to Possess Slaves?" The response? "We hold the negative. . . . This government that vaunts of its freedom and civilization, and that declares this land to be an asylum for all seekers of liberty,—how is it acting to the poor slave?"[10] The immediate issue was the Kansas-Nebraska Act, pending before Congress in February 1854, which would have allowed those two states to vote on whether to permit slavery within their territories. "We cannot characterize that measure other than iniquitous and demoralizing, having for its object the perpetuation of an institution which is condemned by the whole civilized world," *El Mulato* argued. The paper focused directly on the raging conflict exacerbated by the Kansas-Nebraska Act: as the geopolitical boundaries of the Americas were changing in the wake of Manifest Destiny expansionism, which areas would be deemed slave territories? As historians have shown, the fili-bustering expeditions to Cuba and Nicaragua drew some support from U.S. southerners who sought to expand slavery.[11] Some southerners had even signed on to López's expeditions because they wanted to an-nex the island as a slave state.[12] And whatever his intentions, López was not above giving the appearance of proslavery sentiments to draw sup-port from the South.[13] *El Mulato* challenged the willingness to make that kind of political alliance or even to give that impression.

To carry out its program, *El Mulato* portrayed slavery as a scourge to humanity. Discussing the Kansas-Nebraska question, the paper con-ceived of a bleak future: "Ere the refulgent dawn of summer appears, a territory which is called the garden of America will be desolated by that gaunt monster 'slavery.'"[14] The garden metaphor had resonance for Cuba, which was often framed as Edenic in travel accounts. The use of words such as "monster" to describe slavery associated the institution with Spanish despotism, the cause of the dislocation of the paper's staff. In turn, the editors of *El Mulato* deployed their ethos as exiles to mount a concomitant antislavery and anti-Spanish critique: "We are expatriated from our native land for the political principles we profess: but wherever our humble lot may be cast we will never cease to devote our energies to secure our country's independence and the extinction of slavery."[15] *El Mulato* overstated the extent of support for its position by saying that "the majority" of Creoles in Cuba supported abolition and that "on the day the flag of liberty will float from the Morro Castle,— the mandate shall go forth decreeing universal emancipation."[16]

By attacking slavery in the hemisphere rather than just in Cuba, *El Mulato* refused to adopt the tone of obsequiousness toward the United States favored by *La Verdad* and other papers. *El Mulato* also criticized the exile community's overreliance on the United States to change the island's governmental structures. The paper noted disapprovingly, "The cause of the Cuban revolution, it is possible to say, has become completely *Americanized*."[17] In other words, Cubans had come to de-pend on annexation to dislodge Spanish troops from the island, thus creating a kind of indolence toward the revolution. "They want to enter the doors of the republic with a free ticket," the paper noted.[18] Repre-senting a growing sentiment in the New York exile community (includ-ing *El Filibustero*), *El Mulato* promoted separation from Spain first, with annexation as a matter to be taken up only by the Cuban population.

While the paper did not come out clearly against annexation, *El Mulato* was uncompromising in its view that gradual abolition would help Cuba "avoid damages similar to those experienced by the United States for not having approved in due time a measure that would gradually bring about the end of slavery."[19]

Most of the writers who supported López, including Miguel T. Tolón and Cirilo Villaverde, had been willing in 1850 and 1851 to go along with filibustering's tacit acceptance of slavery in Cuba. But their individual positions were more complex. In an 1850 issue of *El Horizonte*, Tolón called for "liberty under Republican rule" for all Cubans: "We love the Humanity of all nations and all races . . . Universal Liberty!"[20] While those beliefs seeped into their articles, most newspapers framed the battle for Cuba almost exclusively as a binary opposition between Spaniards and the Creole elite, cutting out class and race distinctions on the island. Of course, Cuba was a multiracial society, with the 1846 census breaking down the population as 425,767 whites, 323,759 slaves, and 149,226 free colored.[21] In the informal racial taxonomy of Cuba, a person could be viewed as *peninsular* (Spaniard), Creole, *mulato* (sometimes called *pardo*), or black (*negro* or *moreno*). As in the census, *mulatos* and blacks were sometimes grouped together under *de color* (of color), either free or enslaved.[22] In addition, Chinese indentured laborers began arriving in Cuba in 1847.

On what, then, did exile Creoles base their alliance with whites in the United States? I argue that it was on a notion of white republican Americanism (in the hemispheric sense). Exiled Creoles saw themselves as the intellectual descendants of U.S. revolutionaries and in alliance with figures in the U.S. expansionist drama such as John L. O'Sullivan and John Quitman. These types of identifications were possible because Creoles viewed themselves as white. Gaspar Betancourt Cisneros, for example, wrote, "All the white races spring from one trunk, viz. the Caucasian; and that the various tribes or families, the Arabians, the Teutonics, Celts, Greeks, or Latins, are nothing more than shoots from the primitive trunk, the Caucasian."[23] By contrast, some of the U.S. population saw Cubans as a distinct hybrid race, a point I take up in more detail later in this chapter. In public, Creoles argued that they had a right to oversee the political governance of the stretch of land called Cuba because of differences from Spain in location, political tradition (linked to the United States), and culture but not in race. In turn, it was possible to argue for democratic control of a territory (Cuba for Cubans) while perpetuating a racialized labor system that accepted slavery.

El Mulato's call for universal rights to extend to Cuba's slaves was a direct affront to exile leaders playing the card of white Americanism. While most if not all contributors to El Mulato were white Creoles, they held up the newspaper's name as a reminder that Cuba was a mixture of races and cultures.[24] In response, exile groups met on more than one occasion in February 1854 to denounce the newspaper. At one meeting, the editors of El Filibustero, Juan and Francisco Bellido de Luna, joined a group that had called itself the "Junta General de Cubanos" and voted for total reprobation of El Mulato, fearing that people in Cuba would associate exiles with abolitionists. El Filibustero published a favorable account of the junta's actions, arguing that discussions of abolition and socialism were premature and could "muddle" the ultimate goal of gaining freedom for Cuba.[25]

During one of the contentious meetings, Juan Clemente Zenea was shouted down for trying to defend El Mulato. A fiercely independent thinker who was willing to make enemies for his principles, Zenea was silenced twice by the tumultuous crowd. Some accused him of having accepted bribes to write for El Mulato. "Are we in Cuba or in New York?" he responded. "Do we live under despotism or liberty?"[26] When the group calmed down, Zenea defended his "efforts on behalf of the emancipation of slaves" by appealing to "freedom of the press":

No vengo tampoco a preguntar si debo escribir o no en El Mulato. Mi conciencia me dirigirá por la senda del deber. No creo que Uds. se erijan en tribunal para encadenar la libertad de imprenta; esto sería imposible y además ridículo. Es verdad que todavía conservamos algunos vicios aristocráticos, algunos hábitos adquiridos bajo la dominación española, pero todo esto es preciso deponerlo al pisar la tierra de Washington. Yo soy republicano desde que tengo uso de razón, y por eso conozco que la tolerancia es la primera virtud democrática. Jamás he tenido la presunción de creer que el que no piensa como yo está en el error.

[I do not come to ask whether I should write for El Mulato. My conscience will guide me down the path of duty. I do not believe that you would convene a court to shackle freedom of the press;

this would be impossible and even ridiculous. It is true that we still retain certain aristocratic vices, certain habits acquired under Spanish domination. But it is necessary to separate ourselves from all of this upon setting foot on the land of Washington. I have been a republican since I started using reason, and as a result I recognize that tolerance is the primary virtue of a democracy. I have never been so presumptive as to believe that he who does not think as I do is in error.]

Zenea invoked a liberal vision of tolerance to defend his more radical vision of abolition. His use of tolerance resonates with a speech in which George Washington took up the question of religious tolerance. All U.S. citizens, Washington said, possess "liberty of conscience and immunities of citizenship." "It is now no more that toleration is spoken of as if it were the indulgence of one class of people that another enjoyed the exercise of their inherent natural rights, for, happily, the Government of the United States, which gives to bigotry no factions, to persecution no assistance, requires only that they who live under its protection should demean themselves as good citizens."[27] To Zenea, being a good citizen meant debating questions rather than promoting a unitary voice for the exile community.[28] Like Zenea, *El Mulato* questioned whether exiles attacking the newspaper should claim to speak for the best interests of the Cuban people: "Who has told them that in a country where liberty of opinion is respected they have the right to elevate themselves as the sole arbiter of public opinion?"[29]

At times, *El Mulato* seemed more intent on developing an alliance with abolitionist republicans from Europe than with fellow exiles or with Cuba's population. The paper often described its fight for the rights of Cubans in relation to mid–nineteenth century European republican struggles. In one issue, *El Mulato* published an extensive article about a banquet ceremony held at Manhattan's Shakespeare Hotel to celebrate the anniversary of the founding of the French Republic in 1848. According to the newspaper, groups of exiles from Italy, France, Poland, and Cuba marched around the city carrying flags and banners on their way to the dinner and stopped in front of City Hall to hear a band play "Hail Columbia" and "La Marseillaise." "Citizens, misfortune turns us into brothers; I come to offer you my hand, which you have already shaken with kindness, and to offer the sympathy of my heart, sympathy which I offer in the name of all my compatriots," Fernando Rodríguez told the group. "We are all disposed to contribute to the work that you have started, and which today we will call ours."[30] Representatives of exiles from various nations also spoke at the gathering. And then, in a moment that displayed his full range in languages, Miguel T. Tolón delivered an oration in French in which he envisioned a utopian moment: "The day approaches when the difference between languages, as well as all distinctions of nationality, mores, and religion—all that impedes social assimilation—will cease to exist among men. This universal unity will be the achievement of the work of modern civilization, which always advances in spite of the obstacles ignorance and tyranny sow along its path."[31] In an editorial move that showed that *El Mulato* was speaking to well-educated exiles, the newspaper decided not to offer a translation "because we know how common among us is the sweet tongue of Voltaire."[32]

El Mulato developed a republican alliance because it suspected the Cuban exile leadership of protecting race and class interests in its pro-U.S. filibustering posture. Instead, the staff of *El Mulato* comprised intellectuals who argued strongly that natural rights extended to Cuban slaves.[33] The editor was listed on the front page as Carlos de Colins, a Matanzas-born political operative who had worked as a courier for López, carrying communications from New Orleans to Cuba.[34] Francisco Agüero Estrada, the main force behind the newspaper *El Pueblo*, contributed to *El Mulato* and took over as editor after the tenth issue, writing in one article that slavery was the "gangrene of our civilization."[35] After working for *El Mulato*, Agüero went on to call for slaves to be included in the ranks of the revolutionary fighters. Anticipating the positions of leaders during the Ten Years' War, Agüero argued that the revolution would remain a dream until slaves were brought into the program. "Has anyone seen or imagined a revolution without revolution?" he asked, paraphrasing a point made by Jacobins to Girondin compromisers.[36]

One prominent contributor to *El Mulato* was Lorenzo Allo Bermúdez, a lawyer who had studied at the Colegio Seminario de San Carlos under Félix Varela and alongside such notable intellectuals as José Antonio Saco and José de la Luz y Caballero. "If I might obey the desires of my soul," *El Mulato* quoted Allo as saying, "the law of manumission for the slaves of Cuba would be very simple:—*All the slaves*

of Cuba are declared free."[37] Exemplifying the types of political contradictions that emerged during this period, Allo in the 1850s worked
in revolutionary movements in Cuba, supported annexation, and promoted abolition. After López's fatal 1851 filibustering expedition, Allo
made his way to New York, where he worked as a teacher and contributed to various newspapers. He died in March 1854, not long
after *El Mulato* started publishing. In the paper's fifth issue, the front
page's columns were lined in black, a common practice in nineteenth-
century newspapers to signify the death of a notable contributor. "A
virtuous man, a just man, wise and selfless, a modest philosopher,
a patriot through his excellence, a friend of *universal liberty* has dis-
appeared forever from our side," *El Mulato* lamented. The obituary
concluded, "Rest in peace where the tyranny and injustice of men does
not reach."[38]

El Mulato emerged in tandem with Allo's notable pamphlet *La Esclavitud Doméstica en Sus Relaciones con la Riqueza* (1854), which was published in English the following year as *Domestic Slavery in Its Relation
with Wealth*. First delivered as a speech at the Cuban Democratic Athenaeum of New York on New Year's Day 1854, this pamphlet sketched
out arguments that closely resembled those appearing in *El Mulato*,
which sometimes quoted directly from the pamphlet in its articles.
Because it had been written as a speech, *Domestic Slavery* followed the
rhetorical structure of classical orations, opening with an exordium,
proceeding to an argument that "Slavery is antagonistic to wealth,"
continuing to a refutation of arguments in support of slavery, and
concluding with a program for how to abolish slavery in Cuba. In
developing his argument, Allo relied on a mix of Enlightenment reason and Christian morality. The following two passages show how he
drew both from political economy and from Christian teaching:

> The free workman requires, in exchange for his labor, main-
> tenance for himself and his family. The master of the slave must
> needs indemnify himself for the capital which his slave cost him,
> for the interest of that capital, for the expense of maintaining and
> providing for him medical attendance; and for the wages of the
> overseer. . . . Let us also recollect that the slave does not live so
> long as the free worker, and we may draw the deduction that the
> work of the slave costs more than the work of the free laborer.[39]

Jesus Christ taught all the principles which constitute true morality, principles which serve as the foundation of his divine religion, and which have brought to the people wealth, science, progress, and prosperity. Wealth is not merely material; it is likewise intellectual and moral; and material wealth cannot even exist without creating the other two. Therefore, slavery is contrary to the bases of Christianity, whose great doctrines are "Love thy neighbor as thyself," and "Do unto others what you would have others do unto you."[40]

In keeping with this vision, *El Mulato* presented its "socialist doctrine" in relation to the work of Jesus Christ. The newspaper's Christ, however, was a republican at heart, walking the earth to eliminate "oppression, slavery, and misery" while trying to establish "fraternity, equality, and liberty."[41]

Despite his abolitionist stance, Allo continued to push the annexationist line in the *Domestic Slavery* pamphlet, arguing that Cuba should "assure her well-being and safety by becoming allied or annexed to the United States."[42] (*El Mulato*, however, had a more ambivalent position on annexation.) To develop his main economic line of argument, Allo turned to history, arguing that Rome's downfall resulted in part from slavery: "Rome always maintained slavery, and in this we have the explanation how it was that the Teutonic races parceled among themselves her provinces, as birds of prey divide a dead body. The European peoples abolished slavery, and the manumissions were followed by the discovery of the compass, the press, the perfection of agriculture, the commercial exchanges between nations, the development of the arts, schools, political right, and all the elements of wealth."[43] Slavery, Allo argued, stamped out the creativity and resourcefulness of people who had nothing to gain from their labor. "Ah! There are now existing in Cuba five hundred thousand intelligent beings, dead so far as labor is concerned," he wrote.[44] The larger economic panorama was affected because "where slavery exists, domestic service and agricultural and manufacturing employments are degraded and are abandoned by free laborers." Allo then turned to the question of women. He argued that in Cuba and other countries with economies of slavery, women did not have the resources to develop economic independence. And what of women who depended on their families or husbands and then lost that support? "Nothing, gentlemen, nothing remains to these women, not even the humble resource of domestic service, since if they entered into it they would be confounded with slaves."[45] Allo had hit on one of the realities of Cuban society: the inextricable connections among labor, race, and status.

"Substantial Distinction": Racial Views of Cuban Land

El Mulato uncovered what transnational newspapers circulating in the 1850s failed to confront: the ways filibustering was supported by a set of tacit assumptions about the relationship of land, cultural right, and racial labor. As articles in *La Verdad* make clear, exiles sought not only to get rid of Spain in Cuba but also to reverse what they saw as Spain's Africanization of the island through its ongoing introduction of new slaves. This position begins to explain the papers' strong rhetoric against the illegal continuation of the slave trade and against the importing into Cuba of indentured labor from Asia. In 1817, Spain had signed on a treaty with England prohibiting the introduction of new slaves into Cuba and other colonial territories. Despite laws that specified punishments for ship captains and crew involved in the illegal trade, vessels continued to bypass the prohibition and make their way to Cuba.[46] In the 1850s, *filibustero* newspapers ran a steady stream of articles reporting the arrival of new slaves from Africa in violation of the treaty. *El Filibustero* reported on 9 May 1853 that the ship *Lady Suffolk* had "unloaded on the coast of Matanzas a shipment of 600 newly arrived blacks from Africa, mocking the surveillance of English cruisers."[47] Those articles pointed to the cruelty of the slave trade, and exiles were quick to relate conditions aboard a *pirata negrero*, a slave ship, to Spanish abuses of the general Cuban population, echoing the powerful concluding lines of Zenea's poem "El Filibustero." But the articles also betrayed a fear that blacks would take over Cuba.

From the inception of *La Verdad* in 1848 until the late 1850s, transnational newspapers regularly voiced concerns that the illegal slave trade would "Africanize" Cuba and possibly unleash a black revolt. Fear of a black takeover had influenced Creole landowners in Cuba to support annexation in the late 1840s. Pro-Spanish newspapers in Havana and *La Crónica* in New York sometimes tweaked Creole fears by stating flatly that only two scenarios were possible in the future: To remain Spanish or become "African." Exiles responded with lengthy denunciations of Spain's willingness to unleash slave terror on the island rather than give up its colonial hold. The fear of a black-led revolt begins to explain *El Mulato*'s effort to distance itself from calls for black revolution. The paper explained that in calling for abolition, it was not "lighting the fuse of a bomb that will explode with frightening thunder." Instead, the paper argued, by granting the rights of a democratic republic to "all men," Cuba would "alleviate" the suffering of blacks and build a future based on justice for all sectors of society. In other words, *El Mulato* wanted neither Spanish colonialism nor black revolution.[48]

Newspapers such as *La Verdad* and *El Filibustero* also voiced concern about how the arrival in Cuba of indentured laborers from Asia was affecting the island racially and culturally. Spaniards and Creole landowners on the island had started to bring Chinese workers to Cuba in 1847 as a way to ensure a cheap source of labor. More than 23,000 Chinese were taken to the island between 1847 and 1857, with an additional 13,384 arriving in 1858.[49] These workers were purchased for four hundred dollars each and were forced to work at a salary of four dollars a month.[50] With "contracts" lasting eight years, Chinese laborers were practically slaves.[51] *El Filibustero* regularly ran articles criticizing the trade in Chinese laborers, not only because of the treatment of the Chinese but also because of the effect these workers would have on Cuban society. Transnational newspapers pointed to Chinese labor as one of the scandals of Spanish colonialism, in part because exiles believed that Asian workers were not part of the island's culture.

El Mulato's call to empower all of Cuba's classes was at odds with annexation supporters who saw Cuba as a land waiting to be conquered by industrious Anglo-Saxon businesspeople. As I argued in chapter 2, *La Verdad* trained on Cuba an imperialist eye that mapped the island's resources as ripe for the taking by U.S. investors. While *La Verdad* attempted to downplay race and slavery in that picture, some U.S. observers emphasized slavery as a justification for capitalist expansion and filibustering in Cuba. To understand the broader social context here, we can look at William Walker's 1855 filibustering expedition to Nicaragua. Walker held out land as a reward to attract colonists from the United States. Given the ideology of Anglo-Saxon enterprise that fed the Nicaraguan venture, Walker reinstated slavery in 1856 although it had been abolished throughout Central America in 1824, after the region gained independence from Spain. Walker issued a governmental decree that granted 250 acres to any single man and 350 acres to any family that migrated from the United States to Nicaragua. According to Walker, "tropical America" was the place where slavery "finds the natural seat of its empire."[52]

In conjunction with Walker's expedition, books appeared in the United States touting Central America for prospective settlers. William Wells's *Walker's Expedition to Nicaragua* (1856) portrayed the country as a bountiful area replete with a variety of fruits, vegetables, minerals, and animal life that could be of great benefit to colonists and capitalists from the United States. Framed as a collection of "facts and data" and an "authentic, reliable, and correct" picture, the book is filled with lists of agricultural offerings: "There are the orange, lemon, lime, banana, cocoa nut, cocoa plum, alligator pear, guava, plantains, paypayas [sic], marañon, rose apples, granadilla, watermelon, cantelope [sic] . . . potato, okra, yam, sweet potato, pears, Lima, French, and Vanilla beans, squashes, tomatoes, peppers."[53] One effect of such lists, which also emerged in writings about Cuba, is that the fruits of the land appear so bountiful as to be open for the taking of those who would provide the necessary labor—their own or that of slaves—to turn these plants into commodities.

The bounty of raw materials offered by the Nicaraguan land is a central concern in *The Destiny of Nicaragua: Central America as It Was, Is, and May Be* (1856), published anonymously by one of Walker's officers. The book presents the area as a plentiful territory, leaving a discussion of Walker for the final pages. As a result, *Destiny* shifts the debate on Nicaragua from a focus on Walker and the illegitimacy of his filibustering to a consideration of Nicaragua as a territory that could benefit U.S. capitalists. Both in its organization and its content, *Destiny* argues that public reservations about filibustering should give way to business interests. Accordingly, the book argues that the negative view of Walker's expedition resulted from misperceptions about the land's potential: "The mistakes undoubtedly arise from the fact that so little is known, generally, of that garden of the world."[54] The passage calls for "business-like" interests to prevail on the Nicaragua question. In other words, "the American mind" had to learn of the material resources and commodities offered by the region to reach a reasonable conclusion on Nicaragua. Walker's slavery decree was in keeping with a perspective on race and land that promoted the Anglo-Saxon right to govern and make a profit at the expense of the mixed-raced populations of Latin America.

On one level, then, filibuster writings—including a newspaper such as *La Verdad*—functioned as part of what Mary Louise Pratt calls a "capitalist vanguard."[55] Descriptions that fetishized land as an economic resource for the production of commodities can be traced back to early modern "exploration" narratives. But at the same time, the particularities of the filibustering moment prompted a description of the land and its labor conditions in terms specific to the context in the territories. One settler in Nicaragua wrote, "All that has been said of the fertility of the soil and the nature of its productions is quite correct; the one thing needful is its development. When that is effected by the influx of settlers, this country must become the Paradise of North America."[56] This settler repeats the paradise trope introduced by Columbus and so often deployed in writings about the topography of the Caribbean, and particularly Cuba, but he does so in the context of a filibustering venture based on slavery.

In the case of Cuba, the land offered not only resources but also a territory where slavery was already a part of the local economy. A segment of the U.S. population saw in slavery enough of a reason for opposing filibustering and/or annexation. That position was intertwined with sectional debates in the United States. In Richard Henry Dana's *To Cuba and Back: A Vacation Voyage* (1859) and Julia Ward Howe's *A Trip to Cuba* (1860), Cuba is looped into a southern region of slavery with the U.S. South so that an opposition emerges between New England on the one hand and Cuba and the U.S. South on the other. Howe, a poet whose articles about Cuba appeared in the *Atlantic Monthly* and later as a book, argued that slave owners would not voluntarily abolish slavery because the "indolence and mechanical ineptitude which enter into their characters will make them always a people to be waited on."[57] She emphasized regional difference: "Perhaps no nation, living below a certain parallel, would be capable of" abolishing slavery (*Trip* 233). Howe's notion that the ability and willingness to work is tied to region begins to explain Dana's interest in the relationships among race, labor, and land.[58]

In the context of nineteenth-century views on race, Dana and Howe were opponents of slavery who simultaneously held racist views about Cuban blacks, Spaniards, and Cuban Creoles. Slavery was at odds with Dana's notion of a New England work ethic based on the idea that a person reaps what he or she sows. Describing an encounter with an engineer from Lowell, Massachusetts, at La Ariadne plantation, Dana emphasizes that the engineer works for a salary, unlike the plantation owners. It was not uncommon at this time for engineers from the United States to work in Cuba for several months during the cane-harvesting season and then return to their homes. In Cirilo Villaverde's novel, *Cecilia Valdés* (1882), as we will see in the next chapter, the engineer at La Tijana plantation is a "young American man."[59] Dana praises these engineers for taking their knowledge of machinery to a "remote place": "Their skill is of great value, and while on the planta-tion their work is incessant, and they have no society or recreations whatever" (*TC* 60). In the next two sentences, Dana twice describes the engineer as "independent," first implying financial independence from salaried labor rather than a master-slave relationship and then implying political independence from the horrors of the slave system. Dana tries to distance the machinist, who "talked, like a true Yankee, of law and politics," from the more repressive plantations, noting that La Ariadne is "a favorable specimen, both for skill and humanity" (*TC* 60).

Dana's insistence on the difference between Cuba and New England begins to approximate essentialism when he reaches into the earth and contemplates "these strange palm trees everywhere" (*TC* 46). While many trees "look to the eye as if they might grow as well in New England as here," the royal palm "looks so intensely and exclusively tropical" that it has "a strange fascination over the eye and the fancy" (*TC* 47). Emphasizing his perspective, Dana writes, "The palm tree seems a kind of *lusus naturae* to the northern eye—an exotic wherever you meet it" (*TC* 47). By invoking the palm tree, Dana touches the roots of Cuban literary nationalist tropes. The palm had appealed to many of the century's major poets. José María Heredia, in his "Ode to Niagara," wrote of experiencing his own disconnection from the palms on seeing the rushing waters of the falls: "What seeks thy restless eye? Why are not here, / About the jaws of this abyss, the palms— / Ah, the delicious palms."[60] Heredia draws a contrast between the sun, ocean air, and "unspotted blue" sky that surround a Cuban palm tree and the "gran-deur" of Niagara, for which "forest pines / Are fitter coronal." As critics note, Heredia resolves the contrast between northern falls and Carib-bean tropics by invoking a romantic sublime. Dana, however, holds up the palm as floral evidence of the island's distinction in that the tree has "a pride of unmixed blood and royal descent—the hidalgo of the soil" (*TC* 47).[61] Dana's difference is Heredia's familiarity.

The sleight of hand in the discourse of difference on Cuba is in the slippage from race as representative of physical characteristics to race as a people (a common usage in the nineteenth century) to race as cul-ture (a representative set of practices). In U.S. imaginings about Cuba, culture becomes an indication of character. For example, a three-part travel series on Cuba in *Putnam's Monthly Magazine* played into stereo-types that Latin Americans were lazy and implied that sloth was part of Cuba's local character.[62] For many U.S. writers, the question of charac-ter included Cuba's Creole population. Dana framed it in relation to political agency. "You cannot reason from Massachusetts to Cuba," he wrote, arguing that Cubans would not fight for self-government (*TC* 132). Pointing to historical difference, Dana proposed that unlike Cuba, the thirteen colonies had enough autonomy that their people were able to undertake a revolution. In a passage reminiscent of his portrayal of the ship as a republican hierarchical institution in *Two Years before the Mast*, Dana wrote, "The thirteen colonies were ships fully armed and equipped, officered and manned, with long sea experience, sailing as a wing of a great fleet, under the Admiral's fleet signals. . . . But Cuba has neither officers trained to the quarterdeck, nor sailors trained to the helm, the yard, or the gun" (*TC* 132). Ultimately, Dana saw Cuba as full of "evils," "disorder and weakness," and "complication of diffi-culties" related to slavery, the indentured servitude of Asian laborers, and hostilities between Creoles and Spaniards (*TC* 132). In other words, the hybridity of Cuban society was interrelated to continuing colonial government.

The racist writings of antislavery travelers such as Dana and Howe illustrate the full irony of Cuban Creoles' attempts to draw a con-nection between themselves and U.S. whites. Anti-Spanish Creoles such as Gaspar Betancourt Cisneros were willing to develop an alliance with U.S. expansionists in part because the Creoles saw themselves as whites in the Americas fighting a European power. But a segment of the U.S. population, including some antislavery and antiexpansionist writers, saw Creoles as hybrid people incapable of governing themselves. For the rest of the century, Cubans in the United States had to fight an assumption that people on the island were too indolent to fight their own revolution. As late as 1889, Martí had to respond to charges in the U.S. press that Cubans were, like Spaniards, idle and unfit to govern themselves. In a letter to the *New York Evening Post*, Martí wrote, "We are not the people of destitute vagrants or immoral pigmies that the [Philadelphia] *Manufacturer* is pleased to picture; nor the country of petty talkers, incapable of action, hostile to hard work, that, in a mass with the other countries of Spanish America, we are by arrogant travelers and writers represented to be."[63] In other words, while Martí and exiles from the 1850s emphasized cultural and political differences between Cubans and Spaniards, the U.S. press deployed a perspective based on a two-way opposition between self (U.S. white) and other (Cuban/Spaniard). Martí eventually responded in *Patria* with an article about the United States in which he categorically stated, "The entertainment of locating any substantial distinction between the Saxon egotist and the Latin egotist, the generous Saxon and the generous Latin, the Saxon bureaucrat and the Latin bureaucrat—for Latins and Saxons have an equal capacity for virtues and defects—is only for men of prologue and surface."[64] Bringing together the antiessentialist elements of his essays "My Race" and "The Truth about the United States" as well as the antiimperialist dimensions of "Our America," Martí wrote against a binary racial hierarchy that divided the hemisphere between the United States and Latin America. But in the 1850s, most exiles had not reached a point where they could take a critical position on the question of race in Cuba and thus express opposition to U.S. positions justifying expansionism through racial right and slavery. And therein lies the radicalism of *El Mulato*.

"Remembrance of His Pain": Visions of Placid(o)

On April 25, *El Mulato* responded to a letter written by black activist and writer Martin R. Delany and printed in the *Aliened American*, an abolitionist paper published in Ohio. "The letter contains a tissue of invectives directed against Mr. Colins, the Editor of this journal," *El Mulato* said. "We may be permitted to say that the reputation of Mr. Colins reposes on too firm a pedestal to be affected by Delany; and that he, Delany, and his remarks, Mr. Colins can treat with the most sovereign contempt. We should add that the statements contained in Delany's letter are false."[65] Delany certainly had a much different view of Cuba's future than *El Mulato* in that he called for black revolution rather than gradual emancipation. "At the instant of the annexation of Cuba to these United States, it should be the signal for simultaneous rebellion of all the slaves in the Southern States, and throughout that island," Delany wrote in the *North Star*.[66] That view of simultaneous revolution in the United States and Cuba informed Delany's novel *Blake; or, The Huts of America* (1859). Invoking the rights of black and indigenous populations to justify a takeover of Cuba, the novel inverted the racist notions that fueled filibustering expeditions by calling for Anglo-Saxon or white Creole territorial control.[67]

Delany's attack on *El Mulato* points to the circulation of the Cuban paper among African American leaders and emphasizes the very different sociopolitical locations (influenced by individual geographic histories) of Delany and abolitionist Cuban exiles. In exile circles, *El Mulato* was a radical publication. But Delany probably did not believe that the newspaper protected the interests of blacks in Cuba. Furthermore, *El Mulato*'s celebration of a multiracial Cuban subject as exemplified in the poet Plácido was at odds with Delany's insistence on a black leader such as Henry Blake to lead a transnational revolution.[68] In Cuba, free mulattoes such as Plácido interacted with whites, albeit within a system of racial hierarchy that situated the label *negro* at the bottom. The distinction informed Juan Clemente Zenea's rabid defense of his work for *El Mulato*: "I write and will write however many times I want in *El Mulato* or *El Negro*."[69] While there was no such publication as "El Negro," Zenea called forth the figure to thumb his nose at Creoles who would have been scandalized by the idea of celebrating the black race in their publications.

In Plácido, *El Mulato* found a figure that could easily be deployed to attack Spanish colonial rule in Cuba. Plácido (1809–44) was a free mulatto who gained literary fame throughout the Americas both for his verses and for the tragedy of his execution. Friends reported seeing Plácido spend entire days moving from weddings to baptisms to parties, delighting people with his ability to excel at *calamo currente*, a form of poetic improvisation in which the poet was given the concluding line of a short poem and asked to compose extemporaneously a rhymed ten-line stanza or a sonnet leading up to the final line.[70] In 1844, Spanish colonial authorities in Cuba accused Plácido of having been a leader in a plot to overthrow white rule on the island. In response to La Escalera, the colonial government took brutal measures against the population, and a firing squad shot Plácido. In the decade following his death, Plácido became a figure who could be written into a variety of literary-political positions: martyr for the abolitionist cause, politically active rebel, freedom fighter against Spanish colonialism, and poetic genius.[71]

In 1849, the *North American Review* published an article on the poetry of "Spanish America" in which Plácido was glorified not only for his verses but also for his political virtues: "Never have the rights of man found a more heroic martyr than in this despised and humble laborer."[72] The abolitionist collection *Autographs for Freedom* (1853) included an essay by William Allen, a black professor at New York Central College, who presented Plácido as an example that "God hath not given to one race alone, all intellectual and moral greatness."[73] Many writings about Plácido highlighted the circumstances surrounding his execution: Plácido apparently uttered dramatic lines between two sets of volleys by the firing squad. As Allen described the events,

> On the first fire of the soldiers, no ball entered his heart. He looked up, but with no spirit of revenge, no aspect of defiance,— only sat upon his countenance the desire to pass at once into the region where no death is.
>
> "Pity me," he said, "and fire here,"—putting his hand upon his heart. Two balls entered his body, and Placido fell.[74]

By the time Richard Henry Dana went to Matanzas and visited the square where Plácido had been executed, Dana implicitly acknowledged that his description of the square was framed by previous accounts of the poet's death: "At the first volley, as the story is told, he was only wounded. 'Aim here!' said he, pointing to his head. Another volley and it was all over" (*TC* 45). The similarities between Allen's and Dana's passages show that the two were retelling as well as telling, a point that is further emphasized by Dana's phrase, "as the story is told."

Often missing from many accounts of Plácido was the importance of his poetry in developing a sense of Cuba as a land and place distinct from Spain. Plácido was among a group of Cuban poets who, as Frederick Stimson argues, "endeavored to 'Cubanize' poetry by describing island scenery and by utilizing romantic themes such as cockfights and pre-Columbian Indians."[75] In contrast to the *filibustero* writers in the United States, Plácido did not call overtly for the overthrow of the Cuban government. Among his poems are a set known as the blossom poems, which include "La Flor del Café" (The coffee flower) and "La Flor de la Piña" (The pineapple flower). The latter, a seemingly apolitical celebration of a local fruit, takes on anti-Spanish overtones when the pineapple is crowned "queen," thus challenging colonial deference to Spanish monarchy. The "fertile fields" of Cuba proclaim the pineapple as the queen, as opposed to the monarchical lineage of the Spanish queen. Situating the "queen" in Cuba, Plácido eroticizes the pineapple flower, comparing it to a feminine figure, a trope that repeats itself in many of Plácido's nature poems. Vera Kutzinski explores the sociopolitical content of Placido's poems, arguing that "he was wise to the salient ideological contradictions that were part and parcel of the island's sugar and slave economy as he was enamored of Cuba's natural beauty." But as Kutzinski also points out, the dynamic of Plácido's poetry was not nearly as interesting to nineteenth-century readers as the conditions of his imprisonment and execution.[76] When accounts of Plácido in the United States focused on his poetry, they usually turned to his prison poems, written shortly before his execution.

The differences in the way *filibustero* writers deployed Plácido and his treatment in the U.S. press become apparent in two translations of "Despedida a Mi Madre" (Farewell to my mother), a poem that appeared in *El Horizonte* and the *North American Review*.[77] According to *El Horizonte*, this sonnet was "written in the prison chapel a few moments before execution." The *Review* described Plácido writing the poem on a piece of paper the previous night. In offering solace to his mother, Plácido incorporated spiritual elements into the poem, most evident in the line, "Ya de la religión me cubre el manto! [Now religion's mantle covers me]." The *Review*'s translation, which was preceded by Plácido's poem, "Prayer to God," emphasizes the religious vision and concludes with the line "Mother, farewell! God keep thee and for ever!" The original, however, does not include the word "God" in the final line, although the translator might have been playing with the word *adios* (farewell), which sounds like *a Dios* (to God). By contrast, the translation in *El Horizonte* deemphasizes the spiritual tone and concludes with "I bend the neck.—Religion mild appears / And robes me, mother, while I breathe farewell." The differences in the two translations are evident in the way they handle the first four lines of the sonnet's turn:

Sonido dulce, melodioso y santo,
Glorioso, espiritual, puro y divino,
Inocente, espontáneo como el llanto
Que vertiera al nacer. (Plácido)

A strain of joy and gladness, free, unfailing,
All-glorious and holy, pure, divine,
And innocent, unconscious as the wailing
I uttered at my birth. (*Review*)

A sound most holy in its tender swell
Most glorious, melodious, unbound
Spontaneous as childhood's earliest tears. (*El Horizonte*)

While the *Review* translation picks up on the original's intense spirituality by using "holy," "all-glorious," and "divine," the translation in *El Horizonte* provides a more secular swelling of sound. As a political paper committed to furthering republicanism, *El Horizonte* is more interested in Plácido as a martyr.

In that vein, *El Mulato* opted for an overtly political Plácido, printing in the paper's first issue his poem "El Juramento" with an introductory note: "Those who know his death as decreed by the cannibals on the bloody court of the military commission in 1844, those who became acquainted with the talent of the unfortunate poet, his exquisite sensibility, and more than anything, his enthusiasm for the liberty of the human race, will pay tribute with a melancholy remembrance of his pain."[78] The phrase "more than anything" situates Plácido's political commitment at least on equal footing with, if not above, his poetry. In "El Juramento," the speaker recounts making his way to a site in nature, a creek, possibly for a clandestine meeting of some sort, and swearing (*el juramento*) to be the eternal enemy of tyranny. The poem's concluding lines articulate a second commitment: "Y morir a las manos de un verdugo / Si es necesario, por romper el yugo [And to die at the hands of an executioner / If necessary, to break the yoke]." By those terms, Plácido's destiny is to die for the cause. Two months later, *El Mulato* published another poem by Plácido that compares a cat who tortures a mouse out of malice to people who rule in that manner.[79] *La Verdad* also provided a political Plácido, publishing his sonnet about William Tell's killing of Herman Gessler.[80] Whatever their position on slavery, all of Cuba's exiles in the United States clearly held Plácido up as a reason to fight colonialism.

Delany published *Blake* against this backdrop of Cuban anticolonial agitation.[81] The character of Placido (without an accent) kindles revolutionary commitment and inspires Blake, who believes the revolution needs poetry to inspire and promote the cause. But Delany's novel also challenges the assumption that the writer can function effectively to take over territories. By the end of the novel, it becomes clear that Placido has a limited ability to support Blake's effort to acquire and control Cuba. Writing after the failed expeditions of Narciso López and William Walker, Delany was probably aware that filibusters could publish extensively, but if military, economic, and political conditions did not develop along with the writings, filibusters could not hold the land they sought. The anxiety over the efficacy of writing for revolution that emerges in *Blake* is reminiscent of the tension between arms and letters that captivated Cuban *filibusteros*, as I discussed in the preceding chapter. *Blake* seems to recognize that writing cannot compensate for military success; thus, the novel presents a more militant version of Placido than other documents at the time, only to displace him as a factor in revolutionary change.

The emphasis on Cuban land and customs in Plácido's poetry is muted in Delany's Placido. Despite the availability in the antebellum period of English-language translations of Plácido's poems, Delany chose not to use any of those versions. Eric Sundquist argues that Delany's substitution of verses by the African American poet James Whitfield for Plácido's works facilitates the insertion of poetry that "is more overtly antislavery in spirit" and thus helps Delany to demonstrate his "belief in the political function of literature."[82] The substitution of Whitfield for Plácido, I believe, also erases the local Cuban conditions of composition. A trajectory from literature to political positioning can be summed up in lines from twentieth-century Salvadoran poet Roque Dalton: "I came to the revolution by way / of poetry."[83] But in emphasizing poetry's political function, Delany obliterates the literary function of politics. While the political function of literature might be to prompt the emancipation of slaves and bring about equality, the literary function of politics is to change conditions that create new perspectives and open literary culture in society to different types of people, including the marginalized, such as a mulatto poet in nineteenth-century Cuba. The inverse of Dalton's line would be, "I came to poetry by way of the revolution." One of the truly revolutionary challenges that Plácido presented to Cuban society was that a free mulatto with a limited education could infuse the coffee flower and pineapples with a sense of the Cuban nation and could do so in verses that many believed surpassed works written by the poets of Spain.

The last of the recovered chapters of *Blake* presents a brutal rejection of Placido as a poet of the revolution.[84] When Placido enters a bookstore and does not remove his hat, a book dealer becomes furious and grabs Placido by the collar. He responds with a look of "godlike defiance," inspired by the "sacred fire of Heaven which burnt divinely in the poet's soul" (*B* 307). The merchant, a representative of U.S. commercial interests, then deals "a well aimed blow [that] sent the bard of Cuba staggering prostrate upon the pavement in the street" (*B* 307). The wound causes a physical disfigurement and becomes "discolored." Placido moves his hand up to his face and feels "the extent of the cruel mutilation, the left molar bone being badly wounded" (*B* 308). Described as "physically weaker" than the bookseller, "the bard of Cuba" responds to the attack by reciting the following lines: "How long, O gracious God! how long / Shall power lord it over right?" (*B* 308). In the tension between the bookseller and poet, the scene rehearses a confrontation between the commercial aspect of books and the poetic imagination. It emphasizes the physical power of white, northern commercial interests and businesspeople who have a stake in the Cuban economy. After he has beaten Placido, the bookseller feels guilty, but he is moved not so much by Placido's pacifist poetic response but by the realization that the action might have monetary ramifications. The merchant thinks Placido is a preacher and concludes, "I knew several of them while doing business in Baltimore, and always found them good religious black men. They are good customers, always buying costly and large works on divinity" (*B* 308). What ultimately triumphs in this exchange are commercial power and the stronger physical body. The scene almost harks back to the first part of the novel, when Henry Blake imparts that the secret of his organization is "capital, capital." Without the novel's final chapter and without knowing the outcome of the planned revolt, *Blake* ends with a resounding statement on the limits of poetry to stand up to the military and commercial forces vying for control of Cuba.

With that conclusion, *Blake* responds to the type of tension between arms and letters that plagued the Cuban *filibusteros* in the United States and that I discussed in the preceding chapter. Delany's militant anti-slavery novel shares with the newspaper *El Mulato* a vision of Plácido as symbol of Cuban emancipation. But as the novel's narrative progresses, Placido is ultimately displaced from influence in the new government. In that sense, *Blake* offers a skeptical perspective on literature's ability to bring about change in Cuban society. But like Cuban exiles, Blake (and Delany, as author of the novel) does not completely give up on the metaphorical possibilities of literary pieces inspiring a revolution. *El Mulato* viewed fiction as an integral part of the transnational fight against slavery; consequently, the newspaper published a serialized abolitionist novella, *El Negro Mártir*.

El Negro Mártir: Francisco in New York

As a transnational newspaper, *El Mulato* is imbricated in a set of political and cultural entanglements that stretch from Cuba to the United States. To understand how Cuban literary conditions make their way to New York and into *El Mulato*, we can turn to *El Negro Mártir*, which was published anonymously in Spanish in eight installments. Set in 1844 against the backdrop of La Escalera conspiracy, the novel is told in the third person but shifts the narratorial voice at times to slaves who share with one another remembrances of Africa. The martyr of the story is a slave, Francisco, who suffers from having been separated from the love of his life after being taken into slavery. Sentimental in tone, the novel presents African characters weeping and describes the Middle Passage and enslavement as a "holocaust." The first installment ends in Africa with Francisco and his beloved sitting under the moonlight: "I took her hands in mine and asked her to sit by my side, and we remained silent for a long time, then her eyes became wet with tears."[85] After Francisco recounts his kidnapping and arrival in Cuba, the novel begins to focus on a love affair between a Creole involved in a clandestine plot to liberate the island and Margarita, the wife of Francisco's master. A district attorney who has his eyes on Margarita intercepts one of their letters and takes it to the island's captain-general, Leopoldo O'Donnel, a character based on a historical figure, using Francisco as the courier. Government authorities arrest him, although he seemingly knows nothing about the conspiracy. As the intricacies of the plot are developing, the novel ends abruptly in *El Mulato*'s tenth issue, no doubt as a result of questions about whether the paper would continue publishing.

Because the narrative ushers Francisco and Margarita into a quick death, *El Mulato* does not develop fully the intertwined plot of love and conspiracy. Instead, the novel succeeds in its deployment of inflammatory language about the slave trade and rulers in Cuba. Describing the effects on Africans of being kidnapped and taken into slavery, the novel asks, "Who could express the agony that overwhelms the soul of those martyrs of the holocaust who are offered up to the most infamous perversity?"[86] The novel also draws a generational distinction between the youthful Creoles fighting the system and the older supporters of Spanish rule. Don Pedro, the owner of a coffee plantation, is described as seventy-year-old man with "vulgar physiognomy, thin body; he is egotistical, uneducated, cruel to his slaves and frequently perverse."[87] Marked by a romantic dualism, *El Negro Mártir* associates slave owners with evil rulers, in contrast to the Creoles. Margarita, for example, is described as olive-skinned and possessing the "perfect beauty of her ardent country."[88] Slaves are caught between the two opposing sides, and Francisco unwittingly becomes a martyr. In the terms of the novel, Francisco belongs to a "race pursued by too many despots." In a metaphor that invokes the Spanish Inquisition, the narrator says, "You are the errant Jew of the nineteenth century."[89]

The mixture of lyric flights of condemnation, truncated romantic machinations, and Cuban setting make *El Negro Mártir* a curious example of a transnational abolitionist novella. The editors of *El Mulato* were surely aware of the success of *Uncle Tom's Cabin*, which had been translated and published in 1852 as *La Cabaña del Tío Tom* by Andrés A. de Orihuela, whose poem about a republican Cuban peasant graced the front page of *El Eco de Cuba*. While Harriet Beecher Stowe's success might have inspired the inclusion of a novella in *El Mulato*, the paper was also following a tradition of Cuban abolitionist fiction that went back to the 1830s. The name "Francisco" would have resonated with readers familiar with the antislavery politics of the circle tied to Domingo Delmonte, an intellectual who promoted the publication of abolitionist literature in Cuba.[90] "Francisco" invoked the ex-slave Juan Francisco Manzano, whose *Autobiografía* was commissioned by Delmonte and published in England. In addition, Anselmo Suárez y Romero had written a novel, *Francisco*, that was known to the Delmonte circle but did not appear in print until 1880.[91] (In the twentieth century, the importance of "Francisco" in Cuba's history was the focus of Sergio Giral's film, *El Otro Francisco* [1975], a critical interpretation of Suárez y Romero's novel.) As scholars note, the rise of the novel in Cuba was inextricable from the antislavery politics of the Delmonte circle. Given these antecedents, *El Negro Mártir* situated Francisco in New York, bringing together a Cuban literary tradition and the U.S.-based print culture formation of transnational writing by Cubans.

El Negro Mártir occupies an interstitial space between Cuban and U.S. literary histories. Forgotten in the pages of *El Mulato*, the story has not been considered either within the nationalist paradigm of the U.S. abolitionist novel or within the Cuban literary pantheon despite the piece's claim to be a "novela cubana." This might be a matter of formal evaluation but more likely is the result of its obscurity in the pages of a newspaper that is not readily available. Because the novel appeared anonymously, it cannot be pinned to the reputation of a writer and thus cannot be easily integrated into the author-based conventions of literary histories. Considered as a part of the history of Spanish-language publication in the United States, *El Negro Mártir* reminds literary historians of the political function of languages other than English. In his efforts to recuperate the wide-ranging contributions of what he calls "multilingual America," Werner Sollors has rallied scholars to consider the variety of writing that has appeared in the United States in languages other than English. Intervening in debates over "English only," Sollors seeks to develop a comprehensive multilingual literature of the United States.[92] *El Mulato* certainly represents part of this long and varied history, scrambling the division between U.S. and Latin America in abolitionist fiction just as Omar Ibn Said's slave narrative written in Arabic and Victor Séjour's "Le Mulâtre" offer new vistas for the study of African American literature.[93] In *El Negro Mártir*, the Spanish language is more than an inscription of the experiences and histories of communities in the United States. The Spanish language here is connected to Cuba, and the novella thus should be considered in light of *El Mulato*'s transnational political function outside of the United States as well as within it. In other words, multilingual America, in this case, is connected to Cuba.

As part of the transnational literary history of Cuban exiles, *El Negro Mártir* provides a heroic representation of the foresight of the writers associated with *El Mulato*. These writers did not wait to see the failure of filibustering in the 1850s to go public with their opposition to slavery. Not until after the U.S. Civil War did a majority of Cuba's exiles in the United States call widely for abolition, which came to Cuba in the 1880s. In the 1850s, the writers for *El Mulato* risked condemnation from their community of exiles to stand by their convictions. Their production of *El Negro Mártir* as a "novela cubana" published in the United States is part of a history of the Cuban-U.S. novel that spans the century. In 1885, for example, José Martí's *Amistad Funesta* (Baneful friendship) appeared in serialized form in the New York newspaper *El Latino-Americano* and was later published as a book titled *Lucía Jerez*. But perhaps the most curious case of a Cuban-U.S. novel is Cirilo Villaverde's *Cecilia Valdés o La Loma del Angel* (1882). In *Cecilia Valdés*, the political impetus of filibustering becomes part of a literary work that attacks the social and political ills of slavery and racial stratification in Cuba. Unlike the contributors to *El Mulato*, Villaverde waited many years to come out firmly against slavery and against U.S. imperialism. His evolution as a writer in the United States and the publication of his well-known *Cecilia Valdés* is the topic of the next chapter.

A *Filibustero*'s Novel

CECILIA VALDÉS AND A MEMORY OF NATION

In 1883, the New York–based Spanish-language newspaper *El Espejo* (The mirror) ran an advertisement promoting Cirilo Villaverde's *Cecilia Valdés o La Loma del Angel* (Cecilia Valdés; or, The Angel's Hill), a "novel of Cuban customs." *El Espejo* was an unlikely place to advertise what would become a canon of Cuban literature and culture, a text William Luis calls "the most important novel written in nineteenth-century Cuba and perhaps one of the most significant works published in Latin America during the same period."[1] *El Espejo* focused primarily not on literary production but rather on business. Circulated in Latin America, *El Espejo* was a commercial sheet filled with advertisements for U.S.-made export products. Locomotives, wheelbarrows, and pianos were standard fare in the columns of *El Espejo*. Appearing alongside ads for washing machines and plastic sacks, the advertisement for *Cecilia Valdés* touted a "historical" novel that inscribed "true" events and portraits of various "public figures" who had lived in Cuba between 1812 and 1831. *Cecilia Valdés*, the ad went on, was dedicated to "las Cubanas," thus positing a gendered national subject. At the same time, the advertisement touted the book's material attributes, offering readers a six-hundred-page octavo volume printed on "good paper." A new type provided for easy reading, and the book was "adorned" with several engravings. Buyers could purchase the novel at *El Espejo*'s New York offices as well as from booksellers in Madrid, Paris, Key West, and Havana.

The ad notes the commodification of the novel's U.S. apparition but also places this most national of Cuban novels within a print culture history that went back to the early nineteenth century and, more specifically, to the transnational newspapers of the 1850s. *El Espejo*, the newspaper that doubled as publisher of the 1882 *Cecilia Valdés*, was owned and edited by Villaverde's and Emilia Casanova's son, Narciso Villaverde, who had been named after Narciso López. If we consider *Cecilia Valdés* coming off the presses of *El Espejo*, the book becomes part of a history of transnational writing that contradicts the novel's insistence on the Cuban nation as a local formation tied to the island. Produced in New York, the ad and novel complicate a longtime critical insistence on *Cecilia Valdés* as a novel not only about but also of Cuba. Since the 1890s, critics have claimed the novel as Cuban, in part because it captures conditions in Havana in the early nineteenth century.[2] I emphasize the way historical perspective in *Cecilia Valdés* is refracted by Villaverde's work as a *filibustero*. The 1882 edition, which differed dramatically from two earlier versions published in Cuba in 1839, did not appear until Villaverde had lived for more than thirty years in the United States. As I show in this chapter, *Cecilia Valdés* is influenced by the filibustering spirit that animated Villaverde in the 1850s—namely, the attempt to capture territory and thus reterritorialize the exile subject within the island's nation and family.

The textual efforts of the *filibusteros* reached fruition and passed into a full-fledged nation-formation process in the 1882 *Cecilia Valdés*. In its evolution, the novel stretches from Cuba to the United States, thus challenging a notion that nationalist culture stems from a fixed, local territory; however, the novel's content promotes a temporal imagined community that emerges from and can be mapped onto the island of Cuba. *Cecilia Valdés* is an attempt to seize the nation at a moment when it appears to Villaverde that the military battle for the island has been lost to Spain. I begin by tracing how and why Villaverde came to rewrite *Cecilia Valdés*, questions that cannot be separated from his participation in filibustering expeditions and the political evolution of Cuban communities in the United States.

Villaverde: From Fiction to Transnational Newspapers

Literary historians in the United States have started to recognize the importance of Félix Varela and José Martí to U.S. literary and cultural history. The nexus between those two prominent figures is Villaverde, whose work in the United States represents the development of politics and letters in exile from the middle to the end of the century. Long known as a nationalist Cuban novelist, Villaverde's main focus for

years in the United States was the publication of newspapers, not fiction, which prevents the easy integration of his work into literary histories. Many of those newspapers are either lost or not yet recovered, so
what we have at best is a fragmentary record of his work as a polemical
journalist. And yet in that incomplete record we can find the elements
of a transnational life that may account for the way his canonical novel
inscribes a local culture that feeds the discourse of the Cuban nation.

Born in 1812 in Cuba's western Pinar del Río province, Villaverde
grew up on a sugar plantation where his father worked as a doctor and
treated slaves as part of his duties. As a witness to the whippings
administered by overseers, Villaverde saw firsthand the racial and labor hierarchies that facilitated the production of sugar in nineteenth-
century Cuba. Plantation life offered him the seeds of discontent that
would sprout into a growing radical posture against colonial rule. After
his primary education, Villaverde earned a law degree in Havana and
began to move in the city's intellectual circles. Instead of working as a
lawyer, he devoted himself to teaching and writing, publishing fiction
in magazines.[3] During this time, Villaverde became part of the literary
circle of Domingo Delmonte, who, as I noted in the preceding chapter,
was instrumental in developing antislavery novels and a Cuban protonational literary scene. Villaverde dedicated much of the 1830s to the
prolific publication of short fiction, including *La Cueva de Taganana*
(Taganana's Cave) (1837), *La Peña Blanca* (The white cliff) (1837), and
the novel *El Espetón de Oro* (The golden skewer) (1838). These early
efforts were heavily influenced by romanticism and do not contain
the intense mimetic effort of the 1882 *Cecilia Valdés*. Even *Excursión
a Vueltabajo* (Excursion to Vueltabajo) (1838–39), a portrait of Villaverde's native tobacco region, is more idealistic in its portrayal of the
people of the area than the 1882 *Cecilia Valdés*.[4] While the final version
of *Cecilia Valdés* appeared late in his life, the character Cecilia Valdés
was present at the beginning of his career. In 1839, Villaverde published
in a periodical the first version of his best-known work as a two-part
story that differs significantly from the lengthy version published in
New York forty-three years later.[5]

In his twenties, Villaverde saw himself developing a career in letters.
His early success was accompanied by increasing dissatisfaction with
colonial society and a growing political conscience. La Escalera in-
tensified this process. In June 1848, Villaverde met Narciso López dur-

ing a concert in Havana and became active in a conspiracy led by López to overthrow Spanish rule.[6] That same year, Villaverde worked as one of the distributors of *La Verdad* in Cuba and may have contributed to the publication.[7] When U.S. government officials betrayed the López plot to Spanish authorities, the conspirators had to escape from the island or risk being detained.[8] Villaverde was surprised at home in the middle of the night by soldiers, who threw him in jail, where he stayed for six months. A military commission convicted him of conspiracy against Spain, and he was condemned to perpetual incarceration.[9] But in a daring escape worthy of one of his novels, Villaverde walked out of jail with the aid of a prison guard, boarded a ship for Florida, and then made his way to New York. Except for two trips to Cuba during periods when Spain offered amnesty to political opponents, Villaverde lived in the United States until his death in 1894.[10]

In excerpts from a letter published in *La Verdad* and the *United States Magazine and Democratic Review* shortly after his escape from Cuba, Villaverde shows a high regard for the United States: "At last I am resting under the wings of the American Eagle. It may be that you are already apprised of my miraculous escape from the prison of Havana, where, as a man guilty of high treason, and accused of a capital crime by the District Attorney (Fiscal) I was lately watched with the greatest diligence. I see myself free in the land of liberty; and I can hardly believe what I see and touch."[11] The letter inscribes a geography of freedom, with the United States offering a place of liberty as opposed to Cuba and its system of colonial surveillance. Villaverde's use of the article "the" before "land of liberty" positions the United States as the sole guarantor of liberty in the Americas, a point emphasized by the metaphor of the eagle taking in Villaverde under its wings. The passage looks naive when viewed from a contemporary lens, but it also shows the intense faith among Cubans at this period that the United States would help usher in a new governmental system for the island. Villaverde's sense of wonder at what he saw and touched was influenced by idealistic interpretations of the United States as the vanguard of liberty in the Americas. In an 1880 English-language newspaper article, José Martí expressed his own contentment at having arrived in the United States: "I am, at last, in a country where every one looks like his own master. One can breathe freely, freedom being here the foundation, the shield, the essence of life."[12] Martí, of course, was talking of post–Civil

War New York. His reference to "master" points to abolition as a distinguishing characteristic between the United States and Cuba in 1880. Villaverde's omission of slavery as an experience in "the land of liberty" is in keeping with the López campaign's efforts to table the question to draw support for filibustering.

After arriving in New York, Villaverde set aside his work in fiction and devoted himself fully to political activity, serving as López's secretary and contributing to *La Verdad*. In the prologue to the 1882 edition of *Cecilia*, Villaverde explained the turn away from literary pursuits after arriving in the United States: "Once outside of Cuba, I reformed my way of life: I exchanged my literary tastes for more noble thoughts; I passed from the world of illusions to the world of realities."[13] The stated distinction between "illusion" and "reality" separated literature from the field of political engagement that Villaverde believed was necessary to change Cuba's status as a colony. But that illusion-reality distinction did not hold up, not even in this passage. Villaverde explained his transformation in terms of two changes—illusion for reality and literary tastes for more noble thoughts. Reality lines up on the same end as noble thoughts, thus creating a dialectical relationship between the real and the ideal. Nevertheless, Villaverde did not appear to read the situation that way and consequently committed himself to organizing and journalism, which kept him involved in the world of writing and textual production.

Villaverde's work for López brought him in contact with John L. O'Sullivan, a newspaper and magazine editor and Democratic Party insider whom many historians credit with coining the term "Manifest Destiny." O'Sullivan and Villaverde collaborated on articles that exemplify the connection between publication and filibustering. One such article was "General López, the Cuban Patriot," which appeared in the *United States Magazine and Democratic Review* in February 1850 and was published as a separate pamphlet the following year.[14] In the introduction to the pamphlet, Villaverde wrote, "As we have in our possession a pamphlet which gives some brief sketches of the life of General López, which we know to be faithful in their deliniations [sic], and the truth of which none will be found to deny, we have though [sic] the present an opportunity to bring them into notice by means of the public press, that they may have a wider circulation and defeat the machinations, which calumny has raised against a man destined by

Providence to take a prominent part in events of the greatest importance in American history."[15] As the passage implies, Villaverde was
aware that López's expeditions were also fighting public opinion in the
United States. Just as William Walker would later face public attacks
from those who questioned the legitimacy of his Nicaraguan venture,
López encountered the scrutiny of filibustering's opponents. To coun-
ter criticism of López and his enterprise, the pamphlet positioned the
general as a defender of liberty who had "undertaken the noble mission of emancipating Cuba from the yoke and the abomination of
Spanish tyranny, with a view to her entrance into our Union." A biographical overview portrayed López as a fearless military leader who
was widely admired and supported by the Cuban population, in part
because of his "sympathy with the poor and the oppressed."[16] Villaverde's description of López as purveyor of "Providence" and "American history" showed the influence of O'Sullivan's Manifest Destiny
writings on the López pamphlet. It is unclear whether Villaverde actually embraced the tenets of Manifest Destiny, for his later writings
criticize the United States for quelling liberation movements in Latin
America. Villaverde's use of "American" points to a possible duplicity.
Is "American" a metonymic substitution for United States, emphasizing that López was to bring a state into the union? Or is Villaverde
using "American" in the broader sense of the word, meaning that
López is a liberator of the hemisphere? In other writings from this
period, Villaverde used "American" as an adjective for the Americas,
particularly in opposition to Europe. His use of "American" coincides
with the pamphlet's annexationist bent: "His plan for Cuba has always
been Independence and Annexation to the American Union."[17] This
notion of independence and annexation overlapped with La Verdad's
position, which was influenced by antebellum conceptions of states'
rights, as I discussed in Chapter 2. "Independence" here meant independence from Spain, to be followed by Cuba's willful entrance into
the Union.

The "General López" article/pamphlet skillfully glossed over several
episodes in which López showed himself to be more of an opportunist
than a liberator. When Simón Bolívar struck out to liberate Venezuela
from Spain in the 1820s, López fought on the side of Spain; this decision was justified in Villaverde's article by the assertion that López was
responding to a massacre carried out in his town by opponents of

Spain. A second opportunistic move, López's acceptance of a post in Cuba's colonial government as governor and commander in chief of the Central Department in 1839, was explained away as a "personal obligation" to a friend who had assumed the post of captain-general on the island.

As López's secretary, Villaverde was literally the general's right-hand man. When López was killed, Villaverde turned more radical in his opposition to Spain. Taking up the editorship of *La Verdad* from February to April 1852, Villaverde began regularly to use the term "revolución de Cuba" and called for total commitment to armed combat, as exemplified in his "man of action" articles, which I discussed in chapter 3. After his brief stint as editor of *La Verdad*, Villaverde began to move away from the wealthy New York exiles and toward a more independent line. Villaverde's newspaper, *El Independiente*, issued an English-language proclamation against the purchase of Cuba by interested parties: "We are opposed to the purchase of Cuba either by Cubans or by Americans. We believe that Cuba can yet gain her independence by force of arms, the only resource left to downtrodden people, the only one which, through a process of purification, can adequately prepare them to pass from limited despotism to absolute freedom, by purging them of many evils, which otherwise would lurk in the body politic, and the only one which, by enabling them to count the cost, will lead them properly to value and to keep intact the sacred boon of liberty."[18] By purchasing the island, the article implied, wealthy Cubans would retain too much power in society. Rather, Villaverde and his coeditor, Manuel Antonio Mariño, wanted to see Cubans seize agency in their own historical transformation. Although Villaverde had not shed his annexationist leanings, he was beginning to move away from the U.S.–Cuban Creole coalition that had been at the center of efforts by the Cuban Council and Narciso López until 1851. Villaverde had concluded that the people of Cuba must fight to appreciate a hard-won victory for self-rule.

But which people? *El Independiente* was clear: "el pueblo blanco, libre y civilizado [white, free and civilized people]."[19] The newspaper was not calling for the inclusion of slaves or even free people of color into the body politic. Actually, Villaverde and Mariño feared that England and France would pressure Spain to abolish slavery and thus deprive white Cubans of their slaves without monetary compensation. In keeping with this perspective, *El Independiente* critiqued Cubans who called for abolition. Thus the paper helps to establish that Villaverde was not an abolitionist from early on. In fact, his position against slavery was part of his development in the United States, no doubt influenced by the U.S. Civil War and his wife, Emilia Casanova, who was consistent in her abolitionist position. Villaverde grew into an abolitionist position only after working as a transnational writer and editor for *La Verdad, El Independiente, La Voz de la América, El Tribuno Cubano* (New York, 1876), and other newspapers. Conspicuously absent from the group of contributors to *El Mulato*, Villaverde was explicit in *El Independiente* about his concern for the future of Cuban whites rather than free blacks or slaves. As Doris Sommer notes, "It took the U.S. Civil War to produce Villaverde's about-face on the importance of slavery."[20]

Only through the omissions of literary histories and a conflation of the 1839 and 1882 versions of *Cecilia Valdés* can Villaverde be called an antislavery writer. During the U.S. Civil War, Villaverde apparently even flirted with the Confederacy, translating the second edition of Edward Pollard's pro-Southern *History of the First Year of the Southern War*, published as *Historia del Primer Año de la Guerra del Sur* (New York, 1863). The translation, which includes Pollard's preface defending his dual role as an objective historian and supporter of the South, is faithful to Pollard's points but written in Villaverde's lively prose.[21] Villaverde may have worked on the translation to obtain money. Pollard's history went through three editions in two years, so there was probably a demand for a Spanish-language translation in Latin America and the United States. But would a highly political writer such as Villaverde sign on as a ventriloquist to a cause in which he did not believe? That is doubtful, and the translation remains as an indication that Villaverde might have been sympathetic to the rebellion against the Union.

After the Civil War, Villaverde and other exiles returned to organizing and publishing transnational writings to bring about change in Cuba, particularly in support of the revolutionary effort on the island known as the Ten Years' War. When the war broke out in 1868, Villaverde and Emilia Casanova committed to supporting Cuban independence. The war continued intermittently until 1878, only to bring defeat to rebels outgunned by Spanish battalions, which reached a force of almost 100,000.[22] Recounting his activities during this war, Villaverde wrote, "Like before and like always, I exchanged literary occupations for military politics. . . . During the larger part of this period of delirium and patriotic dreams, certainly, the manuscript of the novel was dormant."[23] The failure of the liberation armies in the war drove Villaverde back to *Cecilia Valdés*. He returned to the manuscript when "the memory of the fatherland is soaking in the blood of its finest sons."[24]

Villaverde's ultimate position against slavery developed in tandem with his view of the United States as a power more interested in its own hemispheric ambitions than in Cuban independence. In 1869, Villaverde delivered a political oration in which he accused the United States of betraying liberation movements in Latin America: "What we cannot understand under any circumstances is that Cubans in the United States embrace the hope that by appealing to the greed of Americans to acquire Cuba . . . they will inspire public sympathy and obtain the help of the [American] people with the consent of the government in Washington."[25] Villaverde ultimately renounced annexation, denounced the United States, and wrote critically about slavery, positions that mirrored changes among other Cuban exiles in the United States.[26] This evolution paved the way for a rewriting of *Cecilia Valdés o La Loma del Angel*.

Exchanging Cuba: History, Memory, Novel

Staring down yet another failure in the battle against colonial rule after the Ten Years' War, Villaverde devoted himself for more than two years to rewriting *Cecilia Valdés*. The result was a novel that concerned itself with the construction of race and conditions of slavery in Cuba, topics that Villaverde had once repressed to promote the filibustering platform. The novel looked back to life in Havana and Cuba's slave plantations between 1812 and 1831 and offered, according to Villaverde, a historical "tripartite" vision of physical, moral, and social conditions on the island. In the 120 years since the 1882 edition was published, *Cecilia Valdés* has become a Cuban cultural artifact that has inspired countless studies, a musical theater production, and fictional offshoots. Reinaldo Arenas and Alfredo Antonio Fernández are among the novelists who have incorporated *Cecilia Valdés* into their work, the latter in a novel that brings together Cecilia, Villaverde, and Narciso López as fictional characters.[27] Villaverde's novel also became an elaborately staged six-part film coproduced by the Cuban film institute.[28] Literary critics and historians have described *Cecilia Valdés* as a mimetic historical representation. Pedro Deschamps Chapeaux is among the scholars who have studied the musicians, poets, and military leaders on whom Villaverde's characters are based.[29] In many ways, Villaverde's turn toward realism from his New York residency created nineteenth-century Cuba for twentieth-century readers. In response, Arenas offers an ironic, postmodern rewriting of the characters and social conditions in Villaverde's novel.

Villaverde paints a portrait by bringing together historical figures and the memory of his days as a young man in Cuba. As the novel's full title makes clear, the narrative focus is both Cecilia and the Angel's Hill, a section of Old Havana that functions as one of the local points of Villaverde's conception of nation. The people of the Angel's Hill—musicians, tailors, police officials, and intellectuals—provide much of *Cecilia Valdés'* apparent authenticity. The *mulata* Cecilia Valdés, described as a "little bronze virgin" who bears "perhaps the most beautiful woman's face that existed at that time in Havana" (*CV* 160), symbolizes Cuban womanhood and, more generally speaking, Cuban racial and cultural hybridity.[30] Vera Kutzinski argues that *Cecilia Valdés* is "representative of a racialized and sexualized cultural iconography that offers an alternate mythic foundation: the Cuban cult of the *mulata*."[31] The Cuban *mulata*, a highly sexualized construction tied to the nation, persists today and has even captivated the literary imagination of U.S.-born Cuban American writers such as Oscar Hijuelos.[32] It becomes clear that the *mulata*—not the *mulato*, as the newspaper of that name proposed—became a central figure of the Cuban nation. If we consider the objectification of the Cuban *mulata* in relation to the context of nineteenth-century U.S. exile circles, then Cecilia becomes the object sought by the "men of action." In that sense, Villaverde's novel compensates for the failure of various military operations against Spanish colonialism. The writer's (re)turn to realism through the portrayal of Cuba and Cecilia Valdés is an attempt to offset military loss. Villaverde takes hold of the *mulata* and the island.

The symbolic construction of Cecilia as Cuban woman is accomplished by presenting her within "a multitude of true events," as the *El Espejo* advertisement stated. The inscription of social mores, racial perspectives, political conditions, and economic relationships in Havana and the outlying plantations creates Cecilia as a Cuban character. Villaverde tells readers in the prologue that the major characters appear in the "clothes they wore in life" and that the text mimics "the language they used in historical scenes in which they were involved."[33] The novel's panorama takes in a litany of historical personalities, among them Plácido, Félix Varela, Captain-General Dionisio Vives, and even José Antonio Saco (Villaverde's nemesis in the "man of action" debates). Striving to re-create an epoch, Villaverde goes as far as to apologize in the prologue for having excluded some of Havana's most colorful characters. When the setting moves in the second half of the novel to slave plantations, Villaverde incorporates into his vision of Cuba graphic depictions of the cruel treatment of slaves.

The evolution of the novel in the United States is one of the matters taken up in the prologue to the 1882 edition. Exchange is one of the dominating concepts in the prologue, which elaborates a dialectic of literary production and political activity that is synthesized in the rewriting of *Cecilia Valdés* as a realistic novel. Villaverde noted his transformation from novelist to military organizer, his shift in location from Cuba to New York, and his generic change from romance novels to the journalism of *La Verdad*. Looking back on decades of participation in separatist and revolutionary groups in the United States, Villaverde emphasized that fiction gave way first to his work for López and then in the 1860s to "political agitation." (Villaverde also mentioned the "necessity of providing for the subsistence of my family in a foreign country.") Cuba demands a "faithful picture of its existence," he wrote, just as he faced the possible end of a dream to liberate Cuba militarily.[34] In other words, *Cecilia Valdés* substituted for a bodily loss brought on by efforts to seize control of territory in Cuba. If I can't have Cuba in and of itself, Villaverde seems to say, I will have it as a book.

What Villaverde could not achieve as a political operative—Cuba without colonialism—he developed in fiction that conceived of the nation of Cuba as a historical formation. In this novel, Cuba is not a Spanish colony but rather is its own place. Colonialism represents but one of many parts of the picture and does not define the political subject. The nation appears in this book and inspires desire before the founding of the nation-state on Cuban soil. The novel circulated in Cuba and among exiles for more than fifteen years before the end of colonial rule. Writing in New York in his sixties, Villaverde could not divorce the "period of the history of Cuba" from memory as it emerged in the transnational space of exile. His claim to historical representation was based in part on firsthand experience. He expected readers of his generation to "recognize" the people who populate the novel. To understand Villaverde's attitude toward history, we could say, following Walter Benjamin, that he seizes "hold of a memory as it flashes up at a moment of danger."[35] The danger is the ostensible failure of Cuban independence. Villaverde dusted himself off and returned to the novel form to mount a rearguard attack against the enemy. Villaverde would probably have appreciated Benjamin's comment that "*even the dead* will not be safe from the enemy if he wins."[36] But Villaverde's turn to realism also places him at odds with the Benjaminian view that history cannot be recovered as an objective set of facts. If anything, *Cecilia Valdés* proposes that history can be recovered as it was and inserted into fiction to usher in a future moment of liberation. Realism in a novel ultimately accomplished for Villaverde what the transnational newspapers did not, integration into the Cuban nation.

Villaverde could write a historical novel because the failure of the Ten Years' War created a rupture in the teleological view of history that circulated among exiles as early as the 1850s. Both Villaverde and Casanova saw the liberation of the island and the foundation of a Cuban nation-state as a teleological inevitability, but they were forced to recognize that it was not going to happen in the 1870s. Always seeking new ways to conceive of Cuba's anticolonial future, Villaverde returned to the novel form to account for the island's past. *Cecilia Valdés*'s narratorial perspective was influenced by time and distance, for the late 1870s offered an opportunity that was not available earlier in the century. As the narrative of *Cecilia Valdés* tells us, in the 1830s, "History, which collects and stores all until the opportune moment, was not yet written" (*CV* 166).

Filibustero writers in the 1850s believed that they lacked the necessary materials to write a history of nineteenth-century Cuba. In *Lecciones Orales sobre la Historia de Cuba, Pronunciadas en el Ateneo Democrático Cubano de Nueva York* (1859), Pedro Santacilia stopped his narration of Spanish colonial atrocities at the end of the eighteenth century. Citing a lack of documents and sources, Santacilia fell back on his exile position and noted that colonial conditions prevented him from acquiring the materials necessary to depict events in his century. He vowed to seek sources because he saw history as a pedagogical exercise for revolutionary change. "I have wanted for Cuban youth to read my book meticulously and learn to hate to death the oppressors of their country," Santacilia wrote in a prologue that called for monuments in Cuba to López and others killed by colonial authorities.[37] His use of *odiar* (hate) represents the exile view of writing as a form that could inspire such a strong reaction that people would take up arms. Villaverde, of course, had a more ambivalent relationship to letters as arms, critiquing the assumption that writing would inspire people to battle. In turn, the attempt to capture Cuba in *Cecilia Valdés* gives way at times to the love story.

The novel intertwines historical representation with the soap-operatic narrative of Cecilia's relationship with her half-brother, Leonardo Gamboa. Cecilia is the illegitimate offspring of an adulterous affair between a corrupt, Spanish-born plantation owner and a free *mulata*. Leonardo is the prodigal son of Cándido Gamboa, Cecilia's father, a businessman who makes a part of his fortune from illegal participation in the slave trade. Unaware that she is related to the object of her affection, Cecilia hopes that she can use her charms to marry a "young white man, from a rich family" (*CV* 162) and thus rise in socioeconomic status. After all, the narrator tells us, "gold purifies the most turbid of blood and covers major defects, both physical and moral" (*CV* 162). Leonardo's desire for Cecilia is marked by the hierarchies of racial difference in Havana society. In a joke questioning the purity of his own privileged whiteness, Leonardo tells a friend, "Perhaps it's because I have some *mulato* in me that I like *mulatas* by the handful" (*CV* 136). Leonardo's uncertainty about his own racial genealogy overlaps with the novel's insistence that race is socially and economically marked. As George Handley notes, "Villaverde represents Cuban society's emphasis on the external visibility of social and racial identity as a kind of vulnerability to a corrupt and illegitimate colonial power."[38] While race can be constructed in colonial Cuba, Handley notes, neither inner essences nor genealogical backgrounds are readily apparent, and the result is an incestuous relationship.

The consummation of the relationship between Leonardo and Cecilia allows the reader to experience both possession and prohibition. In other words, it does not permit a complacent seizure of Cecilia-Cuba.

Leonardo ends up with Cecilia Valdés, and the reader ends up with *Cecilia Valdés*, but incest disturbs that connection. For *Cecilia Valdés* to work comfortably as a "novel of Cuban customs," the reader has to move the incest plot to the margins. This is possible because the novel gives ample hints that the lovers are related, and a reader can focus on something other than finding out about the lovers' background. The emphasis on a language of place, apparent in the minutiae of description, reterritorializes the exile memory and the text itself. To put it another way, this novel situates the people of Cuba, even those in exile, on the island. Through narration, *Cecilia Valdés* enacts what the filibusters of the Narciso López era could not, successfully staking a claim on Cuban ground. (*Cecilia Valdés* enters Cuban history; the *filibusteros* fall by the wayside.) The novel's success is accomplished through a spatial imagining that erases the transnational conditions that facilitated that creation. *Cecilia Valdés* appears to come right out of Cuba. To be a novel of the nation, its transnational print culture history has to be bracketed, alongside the incest. Incest, of course, is not a national custom or the theme of one particular nation. But *Cecilia Valdés* perhaps seeks to tell us that the form of incest in a novel—how it plays out and who is involved—provides a window into historical contingencies.

Cecilia Valdés: Transnational Nation

The threat and ultimate union of half-brother and -sister situate *Cecilia Valdés* in a literary tradition outside of the nation—namely, that of novels from throughout the Americas that tapped into the incest trope in the nineteenth century. Similar brother-sister relationships are consummated, threatened, or implied in, to name just a few, Jorge Isaacs's *María* (Colombia, 1867), Herman Melville's *Pierre* (United States, 1852), Juan León Mera's *Cumandá* (Ecuador, 1879), and Eligio Ancona's *El Filibustero* (Mexico, 1856). In these novels, the metaphorical function of incest varies depending on the cultural and political contexts of the books. In *Cumandá*, I believe, the impossibility of an incestuous relationship between the indigenous woman, who is white by birth, and her brother reinforces a geographic and social separation between white elites and indigenous populations, a separation that continues to plague the Ecuadoran state today. In *Cecilia Valdés*, the partners in the incestuous couple provide a window into sexual mores in nineteenth-century Havana but also reflect the racialized division between (most) Creole exiles and a segment of the island's population. We could say that Villaverde finally came to see the wisdom of the *El Mulato* writers who in 1854 had the temerity to claim a racially mixed subject as an important part of their writing program. Villaverde's *mulata* was probably more acceptable than *El Mulato* to the aging men of action and to the new generation that would fight for Cuba as part of Martí's interracial coalition.

Villaverde surely had *mulatas* as well as white and possibly even black women in mind when he dedicated his novel to *las cubanas* (Cuban women). Returning to the trope of *filibustero* poets who positioned Cuban women as a metonym for the island, Villaverde offered a new turn on a common theme by placing a *mulata* at the center of the novel's concerns. His gallant dedication is followed up by a recognition in the prologue that women are not only passive recipients of a writer's affection. Villaverde acknowledges that he owes the uniform and lively tone of the novel to the careful reading of his wife, Emilia Casanova, who commented on each of the chapters.[39] One has to wonder about the extent of Casanova's influence on the final version of the book.

The novel pulls in opposite directions. On the one hand, I have argued that *Cecilia Valdés* captures Cuba and the novel's *mulata* heroine. On the other hand, I have noted that incest prohibits that process and that the novel's transnational production complicates the equation between novel and nation. I want to continue reading against what I see as the novel's dominant thread, the portrayal of Cuban customs. In other words, I want to read against the narrator and against Villaverde's effort to create a *novela cubana*. In addition to the print culture history that situates the book in New York, the narrative contains (between the lines) indications that this novel of Cuba is a transnational production. One of the most suggestive recent analyses takes issue with readers' hasty acceptance of *Cecilia Valdés* as a sociohistorical portrait. Doris Sommer calls attention to the "narrator's apparent ignorance" and emphasizes that he refuses to spell out the novel's interracial incestuous crescendo even as it becomes obvious to the reader. "His hesitation to assimilate information permits competent readers to congratulate themselves on the good job of filling in blanks and tying up loose ends," Sommer writes.[40] The delay in providing information, Sommer argues, dramatizes the limits of knowledge of whites in this slaveholding society. "Black informants," by contrast, can tell the story of Cecilia's parentage. Thus, Sommer's revisionary reading racializes the narrator as a white Creole. While I am reluctant to grant excessive epistemological or speaking force to the novel's black characters, I want to build on Sommer's interrogation of the narrator by taking up two questions that are important to the novel's detour through the United States: When is the narrator writing? Where is he?

The narrator calls attention to his historical perspective by setting the first four chapters in 1812, the mid-1820s, and 1828. The repeated use of phrases noting historical distance, such as "in that period" (*CV* 63), further emphasizes the intended separation between the narrator and events. His historical memory is at best shady, judging from the first sentence of the second chapter, "Some years later, or better, one or two after the fall of the second brief constitutional period" (*CV* 72), a reference to Spain's return to absolutist rule in 1823. In other words, the narrator is unable or unwilling to pinpoint with precision some events in the novel. The union of historical details and sporadic amnesia is in keeping with the perspective of an aging man. It becomes evident through references to occurrences in the 1850s that the narrator is writing several decades after the story's events.

But while we can roughly situate the time of writing, the text is not explicit about "where" the narrator is writing. Readers of the 1882 edition would have located the novel in New York because the prologue is dated, "New York, May 1879." In addition, exiled Cubans in the United States or Europe in the late nineteenth century might well have found a striking parallel between their relationship to Cuba and the narratorial desire to recuperate a place that had been left behind. But the text of the novel, unlike the prologue, does not acknowledge outright that the vision of *Cecilia Valdés'* Cuba detours through New York. Published with a different title page and lacking Villaverde's prologue—as in Raimundo Lazo's popular edition and others—*Cecilia Valdés* can be positioned as a novel solely of Cuba, the ultimate nationalist fiction.[41] My point here is not that the novel should have specified the narrator's location but rather that questioning his whereabouts complicates a facile nationalist frame. If we place the narrator in New York, *Cecilia Valdés* begins to tell stories about Cuban writers in the United States and not just in Cuba.

In the prolific criticism on the novel, readers have largely overlooked several paragraphs that recount a tradition of anticolonial print culture among Cubans in the United States. In chapter 11, the narrator looks back at writers who preceded Villaverde's arrival in New York. The chapter lists a veritable who's who of Cuban intellectuals who lived in or passed through the United States: Félix Varela, José Antonio Saco, and José María Heredia. These writers, the novel tell us, used the United States as a base from which to circulate politically loaded writings. (Like the book's author, we could add.) Outside of Cuba, writers committed themselves to publishing works that would inform readers in Cuba as well as "teach the people their duties and remind them of their rights" (*CV* 166).

Cecilia Valdés points out that for these writers, publication in the United States was a politically militant move that challenged Spanish authorities. Their work could serve the pedagogical function of calling people's attention to Spain's oppression and raising awareness about republican rights:

> A ese fin, entre otros, el virtuoso Padre Varela publicó en Fila-delfia *El Habanero*, de 1824 a 1826; pero el gobierno español le declaró papel subversivo y prohibió su entrada en Cuba. De suerte que puede asegurarse que muy pocos ejemplares circularon en ella. Más tarde, es decir, de 1828 a 1830, emprendió Saco tambien en el Norte de América la publicación de *El Mensajero Semanal*, periódico científico-literario, el cual, por iguales motivos que el anterior, tuvo escasa circulación el la Habana y no ejerció influencia apreciable en las ideas políticas. (*CV* 166)

> [With that goal, among others, the virtuous Félix Varela published in Philadelphia *El Habanero* from 1824 to 1826; however, the Spanish government declared the paper subversive and prohibited its entrance into Cuba. It was their luck that very few copies circulated on the island. At a later date—to be more precise, 1828 to 1830—Saco, who was also in North America, published *El Mensajero Semanal*, a scientific and literary newspaper, which, for the

same reasons as the former, had a small circulation in Havana
and did not have a notable influence on political currents.]

But this acknowledgment of Villaverde's predecessors refuses to celebrate the writings of Varela, Heredia, and Saco. The most politically
successful of those writers, the narrator tells us, was Heredia, the patriot whose verses were memorized by the youth of Havana and recited
at gatherings where there was no danger of persecution from authorities. "But neither those newspapers nor these fiery verses overflowing
with notions of patriotism and freedom could inspire that sense of
motherland and liberty that sometimes impels men to sacrifice themselves by taking up the sword and fighting for their rights" (*CV* 167).[42]
In other words, the poems and other writings were insufficient to bring
about the necessary military action. If we consider that passage in
relation to Villaverde's explanation of why he returned to *Cecilia Valdés*
in the late 1870s, it becomes clear that Villaverde wrote the novel as an
alternative to a military solution.

If we position Villaverde as a bridge between early exiles and the
generation of Martí, we need to consider the inclusion in *Cecilia Valdés*
of several lines from Heredia's "To Emilia" as the epigraph to chapter
11. "To Emilia" is an epistolary written to a woman "from the fatal soil
of his exile." At first, the poet is presented in third person as an exiled
lover of both Cuba and Emilia; he must suffer the separation from both
because of the tyranny of the island's rulers. "To Emilia" was an important part of the literary imagination of Cuban writers involved in filibustering in the 1850s. The poem was included in the collection *El
Laúd del Desterrado*, which featured Heredia alongside exiles from the
1850s. The overall perspective in "To Emilia" is that of someone writing
to Cuba from a distant land:

Mis ojos doloridos
no verán ya mecerse de la palma
la copa gallardísima, dorada
por los rayos del sol en occidente.

[My sorrowful eyes
will not view on the swinging palm
the gallant top, bronzed
by the rays of the western sun.][43]

The inability to see the palms emphasizes the poet's separation from the land and woman he loves. And yet that separation is necessary, as explained in the lines quoted in the epigraph to chapter 11:

De mi patria
bajo el hermoso desnublado cielo
no pude resolverme a ser esclavo,
ni consentir que todo en la natura
    fuese noble y feliz, menos el hombre.

[In the beautiful sunny sky of
my motherland
I could not accept becoming a slave,
nor concur that all in nature
    should be noble and content, except man.][44]

These lines from Heredia comment on Villaverde's position and explain Villaverde's need to write *Cecilia Valdés* just as the former had written "To Emilia." (Curiously, both Villaverde and Miguel Tolón were married to women named Emilia.)

Heredia's use of "slavery" resonates in a novel with scenes in Cuban plantations. But *Cecilia Valdés* comes very late as a critical intervention on slavery in the Americas. By the time Villaverde committed himself to finishing his novel, Cuba had started to move toward abolition, which came in 1886. As such, it is important to take into account the point made by Raimundo Lazo and other critics that slavery in *Cecilia Valdés* is part of a portrait of Cuba but not the main focus of the novel, in contrast to an abolitionist novel such as *Uncle Tom's Cabin*. Perhaps the treatment of slavery in *Cecilia Valdés* has more in common with *Huckleberry Finn*, which offers a critique of slavery as part of a much larger picture of the antebellum United States and does so after slavery has already been abolished. In *Cecilia Valdés*, chapters set on plantations not only depict the brutality of the system but also include lengthy descriptions of the landscape in Villaverde's native Pinar del Río province. Again, the memory of his youth emerges as Villaverde's portrait betrays an intimate knowledge of the area's topography.

But what interests me is how *Cecilia Valdés* also subtly shows the transnational dimensions of slavery. When the novel describes what makes the sugar plantation La Tijana "grandiose," it takes inventory of three hundred slaves, extensive fields, and a "great steam engine with twenty-five horse power, recently imported from North America" for the elaboration of sugar (*CV* 437). That steam engine is operated by a "young American man" (438) for whom living quarters were built on the plantation. With this detail, the novel creates an awareness of how U.S. exports and U.S. labor are implicated in the running of Cuban plantations. The years during which most of the action in *Cecilia Valdés* takes place, 1828–31, coincided with a rise in the number of U.S. investors buying large tracts of land for slave plantations on the island.

But perhaps the most forceful critique of slavery's transnational dimensions emerges in the depiction of the slave trade. The novel accomplishes this through the portrayal of Cándido Gamboa, the Spanish-born father of the ill-fated lovers. A cold man who places profits and personal ambition above the welfare of his family and Cuba, Cándido represents colonial forces in Cuba. Not only does he own slaves, but he continues to bring slaves into Cuba from Africa illegally at a time when Spain has signed on to international laws prohibiting the continuation of the slave trade. Cándido's wife, Rosa, explains to Leonardo that her husband receives slave ships, takes what he needs for his plantations, and sells the rest. In that sense, Cándido can be read as the fictional embodiment of the guilty parties blasted by transnational newspapers such as *El Filibustero* for participating in the illegal slave trade. Leonardo is scandalized and responds by calling his father a kidnapper and adding that the slave trade violates human rights. Even Leonardo, who is more intent on pleasure than ethical conduct, rises above his father's acts. But in the context of the novel's publication date, this critique of the slave trade is dated and perhaps should be read as a retraction of the author's blind spots.

One detail in the novel also connects Cándido to the United States. Cándido's business has turned a profit by importing wood and bricks from the United States. In one narrative sequence, the novel connects the U.S. wood to Cuba's colonial government by noting that wood is used to build a repressive state apparatus linked to the hanging of Cuban patriots. Chapter 9 begins with an attack on capital punishment and proceeds with a description of a Havana field known as La Punta. On one side of the field, several houses made of wood had been constructed, and on the south side stood, "piles of boards and beams imported from the United States of America" (*CV* 142), possibly by

Cándido Gamboa. At La Punta, the Spaniards had constructed a jail, a prison, and quarters for Spanish soldiers. The construction of La Punta with materials from the United States is established as part of a repressive system that will lead to the execution of some of Cuba's most notable patriots. By building the prison so close to the field of execution, colonial authorities positioned political prisoners "two hundred steps" from the site where they would be killed. Among those executed at La Punta, *Cecilia Valdés* tells us, was Eduardo Facciolo, who published the revolutionary sheet *La Voz del Pueblo Cubano*. But most notable for Villaverde, the novel notes that La Punta was the place where an executioner's garrote brought an end to Narciso López. It was the site on which Villaverde's filibustering dreams were cut short.

Although López is mentioned, it is curious that he does not play a more prominent part in the novel's historical reconstruction. For decades after López's death, Villaverde wrote glowingly of the general. In 1866, Villaverde featured López in an issue of the newspaper *La Voz de la América*. The newspaper's front page displayed a lithograph of López planting a Cuban flag on a beach with a caption that described the general as "libertador de Cuba." The articles on that page included a biographical piece about López and a fiery piece with the headline "¡A LAS ARMAS, CUBANOS! [Cubans, arm yourselves!]."[45] The unsigned biographical sketch, probably by Villaverde, described the general as the Cuban people's "Moses, sent by Providence to liberate them from colonial subjection."[46] Villaverde had used the word "Providence" in his introduction to the 1851 "General López" pamphlet. In 1869, Villaverde again invoked López, this time attempting to erase the general's annexationist connections. López, Villaverde wrote, had been maligned by "representatives of conservative principles" who worked for the annexation of Cuba to the United States.[47] From the 1860s until the end of his life, Villaverde argued publicly that he and López did not support annexation, despite their public pronouncements to the contrary in 1851.[48] Given Villaverde's longtime admiration of López, the omission of the filibustering expeditions in *Cecilia Valdés* is representative of the novel's emphasis on local island customs.

Empires remain at the periphery. While Spain is the most offensive empire, *Cecilia Valdés* notes that Washington also contributed to repression on the island by opposing efforts to throw off Spanish colonialism. The novel reminds readers that the United States stood firmly against a plan among troops in Colombia and Mexico to "invade" Cuba and displace Spain in 1826, thus echoing an article published early in the *La Verdad*'s run. U.S. opposition to extending the reach of Latin America's wars of liberation to Cuba in the 1820s was based on a variety of factors, including U.S. designs on possessing the island and fear that the island would emerge as a black-led state in the tradition of Haiti. In 1829, Martin Van Buren wrote that it was in "the interest of the southern section of the Union that no attempt should be made in that island to throw off the yoke of Spanish dependence, the first effect of which would be the sudden emancipation of a numerous slave population, the result of which could not but be very sensibly felt upon the adjacent shores of the United States."[49] Thus U.S. diplomacy in relation to Cuba was influenced not only by expansionist designs but also by efforts to maintain slavery, a point that is not lost in *Cecilia Valdés*. The novel notes that a "rumor" circulated around Havana that "Washington had opposed the invasion of Cuba and Puerto Rico by troops from Mexico and Colombia" (*CV* 167).

I have recuperated transnational dimensions of the production and text of *Cecilia Valdés* to note that they have been overlooked in critical efforts to emphasize Cuba's local history. When readers accept the novel's tendency to emphasize Havana at the level of street life (the first sentence mentions Compostela Street and the last sentence ends with the word "streets"), the local nation becomes dominant at the expense of the metropolitan histories (New York, Madrid) that sheltered so many Cuban writers in the nineteenth century. By creating a "historical" novel with a historian narrator who fails to name where he is standing, Villaverde effectively deemphasizes the transnational dimensions of his text. That is not to say that historical novels, even those with limited-perspective narrators, always do or should specify where the narrator is situated. But given Villaverde's literary-political evolution and his extensive participation in a U.S.-based, Spanish-language print culture, that omission has consequences for the place of *Cecilia Valdés* in literary history. Readers have accepted the sociohistorical depiction offered by the novel and forgotten that Villaverde could publish the novel only after thirty years in exile. His historical re-creation of Cuba is, metaphorically speaking, the ultimate filibustering gesture.

Formerly the proud secretary of the *filibustero* López, Villaverde gives up territory for the textual seizure of the nation. It is not an exaggeration to argue that Villaverde creates not only Cecilia Valdés but nineteenth-century Havana. That is implication of a book, *La Habana de Cecilia Valdés* (1946), by Loló de la Torriente. A masterful performance, Torriente's book blurs the distinctions among novel, nation, personal experience, history, and the geography of Havana. "As a young girl, I used to take my father's hand and walk through the narrow and dusty streets of Old Havana," the book begins. "When I reached an appropriate age, my father gave me the first novel that every Cuban should read: *Cecilia Valdés o La Loma del Angel.*"[50] This nationalist invocation is followed by an extensive interdisciplinary reading of Villaverde's novel, primary and secondary historical documents, the streets of Old Havana, photographs, and the politics of nation formation in the nineteenth century. At times, Havana does seem to belong to *Cecilia Valdés*. At least by Torriente's terms, Villaverde was Cuba's most successful nineteenth-century historian. His novel represented not only a resistance to the Spanish empire and its lengthy hold on Cuba but also a refusal to be swallowed and forgotten within the entrails of the other empire, the one in which he lived for more than half of his life. By returning to the novel of earlier days and marginalizing the novel's transnational connections, Villaverde filibustered Cuba.

Epilogue

José Martí's obituary of Cirilo Villaverde, published in the New York newspaper *Patria* in 1894, establishes political action as a priority in the writer's life. While Martí recognizes Villaverde's contributions to literature, Martí indicates that Villaverde was also an important contributor to the island's independence movement. The obituary opens, "From a long and tenacious life as a complete patriot and useful writer he has passed into death, which must be a worthy prize for this elder who gave Cuba his blood, without regret, and an unforgettable novel."[1] Villaverde's willingness to sacrifice his life for Cuba takes precedence over an "unforgettable novel." The piece's most captivating image recounts a "mortally cold New York night" when Villaverde took into his home a group of downcast young militants and lifted their spirits by urging them to seek new methods to achieve Cuba's independence. Martí remembered the contrast between "the gentleness of his gestures and the scourge and rebellion of his words."[2] Martí also looked back on Villaverde's involvement in the filibustering expeditions of Narciso López, but instead of bringing up the annexationist taint of those efforts, the piece categorizes Villaverde as an elder activist who contributed to the ongoing struggle for Cuban independence. If the article glosses over Villaverde's work as a filibuster, it also portrays his evolution over decades in the United States.

Martí was not as kind to the *filibustero* López. In the prologue to *Versos Sencillos* (Simple verses), Martí associated Narciso López with not only William Walker but also the talons of the "fearsome eagle" Martí perceived as threatening to become Cuba's new master.[3] While *filibustero* writers such as Pedro Angel Castellón had celebrated López as a martyr of Cuba, Martí turned a critical eye on the general. (Nevertheless, Martí, like many later observers, would associate López with the Cuban flag, which was conceived initially for the filibustering expeditions of 1850 and 1851.)[4] Succeeding generations have not always been as kind to López as the many writers who offered verses in his honor in the 1850s. In the 1930s and 1940s, scholars in Cuba were eager to reconsider López as well as the poets of *El Laúd del Desterrado* and Emilia Casanova as nationalist forerunners, but that type of enthusiasm has waned in the post-1959 period. Some commentators even read the López expeditions as forerunners of the Bay of Pigs.[5] Where does that leave writers who committed themselves to filibustering? As I have pointed out at various points in this study, figures such as Villaverde and Juan Clemente Zenea have been monumentalized as literary writers rather than as militant activists tied to a cause that, at least in the 1850s, involved a compromise with the United States. Cuban writers and other exiles traversed a steep learning curve in the nineteenth century so that Casanova and Martí, among others, ultimately recognized that independence was the only option for Cuba and that the United States was more interested in its own geopolitical ambitions than in self-determination for the island's people. We could consider Martí's ultimate transracial platform for independence, devised in the United States, as the culmination of the efforts undertaken by the exiles who preceded him. Such a teleology, while problematic for its privileging of Martí, would have appealed to *filibusteros* such as Pedro Santacilia, who saw the evolution of politics toward Cuban independence as an outgrowth of the nineteenth-century spirit of filibustering and republican principles.

In this book I have demonstrated the depth and complexity of the Cuban exile experience in the United States by focusing on a very specific moment in history. Over the years, I have been asked to reflect on how *filibusteros* can inform our reading of the contemporary Cuban exile condition. I have always approached the question with reluctance, out of concern that the highly vexed and polarizing issues surrounding the Cuban Revolution of 1959 would affect my readings of the mid–nineteenth century. And yet it is only fair that people should wonder about the similarities and differences given an apparent repetition in historical circumstances. Do the *filibusteros*, who allied themselves with U.S. expansionists to end Spanish colonialism, share something with late-twentieth-century exiles who allied themselves with U.S. opponents of communism to combat Fidel Castro's government? Didn't both groups try to enlist the U.S. government in their efforts and hold up concepts such as "freedom" and "democracy" to combat what they see as an illegitimate government in Cuba? It is tempting to draw parallels between two groups from different centuries, but such facile comparisons do not go deep into the specific conditions of each moment and are not particularly attentive to the variety of positions among the players in each drama. Mid-nineteenth-century transnational newspapers engaged in healthy debates over annexation, slavery, and filibustering, issues that are not relevant to the post-1959 period. I do not consider the exiles of either the past or the present as a homogeneous group. If the exile experience appears to repeat, it does so with astounding differences.

I also hesitate to draw a simple connection between transnational writing from the mid–nineteenth century and writing produced after 1959 by Cuban exiles and Cuban Americans. While the contours of Cuban-U.S. literary history could fill several books, I offer a brief impressionistic note on differences between nineteenth-century writers and some of today's best-known figures. Although the exilic longing for Cuba and the painful loss of a home are themes that make their way from one century to the next, marketplace conditions have changed enough that a writer such as Reinaldo Arenas can go into exile and achieve celebrity status. Cuban American writers including Oscar Hijuelos, Virgil Suárez, Gustavo Pérez Firmat, and Cristina García write predominantly for English-speaking audiences in the United States, although they may increasingly find that readers in Cuba are interested in writing of the diaspora. Many of today's writers teach at universities, either full or part time, an option that was not widely available to writers in the mid–nineteenth century. And, most importantly, while today's writers consider the place of politics in the life of Cubans and Cuban exiles, most poets and novelists do not set out to change the government in Cuba through their writings in the way that Zenea, Villaverde, and Miguel T. Tolón did in the nineteenth century.

A final note about the political positions of the *filibusteros*. As someone who has always been interested in the political analysis of texts (particularly in relation to categories of gender, class, ethnicity, and imperialism), I find it necessary to distinguish between politics in writing and writing with an explicit political position. In other words, it is one thing to say that a novel is political because all writing is political, but that is not the same as saying that a piece of writing takes a position on an issue. The distinction is not always so clear, but sometimes it is, particularly when newspaper articles, letters, and pamphlets are part of the writing under consideration. The distinction that I draw here between writing with a position, including poetry, and writing that is more ambiguous or ambivalent is important for efforts to develop new literary histories. Many writers who today would be considered Latinos wrote to support their communities, critique social injustices, and reach readers in other countries. That makes for a much different literary history than one based on the great works of a people. The importance of newspapers that differed from the contemporary daily should not be underestimated.

The writers I have called *filibusteros* and their contemporaries who were not as keen on filibustering raise important questions for American literary and cultural studies. First, they created a type of writing that moved beyond the nation both literally and metaphorically, a point that I have emphasized throughout this study, and they did so in the midst of a battle of empires for control of Cuba. If practitioners of American studies truly intend to become transnational or even global, they can no longer study only writers from the United States. To become transnational is to take seriously other literary histories, political and economic conditions outside the United States, and, most importantly, languages other than English. To do so is to move out of the comforts of disciplinary knowledge, to enter into an uncomfortable place, perhaps akin to what Cuban exiles in the United States called *extraño suelo* (unknown territory or, more literally, strange land). As many of them found, after spending enough time in unknown territory, it might no longer be possible to return to the comforts of a familiar place. A reconstituted American studies that takes into account the plight of ethnic minorities and transnational conditions perhaps should take as its starting point that type of uncomfortable position.

NOTES

Introduction

1. "En el molde de los Estados Unidos, arquetipo de todas las constituciones políticas hasta ahora conocidas" ("Prospecto," *El Horizonte,* 4 July 1850).

2. Tolón, "Fourth of July."

3. Carbonell, *La Poesía Revolucionaria,* 108–10.

4. Montes-Huidobro, *Laúd,* 138; Gruesz, *Ambassadors of Culture,* 148–49.

5. García Carranza and Ponte, *Catálogo de Publicaciones;* Kanellos and Martell, "Comprehensive Bibliography," 143–277.

6. Martí traditionally has been admired both for his contributions to poetry and prose and his work as a militant devoted to achieving Cuban independence; see Franco, *Modern Culture of Latin America,* 22–24. While living in the United States, Martí wrote prolifically, including essays on Ralph Waldo Emerson, Walt Whitman, Ulysses S. Grant, and other aspects of U.S. society; see Martí, *Selected Writings,* 116–29, 193–219. Indications that Martí has crossed disciplinary boundaries from Spanish-language literature and Cuban history to U.S. literary studies include the collection edited by Belnap and Fernández, *José Martí's "Our America,"* and Martí's inclusion in Lauter et al., *Heath Anthology of American Literature.*

7. Martí, "Our America," in *Selected Writings,* 288–96.

8. Saldívar, *Dialectics,* 6.

9. Warner, *Letters of the Republic,* 3.

10. El Amigo de los Hombres [pseud.], *A Todos los Que Habitan las Islas y el Vasto Continente de la América Española,* in Kanellos et al., *Herencia,* 513.

11. See Rocafuerte, *Ideas Necesarias.*

12. Brown, *Agents of Manifest Destiny,* 17–18; *Oxford English Dictionary; A Dictionary of Americanisms on Historical Principles.* Corominos and Pascual, *Diccionario,* note that the Spanish *filibustero* postdates usage in English, but the editors acknowledge that sailors could have used the Spanish form and cite an appearance of the word in print in 1640.

13. The study of filibustering and Cuba in the mid–nineteenth century has until now remained largely within the purview of historians. See, for example, May, *Manifest Destiny's Underworld;* May, *Southern Dream;* Brown, *Agents of Manifest Destiny;* Greene, *Career of William Walker;* Rosengarten, *Freebooters Must Die!* Books by

Central American historians include Bolaños Geyer, *William Walker*; Guier, *William Walker*. The standard history in Cuba of the filibustering expeditions of 1850 and 1851 is Portell Vilá, *Narciso López*. In the United States, Chaffin, *Fatal Glory*, focuses on López's connection to both northerners and southerners in the United States. Owsley and Smith, *Filibusters and Expansionists*, focus on the period 1800–1821 and shift the meaning of "filibuster" to argue that the practice was common decades before the 1850s and was intertwined with the efforts of Jefferson, Madison, and Monroe to expand the borders of the United States. This study focuses on the textuality of filibustering, in terms of both texts produced and the ways that filibusters (re)produced themselves and their historical moment. By recovering the conditions of textual production of Cuban writers, I emphasize that filibustering was intertwined with print cultures that attempted to influence the shifting borders of nations in the Americas.

14. May, *Manifest Destiny's Underworld*, xii.

15. Galeano, *Open Veins*, 121.

16. Poyo, *"With All and for the Good of All,"* 4–5.

17. Pérez, *Cuba and the United States*, 12–14; Rauch, *American Interest in Cuba*, 30.

18. Pérez, *Cuba and the United States*, 38.

19. Jefferson, *Writings*, 15:479.

20. "Cuba," *United States Magazine*, 200.

21. Rauch, *American Interest in Cuba*, 73, 292, 302.

22. Traveling through the Cuban countryside in the 1820s, Massachusetts minister Abiel Abbot wrote of one plantation, "A great invalid is receiving the same generous hospitality with myself" (*Letters*, 9). Abbot's book remained popular for decades.

23. For collections of travel writings about Cuba, see Pérez, *Slaves, Sugar, and Colonial Society*; Olivera, *Viajeros en Cuba*; see also Campuzano, "A 'Valiant Symbol.' "

24. Hurlbert, *Gan-Eden*, 3. This book, loaded with an ideology of Euro-American colonial superiority, includes lines such as, "Before Columbus all human history in Cuba is a blank" (2).

25. For a discussion of Heredia in the United States, see Gruesz, *Ambassadors of Culture*, 30–48.

26. See Leal and Cortina, introduction, vii–xviii; McCadden and McCadden, *Father Varela*.

27. Pérez, *Cuba and the United States*, 36.

28. Rauch, *American Interest in Cuba*, 42; for a detailed analysis of La Escalera, see Paquette, *Sugar Is Made with Blood*.

29. Paquette, *Sugar Is Made with Blood*, 223–24.

30. Benítez Rojo, "Power/Sugar/Literature."

31. For a discussion of Delmonte's correspondence with Everett, see Paquette, *Sugar Is Made with Blood*, 9–10, 197, 263–64.

32. Villaverde to Delmonte, Havana, 9 September 1844, in Villaverde, *Homenaje*, 71.

33. Pérez, *Cuba: Between Reform and Revolution*, 86.

34. Kutzinski, *Sugar's Secrets*, 15.

35. "Por el contrario le han agravado constantemente el bolsillo, además de hacerle perder su tiempo y su trabajo personal" (Mesa, "A Mis Lectores").

36. Chaffin, *Fatal Glory*, 35.

37. Said, *Representations of the Intellectual*, 47, 49.

38. Said, *Culture and Imperialism*, xxvii.

39. Jorge Duany, "Reconstructing Cubanness," argues that Cubanness as expressed in the work of Cuba-based intellectuals has connected territory and nation in ways that differ from the diasporic conceptions of U.S.-based scholars. Recent developments in Cuba suggest that scholars there are beginning to consider the relationship of Cuban literature to emigration and exile; see Fornet, "Cuban Literary Diaspora."

40. The term "Cuban American" is most commonly used in reference to a post-1959 identity construction and what scholars sometimes call the 1.5 generation—people who arrived in the United States at a young age. As Gustavo Pérez Firmat, *Life on the Hyphen*, 3, notes, "It is one thing to be Cuban in America, and quite another to be Cuban American." The adjectival form of the latter incorporates a hyphen; thus, "Cuban-American" implies the ability to cross the hyphen like a bridge from one side to the other or even to "live on the hyphen." My analysis is concerned with political positions that did not correspond to specific identities (for example, support of annexation).

41. See, for example, A. Kaplan and Pease, *Cultures of United States Imperialism*.

42. The parallel revisionary goals of these two projects led to the combined 2002 American Studies/Recovering the U.S. Hispanic Literary Heritage conference, "The Local and the Global: Redefining 'Nuestra América.'"

43. Kanellos et al., *Herencia*, 1.

44. In addition to numerous editions of fiction, poetry, and nonfiction published as part of the Recovering the U.S. Hispanic Literary Heritage Project series, four volumes of essays have been published under the title *Recovering the U.S. Hispanic Literature Heritage*. For significant early studies that contributed to the goals of the Recovery Project, see Padilla, *My History, Not Yours*; R. Sánchez, *Telling Identities*.

45. Studies that focus on the Spanish-language press in New Mexico include Meléndez, *So All Is Not Lost*; Meyer, *Speaking for Themselves*.

46. Gruesz, *Ambassadors of Culture*, xii.

47. Aranda, "Contradictory Impulses," 554.

48. Kanellos et al., *Herencia*, 21–29.

49. Basch, Schiller, and Blanc, *Nations Unbound*, 27. Other studies have moved beyond the duality of a focus on two countries by bringing forth how globalization in its various manifestations influences transnational experiences in the contemporary age (Appadurai, *Modernity at Large*; Kennedy and Roudometof, *Communities across Borders*).

50. Rowe, "Literary Culture and Transnationality," 79.

51. In his model of print culture, Darnton, "History of Books," 5–6, diagrams his circuit in the shape of a sphere with links to various contingent factors: "intellectual influences and publicity," "economic and social conjuncture," and "political and legal sanctions."

52. Said, *Culture and Imperialism*, 336.

Chapter One

1. *Congressional Globe*, 32d Cong., 1st sess., 3 January 1853, 190.

2. As an example of common usage in the nineteenth-century United States, the words "filibuster," "freebooter," and "pirate" were used interchangeably in *Putnam's Monthly Magazine*, "Filibustering." "Buccaneer," "freebooter," and "corsair" had various international etymological histories, but all came to be used interchangeably with "pirate." For a discussion of the variations in these terms, see Gerassi-Navarro, *Pirate Novels*, 16–19.

3. "Filibusterismo."

4. In his "vocabulary of culture and society," R. Williams investigates how social and historical processes play out in debates over the connotations of particular words. "Keywords" are significant to certain activities and indicative of "certain forms of thought," but their importance goes beyond the linguistic realm. Williams writes, "Most of the social and intellectual issues, including both gradual developments and the most explicit controversies and conflicts, persisted within and beyond the linguistic analysis" (*Keywords*, 16).

5. The opening lines of Cardenal's poem complicate a facile vilification of the *filibusteros*. Among them, he writes, were not only thieves and gamblers but also honorable men who responded to necessities and illusions (*Antología*, 40). Those who joined Walker for principles rather than money included Cubans who believed Walker would help them liberate the island.

6. Walker, *War in Nicaragua*, 429.

7. Ibid., 145.

8. Brown, *Agents of Manifest Destiny*, 308.

9. An Officer in the Service of Walker, *Destiny of Nicaragua*, 14–15.

10. Walker, *War in Nicaragua*, 429–30.

11. Whittier, *Complete Poetical Works*, 391.

12. Howe, *Trip*, 85, 43.

13. *Congressional Globe*, 32d Cong., 1st sess., 3 January 1853, 194.

14. "Filibuster" was still used in reference to military expeditions in the early twentieth century. Shipments of arms from the United States to Cuba in the years preceding the Spanish-Cuban-American War were referred to as "filibustering" (Foner, *Spanish-Cuban-American War*, 17–18).

15. S. A. Binder and Smith argue in *Politics or Principle?* that the filibuster has remained a vibrant part of Senate politics not so much because of principles of

extended debate but rather because it protects the personal power of individual senators. In the day-to-day workings of the Senate, the filibuster strengthens individual senators who use the tactic to exert their wills and even demand support for pork barrel projects. The threat of a filibuster is often enough to prompt changes in a bill.

16. For a discussion of *Mr. Smith Goes to Washington* and the creation of citizenship, see Berlant, *Queen of America*, 40–50.

17. Capra, *Mr. Smith Goes to Washington*.

18. "Dos Palabras sobre los Piratas," *La Verdad*, 24 April 1851.

19. Gerassi-Navarro, *Pirate Novels*, 5, reads these contrasting portraits as exemplifying the conflicts between a growing sense of national identity and the residual institutions of colonial Spanish America.

20. Ancona, "El Filibustero," 701. Ancona's *filibustero* character paves the way for a critique of colonial corruption. Pirating becomes an alternative to the graft carried out by Spanish colonial governors and society in the Yucatán. Posing a challenge to the economic stranglehold of the region's upper classes, the *filibustero* even offers a model of economic freedom that is denied by Spanish protectionism. When one of Leonel's friends steals a dress for his mother, who cannot afford to buy one, he justifies his theft by saying, "Siendo España la única que puede comerciar con sus colonias ya sabéis lo caro que cuesta vestirse en la provincia [You know how expensive it is to dress in our province because Spain is the only source of exchange for the colonies]" (666). For a brief discussion of Ancona, see Read, *Mexican Historical Novel*, 140–59.

21. Anderson, *Imagined Communities*, 26–27, discusses Rizal's fiction as exemplifying novelistic conceptions of the temporal simultaneity of imagined communities.

22. In an interesting gloss on Rizal's novel, León M. Guerrero titled the English translation *The Subversive*. The freedom that Guerrero takes in translating *El Filibusterismo* is instructive, for it emphasizes the nationalist insurgency as a version of filibusterism.

23. Guerrero, introduction to Rizal, *The Subversive*, xiv.

24. "Otros dedicados a la piratería y al pillaje, fueron designados por la historia con el nombre de *Filibusteros*, sin pensar que andando el tiempo y corriendo días, uno vendría en que aquel apodo deshonroso habria de convertirse en título honorífico que sirviera para distinguir a los campeones de la democracia, defensores de la libertad" (Santacilia, *Lecciones Orales*, 12).

25. May, "Young American Males," 862.

26. Chaffin, *Fatal Glory*, 6–10.

27. Pérez, *Cuba and the United States*, 47.

28. Chaffin, *Fatal Glory*, 200.

29. Caldwell, *López Expeditions*, 48–50; May, *Southern Dream*, 47–52; Brown, *Agents of Manifest Destiny*, 47–51; May, *Manifest Destiny's Underworld*, 252–54.

30. Chaffin, *Fatal Glory*, 223–24 n.4. Chaffin argues that the López expeditions

were marked by republicanism. Indeed, my readings of the Spanish-language periodical press confirm Chaffin's point. But the internationalist bent of republicanism was tempered by the emphasis within López's inner circle on Cuban self-determination. While the writers closest to López—Villaverde, Tolón, and, Betancourt Cisneros—certainly admired the United States and, in some cases, even longed to see themselves in the Union, these men considered themselves distinctly Cuban, and that self-image emerged in their transnational writing.

31. Portell Vilá, *Narciso López*, 1:8. That debate is likely to circle around the available evidence unless a solid document emerges that can answer the vexed question of intention.

32. Given the presence of Cuban planters in New York annexationist circles, it is no surprise that an estate was listed side by side with life.

33. "Patriotismo Cubano."

34. The idiom "Me quito como el pastelero" can be translated as "I'll get out of the way like the pastry maker" (Sánchez-Boudy, *Diccionario Mayor de Cubanismos*, s.v. "pastelero").

35. "A Nuestros Amigos."

36. Varela, *El Habanero*, 75.

37. Ibid., 17.

38. "Es preciso no perder de vista que en la isla de Cuba no hay *opinión política*, no hay otra opinión que la *mercantil*. En los muelles y almacenes se resuelven todas las cuestiones de Estado" (Varela, *El Habanero*, 16).

39. Betancourt Cisneros to Saco, New York, 3 June 1849, in Betancourt Cisneros, *Cartas a Saco*, 51.

40. See, for example, Betancourt Cisneros, *Thoughts*, 1, 20.

41. Ibid., 5.

42. At first, the Bellidos did not reveal that they were the editors to avoid calling attention to themselves. But after several months, they found that other Cubans were passing off the newspaper as their own work, so the Bellidos publicly claimed the paper; see *El Filibustero*, 8 September 1853.

43. "Adquisición de Cuba."

44. Quoted in Rauch, *American Interest in Cuba*, 293.

45. "EL FILIBUSTERO es un órgano de la libertad de Cuba y los cubanos agotarán todos los medios posibles y honrosos antes de dejar sucumbir un objeto que simbolice la causa santa de su querida patria" ("Reforma de *El Filibustero*," *El Filibustero*, 8 October 1853).

46. "Filibusterismo."

47. "Patriotismo Cubano."

48. Widmer, *Young America*, 197–98.

49. Brown, *Agents of Manifest Destiny*, 105; Rauch, *American Interest in Cuba*, 239.

50. Davis was appointed secretary of war and Cushing attorney general (Rauch, *American Interest in Cuba*, 256–57).

51. "Recepción del Presidente Franklin Pierce."

52. *La Verdad*, 28 February 1853.

53. "El mal en nosotros depende de querer esperarlo todo de los Estados Unidos; y este es un mal gravísimo. . . . Los cubanos de la isla creen que este pueblo les dará la libertad sin que ellos tengan que moverse para nada" ("Cuba," *El Filibustero*, 25 November 1853).

54. "General López."

55. *La Crónica*, 18 August 1849; see also "Isla de Cuba," *La Crónica*, 30 May 1850.

56. For a discussion of the Quitman expedition, see May, *Southern Dream*, 46–67.

57. "Adquisición de Cuba."

58. "No queremos exigir ese sentimiento a los americanos, sería pedir a la naturaleza lo que ella no puede producir" ("Adquisición de Cuba").

59. Quoted in Mott, *American Journalism*, 391.

60. Jensen, *Children of Colonial Despotism*, 102–6.

61. Miguel T. Tolón, "En el Segundo Aniversario de 'La Verdad,'" in Montes-Huidobro, *Laúd*, 39–40.

62. Villaverde, *Cecilia Valdés*, 166–67.

63. Montes-Huidobro, *Laúd*, vii.

64. For a discussion of Heredia in the context of the nineteenth-century United States, see Gruesz, *Ambassadors of Culture*, 1–2, 43–44, 146.

65. Tolón, *Leyendas*, 127–30.

66. Leopoldo Turla, "Canto de Guerra," *El Filibustero*, 6 June 1853.

67. For example, Fernando Rodríguez's "A Cuba" (1853), which concludes with a rousing call to attack the "Iberian despot," is an obvious example of the taste for militaristic language: "Y por fin, si nos basta a ser libres / Preparar con el fuego una brecha, / Apliquemos nosotros la mecha / Y sepamos vencer o morir [At last, if freedom is enough, / Let us prepare a breach with fire, / Let us light the fuse / And learn to triumph or die]" ("A Cuba," *El Filibustero*, 9 May 1853).

68. Pedro Angel Castellón [Cuyaguateje, pseud.], "Al General Narciso López," *La Verdad*, 20 March 1852.

69. Pedro Angel Castellón, "En la Muerte de Julio Chassagne," *El Filibustero*, 6 June 1853; also in Montes-Huidobro, *Laúd*, 90.

70. Gruesz, *Ambassadors of Culture*, 109–10.

71. "Se ha propuesto libar en la bella flor de Cuba, para envenenar su miel y depositarla en asqueroso panal, que solo gusta a los sectarios de la tiranía" ("Al Editor de the New Orleans Bee," *La Verdad*, 10 October 1854).

72. "Castellón fue un forjador de estrofas detonantes que huelen a pólvora recién quemada por la libertad y la bandera" (Carbonell, *Poetas*, 124).

73. Widmer, *Young America*, 198.

74. *El Filibustero*, 4 July 1853.

75. Pedro Angel Castellón, "A Cuba en la Muerte de Varela," *El Filibustero*, 13 June 1853; also in Montes-Huidobro, *Laúd*, 85–88.

76. Scholars have estimated that Castellón died in exile in 1856, but they have

been unable to determine exactly where, how, or when. His tomb has not been found (Carbonell, *Poetas*, 132).

77. Horrego Estuch, *Emilia Casanova*, 12; Montes-Huidobro, *Laúd*, 168.

78. Montes-Huidobro, *Laúd*, 169.

79. Carbonell, *Poetas*, 113–14.

80. Montes-Huidobro, *Laúd*, 168–69; Carbonell, *Poetas*, 119.

81. Tolón, "A Nuestros Lectores."

82. Anonymous, "Himno de Guerra Cubano," *El Horizonte*, 24 September 1850.

83. Casanova de Villaverde, "Cartas," 94.

84. Montes-Huidobro, *Laúd*, 106–12.

85. Ibid., 171.

86. Francisco Agüero Estrada, "Poesía Dedicada a la Memoria de Mi Apreciable Amigo D. Francisco Perdomo Batista, Que Murió en la Heroíca Acción de San Carlos el 13 de Julio de 1851, al Contemplar Su Retrato," *El Filibustero*, 30 May 1853.

87. Ibid.

88. Lezama Lima, *Cantidad Hechizada*, 213.

89. Piñeyro, *Vida y Escritos de Juan Clemente Zenea*, 30.

90. "Diga al Capitán General de Cuba que he escrito, que escribo y que siempre escribiré contra el despotismo," quoted in Lezama Lima, *Cantidad Hechizada*, 201.

91. "El Filibustero," *El Filibustero*, 15 August 1853; "Diez y Seis de Agosto de 1851 en la Habana," *El Filibustero*, 9 May 1853; "En el Aniversario del General López," *El Filibustero*, 1 September 1853; also in Montes-Huidobro, *Laúd*, 93–95, 96–98, 99–100.

92. Zenea, "Esperanza."

93. "Cuba será una patria común para todos, y en su seno hospitalario recibirá con benevolencia a los desgraciados que arriben a sus playas, sin distinción de clase, sexo ni nacionalidad. Cuba, entonces, no será española" (Zenea, "Esperanza").

94. Juan Clemente Zenea, "Fragmento," *El Filibustero*, 15 November 1853.

95. Ibid.

96. "Con él empezamos ya a entender *el misterio de la debilidad* en nuestra poesía y nuestro ser" (Vitier, *Lo Cubano*, 177).

97. Quoted in Olivera, *Cuba en Su Poesía*, 159.

98. Ibid., 160.

99. Chaffin, *Fatal Glory*, 199, 214–15. Montes-Huidobro, *Laúd*, 165–66, reads the historical references in the poem as being in tension with a universal meditation on death as an individual experience rather than a collective political moment.

100. Brown, *Agents of Manifest Destiny*, 87–89.

101. In the lines quoted, the word *cirnióse* appears to be a conjugation of the verb *cerner*, which can be translated as "hover" (Juan Clemente Zenea, "Diez y Seis de Agosto de 1851 en La Habana," in Montes-Huidobro, *Laúd*, 96).

102. Ibid.

103. Barbarito Torres, interview in Wenders and Wenders, *Buena Vista Social Club*, 84.

104. Deleuze and Guattari, *Kafka*, 18–20.

105. For discussions of deterritorialization in the contemporary period, see Appadurai, *Modernity at Large*, 37–39; see also C. Kaplan, "Deterritorializations," 187–98. For a discussion of deterritorialization in relation to the cultural production of the U.S.-Mexico borderlands, see Hicks, *Border Writing*. Hardt and Negri, *Empire*, 295–96, 346–47, focus on deterritorialization in relation to the increased mobility of capital and the growth of what they call "immaterial labor," as exemplified by communications workers, whose networks supersede national sovereignty.

106. "El Filibustero," *El Filibustero*, 15 August 1853; also in Montes-Huidobro, *Laúd*, 93–95.

107. Cubans in the United States kept up their military organizing against Spain after the failure of the original efforts to filibuster Cuba. If anything, the filibustering fifties were a prelude to the efforts of Cuban communities in the United States for much of the century. In 1870, for example, one of the leaders of exiled Cubans in the 1850s, Domingo Goicuría, took part in a filibustering attack on the island that cost him his life when he was captured and publicly garroted; see Thomas, *Cuba*, 257.

108. When the ship went down, Crane ended up on a boat struggling back to land—the plot of "The Open Boat." "Stephen Crane's Own Story" and "The Open Boat" differ significantly not only in style but also in content, for the story begins where the article trails off. Crane ends his newspaper story with the following: "The history of life in an open boat for thirty hours would no doubt be instructive for the young, but none is to be told here and now" (Crane, *Prose and Poetry*, 883).

109. Crane, *Prose and Poetry*, 876.

110. Filibustering is cut out of "The Open Boat," along with the Cubans. Instead, Crane's story focuses on the naturalistic and terrifying power of the ocean, which leaves little agency for the participants. The literary piece erases military and political conditions, yet the deterritorialized sense of the filibuster at the mercy of the ocean informs the naturalist sense of "The Open Boat." Similarly, the danger of the ocean informs Crane's sense of what makes up the filibuster.

111. "Nuestros esfuerzos son casi nulos y nuestra cooperación del todo innecesaria en las presentes circunstancias; cuando estamos persuadidos, que la revolución de Cuba no debe hacerse ya con impresos y papeles, sino con armas, pólvora y balas" ("A Nuestros Amigos").

Chapter Two

1. "El objeto de esta publicación no es otro que depellejar sin misericordia a todos aquellos reptiles que por espíritu de adulación o por una cobardía vergonzosa, se arrastran ante el poder español de Cuba, olvidandose que son hombres y convirtiéndose en bestias miserables" (*El Guao*, 7 June 1853, p. 1).

2. Santacilia, *El Arpa del Proscripto*, 114.

3. Santacilia lived in New York and New Orleans, where some of his most important publications appeared, before settling in Mexico and working as a government official and as secretary to President Benito Juárez. In Mexico, Santacilia worked with activist groups supporting Cuban independence; see Montes-Huidobro, *Laúd*, 152; see also Santacilia, *Lecciones Orales*.

4. I could find only the first issue, which is held at the José Martí National Library in Havana.

5. Kanellos, "Brief History," 6.

6. Cuba was the main focus of the following papers from the 1850s: *La Verdad, El Filibustero, El Pueblo, El Mulato, El Guao, El Cubano, El Papagayo, El Cometa, El Horizonte, El Eco de Cuba*, and *El Independiente*. Other papers probably also circulated. During this period, two Spanish-language papers, *La Crónica* and *La Patria*, opposed the political platforms of papers edited by Cuban exiles.

7. Tolón published six issues numbered continuously between 15 February and 6 April 1855. The last issue noted that the periodical was being transformed into a newspaper-size publication named *El Cometa* (The comet). Tolón might have had that change in mind from the beginning. In the first issue of *El Papagayo*, he wrote that in time "the 'Papagayo' will take such flight that it rises to become a comet" ("Al Lector," *El Papagayo*, 15 February 1855). The six issues of *El Papagayo* are in the José Martí National Library in Havana, and a microfilm copy is held by the Recovering the U.S. Hispanic Literary Heritage Project in Houston. I thank Nicolás Kanellos and Alejandra Balestra for making the microfilm available.

8. Poyo, *"With All and for the Good of All,"* 2.

9. De la Cova, "Filibusters and Freemasons."

10. Quoted in ibid., 100.

11. De la Cova, "Filibusters and Freemasons," 106, notes that the five-pointed stars of the Texas and Cuban flags are also a reference to the Masonic five points of fellowship.

12. The Soles y Rayos de Bolívar movement was led by José Francisco Lemus and included the participation of poet José María Heredia. The group's goal was to prompt an uprising of slaves and Creoles in Cuba on the assumption that they would receive military support from an army led by Simón Bolívar. The plot was discovered by Spanish authorities (Thomas, *Cuba*, 101–4).

13. Letter to the editors, *El Filibustero*, 15 January 1854.

14. Censorship in Cuba had been constant, except for brief periods in 1812 and from 1820 to 1823. After Narciso López's 1851 attack, Cuba's captain-general shut down one of Havana's newspapers, *El Faro Industrial* (The industrial beacon), and eliminated royal censors in favor of a clerk who would work under the captain-general's direction (Caldwell, *López Expeditions*, 9).

15. Fornet, *El Libro en Cuba*, 34.

16. For a study of the periodical press and censorship in Cuba prior to 1840, see Jensen, *Children of Colonial Despotism*.

17. Dana, *To Cuba and Back*, 115.

18. Fornet, *El Libro en Cuba*, 32.

19. Ibid., 32–34.

20. My analysis is based on the copy of the first issue held at the José Martí National Library in Havana. The issue appeared on 13 June 1852 as a single-sided sheet. Below the newspaper's name was the phrase "Organo de la Independencia (organ of independence)". Two columns featured three articles: one introduced readers to the publication, another recounted political conditions on the island, and the third ridiculed the cowardice of a Spanish general who had failed to show up for a duel against a revolutionary. *La Voz del Pueblo Cubano* pledged to shed light on "all political events hidden from us by the Spanish government; all the acts of injustice, despotism, and tyranny that it will commit against our compatriots" ("A Nuestros Lectores").

21. "Multitud de criollos se han trasladado a los E.U., y han armado, arman, y armarán expediciones para invadir esta isla y luchar en ella para alcanzar su independencia de la injusta metrópoli" ("Situación del País," *La Voz del Pueblo Cubano*, 13 June 1852).

22. "La Voz del Pueblo Cubano," *La Verdad*, 30 June 1852.

23. Ibid.

24. "A Nuestros Lectores."

25. Fornet, *El Libro en Cuba*, 32–34.

26. "D. Eduardo Facciolo."

27. Warner, *Letters of the Republic*, 118–19.

28. Anderson, *Imagined Communities*, 62.

29. A more relevant theoretical concept is Homi Bhabha's notion of the nation as barred, separated from the discourses that generate its existence. Bhabha, *Location of Culture*, 148, notes that the signifying space of the nation is *"internally* marked by the discourses of minorities, the heterogeneous histories of contending peoples, antagonist authorities and tense locations of cultural difference."

30. Tolón, for example, believed that military conditions on the island influenced the temporal development of the colony, writing, "Maturity in colonial language is not measured by time but by power" (Miguel T. Tolón, "Cuestión del Dia," *El Cometa*, 25 April 1855).

31. My analysis is based on issues published between June 1855 and February 1856. The originals are in the José Martí National Library and are on microfilm at the Recovering the U.S. Hispanic Literary Heritage Project at the University of Houston.

32. José Mesa, editor's introduction, *El Eco de Cuba*, 22 June 1855.

33. Mesa also printed *El Filibustero* for Juan Bellido de Luna.

34. José Mesa, editor's introduction, *El Eco de Cuba*, 22 June 1855.

35. *El Eco de Cuba*, 22 June 1855.

36. "Anuncios," *El Eco de Cuba*, 22 June 1855.

37. A. A. de Orihuela, "El Guajiro Independiente: Cantos Populares Cubanos," *El Eco de Cuba*, 22 June 1855.

38. Instituto, *Perfil*, 247–54.

39. José Mesa, editor's introduction, *El Eco de Cuba*, 22 June 1855.

40. "Correspondencia: Isla de Cuba," *El Eco de Cuba*, 22 June 1855.

41. *El Horizonte*, which vowed to report on commerce, literature, and politics, appears to have run only for a few months in 1850. My analysis is based on issues from 4 July and 25 July 1850, both at the José Martí National Library, and a one-page supplement dated 24 September 1850 at the Duke University Rare Book, Manuscript, and Special Collections Library.

42. "Adición a Nuestro Prospecto," *El Horizonte*, 4 July 1850.

43. "Cuba, Great Britain, and the United States."

44. Tolón, *Elementary Spanish Reader and Translator*. New editions of this book appeared in 1882, 1901, 1905, and 1912.

45. Miguel T. Tolón, "Remembrance of Home," *El Cubano*, 15 May 1853.

46. "Our Terms," *La Verdad*, 10 August 1852.

47. "Puerto Rico," *La Verdad*, 20 September 1852.

48. The union of Cuban and Puerto Rican intellectuals in New York is exemplified in the work of Lola Rodríguez de Tió (1843–1924), whose poetry included memorable lines comparing the two islands to the two wings of a bird. Her ode "10 de Octubre" is in Kanellos et al., *Herencia*, 560–63.

49. Kanellos, "Brief History," 19.

50. *La Verdad*, 3 April 1849, 1.

51. Rauch, *American Interest in Cuba*, 65.

52. Ibid., 55; Chaffin, *Fatal Glory*, 12–15.

53. Portell Vilá, *Narciso López*, 2:40; Thomas, *Cuba*, 83, 208.

54. "La Verdad," *La Verdad*, 9 January 1848.

55. "La adopción de un sistema general, de un principio único, y de una política enteramente distinta de la política de Europa" ("Prospecto," *La Verdad*, 9 January 1848).

56. "Will the Annexation of Cuba Add to Our Strength as a Nation?" in *A Series of Articles*, 1. The editors of *La Verdad* printed English-language pamphlets containing the newspaper's most important articles. The series of articles, "Of the Advantages Which the Annexation of Cuba Offers to America, and in Particular to the People of the United States," appeared in English and Spanish in February and March 1849. They were subsequently published in an English-language pamphlet held in the Library of Congress and bound as *A Series of Articles on the Cuban Question*.

57. Ibid., 3.

58. Ibid., 2.

59. Cora Montgomery, "Cuba: The Key to the Mexican Gulf," in *A Series of Articles*, 12.

60. "Of the Advantages," in *A Series of Articles*, 9.

61. Ibid., 10.

62. Rauch, *American Interest in Cuba*, 61–64; Chaffin, *Fatal Glory*, 43. Portell Vilá,

Narciso López, 2:44, also notes that *La Verdad* was without a doubt annexationist and proslavery, but he provides background on the Cuban involvement in the paper.

63. *La Verdad* became one of numerous newspapers printed by the *Sun*, which also published a weekly summary of news, the *American Sun*, for circulation overseas, and the *Extra Sun*, "published immediately on the receipt of any important news." See "A Visit to Our Press Room," *New York Sun*, 6 June 1848.

64. Gerald Poyo, *"With All and for the Good of All,"* 7, argues that this sector of the Cuban elite backed annexation in part to maintain white domination of the island and stave off abolition as well as what they perceived as a growing "Africanization" of the island as a result of Spain's ongoing illegal participation in the slave trade.

65. "Of the Advantages," in *A Series of Articles*, 6.

66. "A Nuestros Lectores," *La Verdad*, 3 April 1849.

67. "Cuba and Her Destiny," in *A Series of Articles*, 9.

68. "Will the Annexation of Cuba Benefit the Domestic Interests of the Union?" in *A Series of Articles*, 10.

69. Pedro Santacilia, "A Una Nube," *La Verdad*, 15 October 1855.

70. "El Gobierno de los Estados Unidos, la Isla de Cuba y Puerto Rico," *La Verdad*, 1 May 1849.

71. Quoted in Thomas, *Cuba*, 103.

72. Ibid., 104.

73. Meléndez, *So All Is Not Lost*, 42–44.

74. Brady, *Extinct Lands*, 38–42.

75. Betancourt Cisneros, *Thoughts*, 19. Betancourt Cisneros's article appeared in an English-language pamphlet, which I cite here.

76. Ibid., 20.

77. McDonald, *States' Rights and the Union*, viii.

78. Ibid., 4.

79. See Bueno, *Costumbristas*.

80. Rauch, *American Interest in Cuba*, 79.

81. In a letter quoted by historian Herminio Portell Vilá, Betancourt rallied Tolón and Villaverde to proceed with the September 1851 issue, which followed the capture of Narciso López in Cuba, but cautions against inflammatory material that could hurt the captured filibusters or Cubans suspected of collaboration with López: "We are safe, but they are in grave danger" (Portell Vilá, *Narciso López*, 2:41).

82. Betancourt Cisneros, *Thoughts*, 20.

83. Saco, *Situación Política*, 175.

84. Betancourt Cisneros, *Cartas a Saco*.

85. Betancourt Cisneros, *Thoughts*, 17.

86. In a study of Montgomery's life and work, Linda S. Hudson, *Mistress of Manifest Destiny*, 60–64, argues that Montgomery, and not John L. O'Sullivan, coined the phrase "Manifest Destiny" and wrote expansionist articles for the *United States Magazine and Democratic Review*.

87. Brown, *Agents of Manifest Destiny*, 350–51.

88. Portell Vilá, *Narciso López*, 2:42.

89. Cora Montgomery, "Cuba: The Key to the Mexican Gulf," in *A Series of Articles*, 14.

90. Hudson, *Mistress of Manifest Destiny*, 99.

91. Cora Montgomery, "Cuba: The Key to the Mexican Gulf," in *A Series of Articles*, 12.

92. Ibid., 13.

93. Dana, *Two Years before the Mast*, 125.

94. Mather, *Fe del Christiano*, 12.

95. S. Williams, *Spanish Background*, 17–19.

96. Ibid., 3.

97. Hillgarth, *Mirror of Spain*, 317–24.

98. J. P. Sánchez, *Spanish Black Legend*, 8.

99. Ibid., 8–13; Kanellos, *Thirty Million*, 58–59.

100. J. P. Sánchez, *Spanish Black Legend*, 12–13.

101. Suzanne Oboler, *Ethnic Labels, Latino Lives*, 32–36, is among the scholars who note that Manifest Destiny contributed to a view of a homogeneous nineteenth-century Latin American population.

102. Santacilia, *Lecciones Orales*, 10.

103. Ibid., 9.

104. Miguel T. Tolón, "Al Pan de Matanzas," *La Verdad*, 4 June 1851; also in Montes-Huidobro, *Laúd*, 27.

105. Instituto, *Perfil*, 223.

106. Francisco Sellén, *Hatuey*, in Kanellos et al., *Herencia*, 569.

107. Santacilia, "A España," in Montes-Huidobro, *Laúd*, 79.

108. "Tiempo es ya que desechemos para siempre las mendaces ilusiones de lo pasado" ("Primero de Setiembre de 1855," *La Verdad*, 5 September 1855).

109. *La Crónica*, 30 May 1850. My analysis of *La Crónica* is based on the holdings in the Library of Congress.

110. "Ciertos cubanos desafectos o especuladores, en su mayor parte residentes en este país, y solamente buenos patriotas al salir del suyo, en unión de ciertos especuladores americanos y refugiados europeos, han sido inducidos a formar lo que ellos llaman un gobierno provisional, a contratar empréstitos, y alistar tropas y oficiales, en nombre del pueblo o la república imaginaria de Cuba" ("Las Expediciones Piráticas de Ciudadanos Americanos Contra la Isla de Cuba," *La Crónica*, 24 January 1852).

111. "Ninguna nación del mundo ha poblado con sus hijos, ha gobernado con sus leyes y ha defendido con su sangre a provincias tan magníficas y prósperas como Cuba, Puerto Rico, y las Filipinas" (*La Crónica*, 29 June 1849, p. 1).

112. "Los Estados Unidos apoderado de las arterias principales de la navegación del Nuevo Mundo" (*La Crónica*, 29 June 1849, p. 1).

113. For a discussion of *La Patria*, see Gruesz, *Ambassadors of Culture*, 112–20, 126–27, 136–45.

114. "A 'La Patria' de Nueva Orleans," *La Verdad*, 18 May 1850.

115. The variety of positions that emerged in the periodical press of the mid-1850s supports historian Herminio Portell Vilá's division of annexationists into three groups: those who supported annexation for economic reasons, those who supported it for patriotic reasons, and those who supported it for various other reasons. In the case of the patriotic group, annexation was viewed as a necessary compromise and even a step toward an independent Cuba (Portell Vilá, *Narciso López*, 1:186–209).

116. Porfirio Valiente, one of the leaders of the New York Cuban Junta in 1853, published a letter in *El Filibustero*, 25 July 1853, condemning a purchase plan: "Siempre he protestado contra la consumación de esta idea americana como una calamidad para Cuba y una desgracia para los cubanos, y yo por mi parte antes prefiero sufrir la servidumbre de España que alcanzar la libertad por medio de la compra y al precio de la deshonra de los cubanos [I have always argued against the consummation of this American idea, which would be a calamity for Cuba and a disgrace for Cubans, and as far as I'm concerned, I would rather suffer servitude under Spain than attain liberty through a purchase that would bring dishonor upon Cubans]."

117. The prospectus for *El Independiente*, held at the José Martí National Library, is undated. It probably circulated at the end of 1852 or at the start of 1853, since the second issue is dated 20 February 1853.

118. Rauch, *American Interest in Cuba*, 51–52.

119. Chaffin, *Fatal Glory*, 73–74.

120. "Actas Electorales de la Junta Cubana," *La Verdad*, 20 October 1852.

121. Villaverde and Mariño "La Cuestión de Cuba," *El Independiente*, 20 February 1854.

122. Villaverde and Mariño, "To the Public."

123. It is unclear how many issues of *El Independiente* were published. My analysis is based on the prospectus and a copy of the 20 February 1853 issue, which is in the Duke University Rare Book, Manuscript, and Special Collections Library.

124. "Que Aremos?" *El Pueblo*, 19 June 1855.

125. Ibid.

126. "Nosotros hemos creído desde el principio que no era en los Estados Unidos donde debíamos trabajar de preferencia por la libertad de nuestra patria: no era este el lugar más a propósito para establecer el punto de apoyo de nuestra palanca revolucionaria. En cuanto a la anexión, jamás nos hemos persuadido de que este mal sea necesario" (Publícola [pseud.], "Errores de la Revolución Cubana").

127. "La Venta de Cuba."

128. Francisco Agüero Estrada, "Cubanos," *El Pueblo*, 20 August 1855.

129. Ibid.

130. Poyo, *"With All and for the Good of All,"* 13–17, discusses briefly the shift in the mid-1850s from annexation to a call for a revolution of the Cuban people.

131. "Advertencia," *El Pueblo,* 19 June 1855.

132. Note to readers, *El Independiente,* 20 February 1853.

133. Meléndez, *So All Is Not Lost,* 20.

134. "En esta colección no presentamos ningún nombre que no sea ventajosamente conocido en la república de las letras cubanas" (J. E. Hernández, preface to *El Laúd,* ed. Montes-Huidobro, 4).

135. Note to correspondent, *El Cometa,* 5 July 1855.

136. Portell Vilá, *Narciso López,* 2:42–43.

137. Tolón, "Cuarto Aniversario."

138. Canito [pseud.], *La Verdad,* 11 February 1851.

139. "Los hechos prueban que los habitantes no han querido hasta hoy la revolución. No nos alucinemos los que la deseamos: esta es una verdad" ("Cuba de Hoy: Cuba de Mañana," *El Pueblo,* 19 June 1855).

Chapter Three

1. Fernando Rodríguez, "Manes Sagrados," *La Verdad,* 10 September 1853.

2. "Ceremonia Fúnebre en Honor de la Memoria de los Mártires de la Independencia de Cuba," *El Filibustero,* 8 September 1853.

3. Quoted in Ramos, "Repose of Heroes," 358. Ramos notes that the topos of arms and letters informs the writings of Martí, Bolívar, and Sarmiento.

4. Cervantes Saavedra, *Don Quixote,* 343.

5. "D. Eduardo Facciolo."

6. Ramos, "Repose of Heroes," 358.

7. Montes-Huidobro, *Laúd,* 47.

8. "Acá desplegaban la pluma y la palabra al menos la misma vehemencia que allá el rifle y el machete" (Villaverde, prologue to *Cecilia Valdés,* 5).

9. Paine, *Common Sense,* in *Collected Writings,* 21.

10. Ibid., 20.

11. The articles appeared in *La Verdad* between 10 February and 20 April 1852.

12. Lugo-Ortiz, *Identidades Imaginadas.*

13. Diner, "Irish City," 87; see also F. M. Binder and Reimers, *All the Nations,* 41.

14. Lee, "Daniel O'Connell," 2.

15. Villaverde, "El Sr. Saco.".

16. Quoted in De La Cova, "Ambrosio José Gonzales," 225. De La Cova cites a January 1853 letter. For a biography of Gonzales that includes a discussion of his activities as a filibuster, see De La Cova, *Cuban Confederate Colonel.*

17. Gonzales, *Manifesto,* 16.

18. Ibid., 10.

19. Ibid., 11.

20. Ibid.

21. Saco, "Análisis," 204.

22. "Dos son los móviles principales que impelen a una parte del pueblo americano a la adquisición de Cuba; el deseo de engrandecerse, y el interés de la esclavitud" (Saco, *Situación Política*, 152, 151).

23. Gaspar Betancourt Cisneros was among the writers who preceded Villaverde in attacking Saco; see *Thoughts*.

24. Villaverde, "El Sr. Saco."

25. Sommer, *Proceed with Caution*, 199.

26. Villaverde's critique of Saco unravels under the weight of its internal contradiction. Isn't Villaverde turning to letters by seeking to reign victorious over a man of words? Even as he disparages words, Villaverde never loses some faith in them. He writes that O'Connell "delighted in watching the magical effect" that his words had "on the public masses." And Villaverde points to *La Verdad* as a newspaper founded to "promote" the goals of annexationists in the United States and to "intercede" on behalf of the trampled interests of Cuba, thus implying that the newspaper was involved in a form of action (Villaverde, "El Sr. Saco").

27. Villaverde's venture into Saco's personal life drew the opprobrium of Villaverde's friends in New York and Europe. For a discussion of the personal dimension of this polemic and how Villaverde's friends responded, see Portell Vilá, *Narciso López*, 1:78–80.

28. Saco, *Situación Política*, 176.

29. "Isla de Cuba," *La Crónica*, 17 February 1849.

30. May, "Young American Males," 873–74.

31. "Kossuth y Los Patriotas Cubanos de Nueva York," *La Verdad*, 10 January 1852.

32. "To the Poets and Prose Writers of Cuba," *La Verdad*, 10 January 1852.

33. This book is not listed in databases, nor is it in the José Martí National Library in Havana. I have not seen any references in bibliographies. On more than one occasion, writers at *La Verdad* announced forthcoming books that either were never published or have not been recovered.

34. Miguel T. Tolón, "En la Muerte de Narciso López," *La Verdad*, 28 October 1851; Juan Clemente Zenea, "Diez y Seis de Agosto de 1851 en La Habana," *El Filibustero*, 9 May 1853; Juan Clemente Zenea, "En el Aniversario del General López," *El Filibustero*, 1 September 1853; Leopoldo Turla, "A Narciso López," *El Filibustero*, 1 May 1853. Other poems include Lorenzo Allo [El Peregrino, pseud.], "A la Memoria del General López, Mártir de la Libertad de Cuba," *La Verdad*, 10 January 1852; Pedro Angel Castellón [Cuyaguateje, pseud.], "Al General Narciso López," *La Verdad*, 20 March 1852; Carenas [pseud.], "Al General Narciso López," *La Verdad*, 10 March 1852; Miguel T. Tolón [Lola, pseud.], "Cantar de las Matanzeras en la Muerte del General Narciso López, Mártir de la Libertad de Cuba," *La Verdad*, 28 October 1851; two untitled poems by Fernando Rodríguez published in *La Verdad*, 20 May, 10 September 1853. Compositions to López prior to his death include Una Cubana [pseud.], "Al General López," *El Horizonte*, 5 August 1850; "En Ocasión de Presen-

tarse al General López Una Espada y Una Bandera, por Patriotas de Cuba," *La Verdad*, 27 August 1850.

35. "Adieu, Dear Cuba," *La Verdad*, 10 March 1852.

36. Pedro Angel Castellón, "En la Muerte de Julio Chassagne," *El Filibustero*, 6 June 1853; Pedro Angel Castellón, "A Castañeda, por Haber Entregado al General Narciso López," *El Filibustero*, 24 October 1853; Francisco Agüero Estrada, "Poesía Dedicada a la Memoria de Mi Apreciable Amigo D. Francisco Perdomo Batista, Que Murió en la Heroíca Acción de San Carlos el 13 de Julio de 1851, al Contemplar Su Retrato," *El Filibustero*, 30 May 1853; Antonio M. Betancourt, "El Pabellón Cubano Vencedor en Cárdenas," *El Cubano*, 19 May 1853.

37. Juan Clemente Zenea, "Diez y Seis de Agosto de 1851 en la Habana," in Montes-Huidobro, *Laúd*, 96–97.

38. "General López."

39. Leopoldo Turla, "A Narciso López," in Montes-Huidobro, *Laúd*, 115.

40. Lorenzo Allo [El Peregrino, pseud.], "A la Memoria del General López, Mártir de la Libertad de Cuba," *La Verdad*, 10 January 1852.

41. Quoted in Chaffin, *Fatal Glory*, 200.

42. "Yo te amaba como se ama al padre de la patria. Cuando lanzados de Cuba a un mismo tiempo, me honraste con tu confianza, yo en el fondo de mi corazón consagré a ti, como emanación de la santa causa de mi patria, todo mi ser, para entonces y para siempre" (quoted in Carbonell, *Poetas*, 39).

43. Lorenzo Allo [El Peregrino, pseud.], "A la Memoria del General López, Mártir de la Libertad de Cuba," *La Verdad*, 10 January 1852.

44. Juan Clemente Zenea, "En el Aniversario del General López," in Montes-Huidobro, *Laúd*, 99.

45. Chaffin, *Fatal Glory*, 211–12.

46. "Narciso López," *El Eco de Cuba*, 1 February 1856.

47. Ibid.

48. One newspaper advertised the sale of 1,000 copies of a lithograph of López pictured in his "Cuban" uniform.

49. May, *Manifest Destiny's Underworld*, 66. Chaffin, *Fatal Glory*, 2, best sums up the range of responses to López: "While expansionist zealots in the United States lionized López as a republican hero, critics saw only lawlessness, hypocrisy, and greed. But celebrated or vilified, López's name became a fixture of a mid-nineteenth-century popular culture enthralled with tales of expansionist derring-do."

50. Pickens, *Free Flag*, 57.

51. Dana, *To Cuba and Back*, 138.

52. Ibid., 110.

53. Burton and Burton, introduction to Pickens, *Free Flag*, 30–38.

54. Pickens, *Free Flag*, 57.

55. Ibid., 71.

56. Ibid., 211.

57. "General López, the Cuban Patriot," 99–101.

58. Lorenzo Allo [El Peregrino, pseud.], "A la Memoria del General López, Mártir de la Libertad de Cuba," *La Verdad*, 10 January 1852.

59. Fernando Rodríguez, "Manes Sagrados," *La Verdad*, 10 September 1853.

60. Tolón, "A las Cubanas."

61. Morales y Morales, *Iniciadores*, 2:42, notes that Allo was an intimate friend and admirer of Gómez de Avellaneda.

62. Gertrudis Gómez de Avellaneda, "Al Partir" and "A Washington," *La Verdad*, 20 March 1852, in Gómez de Avellaneda, *Obras*, 237, 259.

63. Among the interesting criticism on Gómez de Avellaneda, Ianes, "Metaficción y 'Elaboraciones al Vapor,' " argues that *Guatimozín* contains elements of metafiction as exemplified in narratorial intrusions that discuss the writer's reading of historical texts.

64. Gómez de Avellaneda was a complex figure with strong ties to Spain as well as to the island where she was born (Harter, *Gómez de Avellaneda*, 30–31).

65. Sofía Estévez is the only woman included in José Martí's collection *Los Poetas de la Guerra*, published originally in New York in 1893.

66. "Y es que, aunque Luisa Pérez no aspirara a ser poeta social ni esa tendencia fuera la más adecuada a su temperamento soñador, desde sus primeros balbuceos poéticos asumió una posición ideológica contraria a toda opresión o tiranía, sea la del rico que explota al pobre, sea la del fuerte que aniquila al débil" (Henríquez Ureña, *Panorama Histórico*, 313).

67. Pérez de Zambrana was one of several distinguished women poets of the 1850s. Cuba's literary magazines also featured some notable but lesser-known poets, including Adelaida del Mármol (1840–57). Her brief life span roughly mirrored the rise of *filibustero* poetry, but her verses do not appear to have touched anything approaching revolutionary consciousness. "La Paz en Nuestro Hogar" (Peace in our household), a poem dedicated to her brothers, offers a vision of an internal living space that resists the "futile pleasures" and "seducers" of society; see González Curquejo, *Florilegio de Escritoras Cubanas*, 1:207–15.

68. When Gómez de Avellaneda returned to Havana, Pérez de Zambrana presided over a ceremony honoring Gómez. In turn, she wrote a prologue to Pérez's second volume of poetry connecting the book to questions of gender and the country of Cuba. As a woman poet, Gómez wrote, Pérez was privileged with an idealistic vision; thus, the book's pages provided an especially interesting image of "the moral and intellectual state of the young country to which the author belongs." In attempting to unify the particular Cuban and universal spirits of poetry, Gómez proposed that Pérez had engaged with the "treasures of her inspiration," the region of her birth, to produce a poetry that was worthy of the universal spirit of the age (Gómez de Avellaneda in Pérez de Zambrana, *Poesías Completas*, 433–34).

69. Miguel T. Tolón, "A Cuba," *La Verdad*, 30 January 1852.

70. Angel Huete, introduction to Pérez de Zambrana, *Poesías Completas*, xvi–xvii.

71. Martí de Cid, "Comparación Estilística," 57.

72. "Es Luisa Pérez pura criatura, a toda pena sensible y habituada a toda deli-

cadeza y generosidad. Cubre el pelo negro en ondas sus abiertas sienes; hay en sus ojos grandes una inagotable fuerza de pasión delicada y de ternura" (Martí, "Luisa Pérez," in Pérez de Zambrana, *Elegias Familiares*, 9).

73. Ibid., 11.

74. Gruesz, *Ambassadors of Culture*, 149.

75. Miguel T. Tolón [Lola, pseud.], "Cantar de las Matanzeras en la Muerte del General Narciso López," *La Verdad*, 28 October 1851.

76. Tolón, "A las Cubanas."

77. "Decir vamos a estudiar, no quiere decir, no vayamos a pelear. Las letras no se oponen a las armas, antes bien las ayudan. La cabeza ilustrada no embarga el brazo valiente: al contrario le da el vigor de la razón y la conciencia recta que le dirige" (quoted in Francisco Agüero Estrada, "Ateneo Democrático Cubano").

78. "Le jour approche où les mots 'l'oppression, l'esclavage' vont être à jamais effacés par la poussière des débris de la Monarchie" (Tolón, "Discours").

79. Figarola-Caneda, *Diccionario Cubano de Seudónimos*, s.v. "Juan Clemente Zenea."

80. "Mon nom révèle bien qu'il y a du sang des Galois qui coule dans mes veines. Quelques uns de mes ancêtres ont vu le jour sous le beau ciel de la Provence; mais moi, je suis né dans une île des mers de l'Amérique, malheureusement opprimée jusqu'à présent" (Tolón, "Discours").

81. Meléndez, *So All Is Not Lost*, 170.

82. "En todo su semblante reinaba una expresión de poética melancolía que hubiera despertado el interés en el alma más prosaica" (Tolón, *Lola Guara*, 7). Tolón published the first part of the novel, sixty-nine pages, in 1846. The rest of the novel has not been found (and possibly was never published), even though *La Verdad* ran a series of advertisements asking for subscriptions to a New York printing of the entire work.

83. "Pues, cuando quiera que Emilia conseguía uno de ellos, lo leía con avidez, lo comentaba y lo pasaba a sus amigos, a fin de que las noticias e ideas nuevas tuviesen la mayor circulación" (Villaverde, *Apuntes Biográficos*, 12).

84. One edition of these letters available in the United States is bound with Cirilo Villaverde's biography of Emilia Casanova, published as *Apuntes Biográficos de Emilia Casanova de Villaverde* under the pseudonym "Un Contemporáneo." Because of a discrepancy between the publication date of Villaverde's biography (1874) and dates of Casanova's letters in 1876, it appears that two publications were bound into one with continuous pagination. The book devotes 188 pages to a section titled "Cartas de La Correspondencia de Emilia C. de Villaverde (1869–1876)" (Letters and correspondence of Emilia C. de Villaverde) Hereafter, I cite Casanova's "Cartas" parenthetically in the text as *C*.

85. See, for example, Santovenia, *La Bandera*, 18; Gay Calbó, "La Bandera y el Escudo," 126; Horrego Estuch, *Emilia Casanova*, 13–14.

86. Villaverde, *Apuntes Biográficos*, 9.

87. "Desde esa fecha memorable se consagró Emilia a la causa de la libertad e

independencia de su patria. Todos sus gustos, sus pensamientos, hasta sus placeres se concentraron en esa idea primordial, que llegó a ser la religión de su alma, y que le dio nuevo impulso, la revistió de nuevo carácter y la hizo nacer a nueva vida" (Villaverde, *Apuntes Biográficos*, 9).

88. Cairo, "Emilia Casanova," 241.

89. Horrego Estuch, *Emilia Casanova*, 29.

90. Although he notes that she was not a "literary figure," Antonio González Curquejo includes her in his three-volume anthology of Cuban women writers, *Florilegio de Escritoras Cubanas*, because of the importance of letters she wrote in support of the Cuban revolution.

91. "Vengo observando la prensa europea por si encontraba una palabra siquiera de aliento en favor de los cubanos del heróico Garibaldo, que jamás y en ningún caso ha negado su espada, ni apoyo o influencia de su gran nombre, a ninguno de los pueblos que han luchado por su libertad."

92. "En este asunto, general, yo no soy sino el conducto por donde una buena porción de sus conciudadanos en Nueva York, desean dar a Vd. un público testimonio de la gratitud y admiración que esperimentan al recordar los servicios que acaba Vd. de prestar a la patria."

93. "Ante una concurrencia relativamente numerosa, presenciamos un acto enteramente nuevo para nosotros, que no estamos acostumbrados a ver al bello sexo figurar para nada en las escenas públicas de la vida social" (quoted in Casanova de Villaverde, "Cartas," 79).

94. Thomas, *Cuba*, 258–59.

95. Montes-Huidobro, *Laúd*, 164.

96. Villaverde, *Apuntes Biográficos*, 14.

Chapter Four

1. *El Mulato*, 20 February 1854, p. 1.

2. Lorenzo Allo, *El Mulato*, 11 March 1854. I quote an English translation of the passage in Allo, *Domestic Slavery*, 9.

3. The last known issue is number 13, held at the José Martí National Library in Cuba. My analysis is based on issues 1–7, 9–11, and 13, some of which are in U.S. libraries.

4. "Si los patriotas blancos lloran al general LOPEZ y a sus compañeros de infortunio, los patriotas de color no pueden jamás olvidar la memoria del sublime poeta Plácido" ("Le Républicain," *El Mulato*, 6 March 1854).

5. See, for example, Sundquist's discussion of Herman Melville and Martin Delany in *To Wake the Nations*, 135–221.

6. The first scholar to note the polemics over *El Mulato* was Poyo, "*With All and for the Good of All*," 17.

7. Ferrer, "Rethinking Race and Nation," 60–61; for a more detailed discussion of race and Cuba's nineteenth-century revolution, see Ferrer, *Insurgent Cuba*.

8. For an insightful journalistic comparison of the ways race was constructed differently in Cuba and the United States in the late twentieth century, see Ojito, "Best of Friends."

9. See Horsman, *Race and Manifest Destiny*; Hietala, *Manifest Design*, 11–54.

10. "Ought a Free Republic to Possess Slaves?"

11. May, *Manifest Destiny's Underworld*, 111, 252–54.

12. Ibid., 254.

13. Chaffin, *Fatal Glory*, 7–10

14. "Ought a Free Republic to Possess Slaves?"

15. Ibid.

16. Ibid.

17. "La causa de la revolución cubana bien puede decirse que se ha *americanizado* completamente" (*El Mulato*, 27 March 1854, p. 1).

18. "Quieren entrar por las puertas de la república con papeleta gratis" (*El Mulato*, 27 March 1854, p. 1).

19. "Deseando evitar daños semejantes a los que hoy experimentan los Estados Unidos por no haber procurado a su tiempo marcar un medio que acabase *lentamente* la esclavitud" (*El Mulato*, 27 February 1854, p. 1).

20. "Prospecto," *El Horizonte*, 4 July 1850.

21. Pérez, *Cuba: Between Reform and Revolution*, 86.

22. For a discussion of nineteenth-century usage of racial labels, see Ferrer, *Insurgent Cuba*, 10–12.

23. Betancourt Cisneros, *Thoughts*, 18.

24. While these writers called for equality of political rights, their beliefs about racial difference were influenced by racist discourses circulating in the mid–nineteenth century. Tolón, for example, argued in one article, "If she [Cuba] becomes really independent, the whites who are but little inferior in numbers to the blacks, will maintain the ascendancy by their superior intelligence, and slavery will probably be abolished by slow degrees" (*El Cubano*, 25 May 1853).

25. *El Filibustero* responded to charges that the revolution had become "Americanized" by echoing *El Mulato*'s platform that annexation was not a real plan but rather a theoretical possibility to be decided at a later date ("Junta General de Cubanos").

26. Zenea, "Meeting Cubano."

27. Quoted in Rahe, *Republics*, 752.

28. Some critics who lament divisions within the exile community are missing the point that exiles such as Zenea believed in the need for debate and dissent rather than compromise for unity. That spirit animated the publication of *El Mulato*.

29. "A Nuestros Lectores," *El Mulato*, 27 February 1854.

30. "Celebración del Aniversario."

31. "Le jour approche où la différence de langues, ainsi que toute distinction de nationalité, de moeurs et de religion—tout ce qui empêche l'assimilation sociale, cessera d'exister parmi les hommes. Cette UNITÉ UNIVERSELLE sera le complément de l'oeuvre de la Civilisation Moderne, qui avance toujours malgré les obstacles dont l'ignorance et la Tyrannie sèment sa route" (Tolón, "Discours").

32. Ibid.

33. Morales y Morales, *Iniciadores*, 2:58, notes that *El Mulato* was founded and edited by Santiago Bombalier, a lawyer who was one of López's conspirators in Cuba. Bombalier's name does not appear on the extant issues of the paper, but he might have written some of the unsigned articles.

34. De la Cova, "Ambrosio José Gonzales," 168.

35. Agüero Estrada, "Pobres Cubanos."

36. Agüero Estrada, "Cubanos."

37. Allo, *Domestic Slavery*, 11. Allo was quoted in an untitled article in *El Mulato*, 11 March 1854, p. 1. Here I cite the English-language translation of his pamphlet, which contained the same line.

38. *El Mulato*, 18 March 1854, p. 1.

39. Allo, *Domestic Slavery*, 6.

40. Ibid., 5.

41. "Doctrina Socialista de Jesús Cristo," *El Mulato*, 1 April 1854.

42. Allo, *Domestic Slavery*, 13.

43. Ibid., 5–6.

44. Ibid., 7.

45. Ibid.

46. Pérez, *Cuba: Between Reform and Revolution*, 105.

47. "Isla de Cuba," *El Filibustero*, 9 May 1853.

48. *El Mulato*, 6 March 1854, p. 1.

49. Yun and Laremont, "Chinese Coolies," 113.

50. Dana, *To Cuba and Back*, 45.

51. Yun and Laremont, "Chinese Coolies," 114.

52. Walker, *War in Nicaragua*, 280.

53. Wells, *Walker's Expedition*, 109–10.

54. An Officer in the Service of Walker, *Destiny of Nicaragua*, v.

55. M. L. Pratt, *Imperial Eyes*, 146–49, discusses European writers who traveled to the Southern Cone after the wars of independence and shows how their writings consecrated imperialist economic aspirations by presenting the area in pragmatic economic terms.

56. Quoted in Wells, *Walker's Expedition*, 118.

57. Howe, *Trip*, 233; hereafter cited parenthetically in the text as *Trip*.

58. Discussing a sugar plantation, Dana, *To Cuba and Back*, 66, compares slaves to machines who work while the ultimate power goes to a master who is "enthroned in the labor of another race, brought from across the sea." Dana explains that "the

land and the agricultural capital of the interior are in the hands of an upper class, which does no manual labor" (51). *To Cuba and Back* is hereafter cited parenthetically in the text as *TC*.

59. Villaverde, *Cecilia Valdés*, 438.

60. Heredia, *Selected Poems*, 33–37.

61. The use of "unmixed blood" and the metaphor of the hidalgo, which connotes nobility but more literally "hijo de algo" (son of something), is in keeping with the book's repeated invocations of race and blood. By contrast, Dana described the hybridity of the people. In that vein, Howe noted racial mingling: "The black and white races are, by all accounts, more mingled in Cuba, than in any part of our own country. . . . [S]ome of the wealthiest and most important families are of mixed blood" (*Trip* 216). Howe was hostile to the darker-skinned people she saw, describing them as "Spanish flies" (*Trip* 30), a "superannuated Mexican" (*Trip* 36), and "half-breed waiters" (*Trip* 42). In the writings of both Dana and Howe, New England stands as the opposite of Cuba, with the latter framed either as pure tropicalism (palm) or hybrid (people in Cuba).

62. "The Habaneros themselves walk their streets at all times. But do not imagine that they locomote after the fashion of an American in Broadway. . . . The Spaniards are decidedly not 'fast'" ("How They Live in Havana," 292).

63. Martí, *Selected Writings*, 264.

64. Ibid., 329.

65. *El Mulato*, 25 April 1854.

66. Martin Delany, "Annexation of Cuba," *North Star*, 27 April 1849.

67. Sundquist, *To Wake the Nations*, 135–221, and Levine, *Martin Delany, Frederick Douglass*, 203–4, situate Delany's novel in relation to filibustering movements. Noting a resemblance between the character of Henry Blake and William Walker, Levine asks, "What is the relationship of the indigenous people to the emerging black nation(s) that Blake hopes to bring forth. Or, to put things another way, what makes Blake in Cuba less of a filibuster—or less of an imperialist—than Walker in Nicaragua?" But, as Levine points out, Blake was born in Cuba, which establishes a vexed genealogical link to the island. In addition, Blake can be read as a leader who offers an alternative to the exiled Creoles who Delany knew were working in New York City.

68. For a discussion of the politics of a black versus a mulatto leader in *Blake*, see Levine, *Martin Delany, Frederick Douglass*, 205–6.

69. Zenea, "Meeting Cubano."

70. Stimson, *Cuba's Romantic Poet*, 54.

71. For articles and books about Plácido, see Stimson, *Cuba's Romantic Poet*, 89–102; Kutzinski, *Sugar's Secrets*, 225 n.14.

72. Hurlbert, "Poetry," 148–49.

73. Allen, "Placido," 263.

74. Ibid., 261.

75. Stimson, *Cuba's Romantic Poet*, 115.

76. Kutzinski, *Sugar's Secrets*, 85.

77. A Spanish-language version of the poem is in Valdez, *Poesías Completas*, 379; "To My Mother," *El Horizonte*, 5 August 1850; Hurlbert, "Poetry," 149.

78. Plácido, "El Juramento," *El Mulato*, 20 February 1854.

79. Plácido, "Décima," *El Mulato*, 25 April 1854.

80. Plácido, "La Muerte de Gesler," *La Verdad*, 20 March 1852.

81. Delany, *Blake*. Hereafter cited parenthetically in the text as *B*.

82. Sundquist, *To Wake the Nations*, 204, 209.

83. Dalton, "Dear Jorge," in *Poems*, 11.

84. Scholars believe that the final six chapters of *Blake*, which was serialized, have not been found. See Miller, "Note on This Edition," in Delany, *Blake*, ix.

85. "Tomé sus manos entre las mías, le dije que se sentara a mi lado y estuvimos sin hablar largo rato hasta que sus ojos se mojaron con algunas lágrimas" (*El Negro Mártir*, *El Mulato*, 20 February 1854).

86. "¿Quién podrá expresar la agonía que agobia el alma de esos mártires ofrecidos en holocausto a la más infame perversidad?" (*El Negro Mártir*, *El Mulato*, 27 February 1854).

87. Ibid., 11 March 1854.

88. Ibid.

89. "Tú eres el judío errante del siglo XIX" (*El Negro Mártir*, *El Mulato*, 6 March 1854).

90. Delmonte offered guidance to young literary talent and promoted the publication of antislavery writing. He also developed contacts with British abolitionists and established seminal relations with U.S. government officials that contributed to the annexationist movement. For a discussion of Delmonte's relationship with the administration of Martin Van Buren (1837–41), see Paquette, *Sugar Is Made with Blood*, 188–205.

91. The influence of this book is evident in a curious turn of publication history: Antonio Zambrana rewrote Suárez y Romero's book and published it as *El Negro Francisco* (1873) in Chile. For an excellent discussion of *Francisco* in the context of antislavery novels in Cuba in the 1830s, see Luis, *Literary Bondage*, 39–58.

92. See Sollors, *Multilingual America*, 7; Shell and Sollors, *Multilingual Anthology*.

93. Sollors, introduction to *Multilingual Anthology*, 5.

Chapter Five

1. Luis, *Literary Bondage*, 100.

2. See, for example, De La Cruz, "*Cecilia Valdés*"; De La Cruz, "Cirilo Villaverde." Lufriu, *Letras y Nacionalismo*, 115, writes that *Cecilia Valdés* "is and will always be, despite its serious defects in technique and style, the first Cuban novel."

3. Lazo, "Estudio Crítico," xi.

4. For an analysis of *Excursión a Vueltabajo*, see Benítez Rojo, "Cirilo Villaverde."

For a fascinating reading of Villaverde's *Excursión* in relation to *Viaje a la Habana* by María de las Mercedes Santa Cruz y Montalvo, the Comtesse de Merlin, see Méndez Rodenas, *Gender and Nationalism*, 120–28.

5. In the 1839 short story, the *mulata* Cecilia Valdés disappears from her home in Havana after being seduced by a young white man from a prominent family. The second version, also published in 1839, was a 246-page novel that expanded on the short story by adding lengthy descriptions of a popular festival known as Ferias del Angel. But not until the 1882 New York edition did Villaverde add an extensive cast of characters and entire chapters devoted to the political and social conditions in Havana during the early part of the century. For a discussion of the differences among the three versions of the novel, see Luis, *Literary Bondage*, 100–119. The 1839 short story was published as "La Primitiva Cecilia Valdés" in *Homenaje a Cirilo Villaverde*, 232–51.

6. Chaffin, *Fatal Glory*, 39.

7. Portell Vilá, *Narciso López*, 2:45. Because many of the articles in *La Verdad* were not signed and many issues apparently have been lost, it is difficult to determine Villaverde's exact contributions.

8. Rauch, *American Interest in Cuba*, 77.

9. Villaverde, prologue to *Cecilia Valdés*, 4.

10. Villaverde returned to Cuba in 1858 and published a new edition of his novel *Dos Amores*. He began to reconsider his relationship to fiction and planned to publish a new edition of *Cecilia Valdés* but had to leave the island again for New York as a result of political conditions; see his prologue to *Cecilia Valdés*, 5.

11. Quoted in "Cuba," *United States Magazine*, 201.

12. Quoted in Kirk, *José Martí*, 48.

13. "Fuera de Cuba, reformé mi género de vida: troqué mis gustos literarios por más altos pensamientos: pasé del mundo de las ilusiones al mundo de las realidades" (Villaverde, prologue to *Cecilia Valdés*, 4).

14. O'Sullivan founded the *Review* in 1837 and sold it in 1846 but remained associated with the magazine as an editor until at least 1852; see J. W. Pratt, "John O'Sullivan."

15. The article "General López, the Cuban Patriot" in the *Democratic Review* and the pamphlet by the same title are identical except that the latter contains an introduction, "To the Public," with Villaverde's initials. Some bibliographies and the U.S. Library of Congress cite Villaverde as the author of the "General López" pamphlet; however, Villaverde's English introduction differs in style and syntax from the article, which implies that Villaverde, although fluent in English, probably worked with O'Sullivan on the article. Here I cite the pamphlet version.

16. *General López*, 16, 6.

17. Ibid., 10.

18. Villaverde and Mariño, "To the Public."

19. Cirilo Villaverde and Manuel Antonio Mariño, "La Cuestión de Cuba," *El Independiente*, 20 February 1853.

20. Sommer, *Proceed with Caution*, 199–200.

21. See, for example, Pollard, *Historia*, 3–6.

22. Rebels who established a provisional republic in 1868 demanded representative government, free trade, and an end to Spain's taxation policies; see Pérez, *Cuba: Between Reform and Revolution*, 121–26.

23. Villaverde, prologue to *Cecilia Valdés*, 5.

24. Ibid., 5.

25. "Lo que no comprendemos de ninguna manera es que los cubanos hoy en los Estados Unidos abriguen la esperanza, de que halagando la codicia de los americanos por la adquisición de Cuba. . . . [S]e logrará no sólo interesar las simpatías, sino obtener la ayuda del pueblo y cuando menos la aquiescencia del gobierno de Washington" (Villaverde, *La Revolución de Cuba*, in *Homenaje a Cirilo Villaverde*, 47).

26. For a discussion of the changing political positions of Cubans in the United States during the nineteenth century, see Poyo, *"With All and for the Good of All,"* 14–19.

27. Arenas, *La Loma del Angel*; A. A. Fernández, *Lances de Amor*.

28. The film *Cecilia*, billed as an adaptation of Villaverde's novel, was directed by Humberto Solás.

29. Deschamps Chapeaux, "Autencidad de Algunos Negros," 220–32.

30. Quotations from *Cecilia Valdés o La Loma del Angel* are my translations of Jean Lamore's edition. I cite these parenthetically as *CV*. For a translation that omits the historical sections, see Villaverde, *The Quadroon; or, Cecilia Valdés*.

31. Kutzinski, *Sugar's Secrets*, 21.

32. In Hijuelos's novel *A Simple Habana Melody*, Rita Valladares is an idealized memory of the *mulata*.

33. Villaverde, prologue to *Cecilia Valdés*, 6.

34. Ibid., 5.

35. Benjamin, "Theses on the Philosophy of History," in *Illuminations*, 255.

36. Ibid.

37. Santacilia, *Lecciones Orales*, x.

38. Handley, *Postslavery Literatures in the Americas*, 53.

39. Villaverde, prologue to *Cecilia Valdés*, 7.

40. Sommer, *Proceed with Caution*, 190.

41. Lazo, "Estudio Crítico," xiii.

42. "Pero ni aquellos periódicos, ni estos fogosos versos, magüer que rebosando en ideas libres y patrióticas, bastaban a inspirar aquel sentimiento de patria y libertad que a veces impele a los hombres hasta el propio sacrificio, que les pone la espada en la mano y los lanza a la conquista de sus derechos."

43. José María Heredia, "A Amilia," in Montes-Huidobro, *Laúd*, 14.

44. Ibid., 15.

45. *La Voz de la América*, 21 May 1866, p. 1.

46. "Reseña Biográfica del General López," *La Voz de la América*, 21 May 1866.

47. Villaverde, *La Revolución de Cuba*, in *Homenaje a Cirilo Villaverde*, 33.

48. Villaverde and López supposedly took an annexationist posture to drum up support for filibustering, but they were actually seeking independence. That is the basis for the argument leveled by Herminio Portell Vilá decades ago. Portell Vilá wrote that he purchased Villaverde's papers from the writer's son, Narciso Villaverde and that those documents included Villaverde's diary from the filibustering period. Portell Vilá quoted the diary in his study (*Narciso López*, 3:2). Historians say Villaverde's diary is lost.

49. Quoted in Pérez, *Cuba: Between Reform and Revolution*, 109. Pérez discusses how slavery and U.S. imperial designs led Washington to oppose Cuban independence for much of the nineteenth century.

50. De la Torriente, *La Habana de Cecilia Valdés*.

Epilogue

1. "De su vida larga y tenaz de patriota entero y escritor útil ha entrado en la muerte, que para él ha de ser el premio merecido, el anciano que dio a Cuba su sangre, nunca arrepentida, y una inolvidable novela" (Martí, *Obras*, 5:241).

2. Martí, *Obras*, 5:242.

3. Martí, *Selected Writings*, 270–71.

4. Martí, *Obras*, 4:386, 5:430.

5. That is the point of the full title, *Fatal Glory: Narciso López and the First Clandestine U.S. War against Cuba*. Chaffin, *Fatal Glory*, xi, opens his preface with a reference to the Bay of Pigs.

BIBLIOGRAPHY

Newspapers

El Cometa (New York, 1855)
La Crónica (New York, 1848–51)
El Eco de Cuba (New York, 1855–56)
El Filibustero (New York, 1853–54)
El Guao (New York, 1853)
El Horizonte (New York, 1850)
El Independiente (New Orleans, 1852)
El Mulato (New York, 1854)
El Papagayo (New York, 1855)
El Pueblo (New York, 1855)
La Verdad (New York, 1848–60)
La Voz de la América (New York, 1866)
La Voz del Pueblo Cubano (Havana, 1852)

Pamphlets and Selected Newspaper Articles by Cuban Exiles

"Adquisición de Cuba." *El Filibustero*. 15 August 1853.

Agüero Estrada, Francisco. "Ateneo Democrático Cubano." *El Filibustero*. 15 November 1853.

———. "Cubanos." *El Pueblo*. 20 August 1855.

———. "Pobres Cubanos." *El Mulato*. 18 March 1854.

Allo, Lorenzo. *Domestic Slavery in Its Relation with Wealth: An Oration Pronounced in the Cuban Democratic Athenaeum of New York, on the Evening of the 1st of January, 1854*. New York: Tinson, 1855.

———. *La Esclavitud Doméstica en Sus Relaciones con la Riqueza: Discurso Pronunciado en el Ateneo Democrático Cubano de New York en la Noche del 10 de Enero de 1854*. New York: J. Mesa, 1854.

Betancourt Cisneros, Gaspar. *Thoughts upon the Incorporation of Cuba into the American Confederation, in Contra-Position to Those Published by José Antonio Saco*. New York: La Verdad, 1849.

"Celebración del Aniversario de la República Francesa." *El Mulato*. 6 March 1854.

"Cuba, Great Britain, and the United States." *El Horizonte*. 25 July 1850.

"D. Eduardo Facciolo." *La Verdad.* 10 October 1856.

"Filibusterismo." *El Filibustero.* 24 April 1853.

"General López." *El Filibustero.* 25 November 1853.

General Lopez, the Cuban Patriot. New York, 1851.

"El Gobierno de los Estados Unidos, la Isla de Cuba y Puerto Rico." *La Verdad.* 1
   May 1849.

Gonzales, Ambrosio José. *Manifesto on Cuban Affairs Addressed to the People of the
   United States.* New Orleans: Daily Delta, 1853.

"Junta General de Cubanos: Actas y Resoluciones." *El Filibustero.* 15 February 1854.

Madan Madan, Cristóbal [Un Hacendado, pseud.]. *Llamamiento de la Isla de Cuba a
   La Nación Española.* New York: Estevan Hallet, 1854.

Mesa, José. "A Mis Lectores." *El Eco de Cuba.* 1 February 1856.

El Negro Mártir: Novela Cubana. El Mulato. 20, 27 February, 6, 11, 25 March, 1, 8, 17,
   25 April 1854.

"A Nuestros Amigos y Compatriotas." *El Filibustero.* 25 February 1854.

"A Nuestros Lectores." *La Voz del Pueblo Cubano.* 13 June 1852.

"Ought a Free Republic to Possess Slaves?" *El Mulato.* 27 February 1854.

"Patriotismo Cubano, Sus Grados y Dominaciones." *El Filibustero.* 5 December
   1853.

Publícola [pseud.]. "Errores de la Revolución Cubana." *El Pueblo.* 15 June 1855.

"Recepción del Presidente Franklin Pierce en Nueva York." *El Filibustero.* 18 July
   1853.

Santacilia, Pedro. Editor's introduction. *El Guao.* 7 June 1853.

A Series of Articles on the Cuban Question. New York: La Verdad, 1849.

Tolón, Miguel T. "A las Cubanas." *El Papagayo.* 25 February 1855.

——. "Cuarto Aniversario de 'La Verdad.'" *La Verdad.* 10 January 1852.

——. "Discours Prononcé devant l'Assemblée des Exilés de Toutes les Nations,
   Convoquée pour Célébrer le Sixième Anniversaire de la République Française
   1848." *El Mulato.* 6 March 1854.

——. "The Fourth of July." *El Horizonte.* 4 July 1850.

——. "A Nuestros Lectores." *El Cubano.* 15 May 1853.

"La Venta de Cuba." *La Verdad.* 10 December 1858.

Villaverde, Cirilo. "El Sr. Saco Con Respecto a la Revolución de Cuba." *La Verdad.*
   10, 20 February, 10, 30 March, 20 April 1852.

Villaverde, Cirilo, and Manuel Antonio Mariño. "To the Public." *El Independiente.*
   20 February 1853.

Zenea, Juan Clemente. "Esperanza." *El Filibustero.* 13 June 1853.

——. "Meeting Cubano." *El Mulato.* 20 February 1854.

Books, Articles, and Dissertations

Abbot, Abiel. *Letters Written in the Interior of Cuba, between the Mountains of Arcana,
   to the East, and of Cusco, to the West, in the Months of February, March, April, and
   May 1828.* Boston: Bowles and Dearborn, 1828.

Allen, William G. "Placido." In *Autographs for Freedom*, edited by Julia Griffiths, 256–63. 1853. Reprint, Miami: Mnemosyne, 1969.

Alvarez Borland, Isabel. *Cuban-American Literature of Exile: From Person to Persona.* Charlottesville: University Press of Virginia, 1998.

Alvarez García, Imeldo, ed. *Acerca de Cirilo Villaverde.* Havana: Editorial Letras Cubanas, 1982.

Ancona, Eligio. "El Filibustero." In *La Novela del México Colonial*, edited by Antonio Castro Leal, 1:619–792. Mexico City: Aguilar, 1964.

Anderson, Benedict. *Imagined Communities: Reflections on the Origin and Spread of Nationalism.* 2d ed. New York: Verso, 1983.

Appadurai, Arjun. *Modernity at Large: Cultural Dimensions of Globalization.* Minneapolis: University of Minnesota Press, 1996.

Aranda, José. "Contradictory Impulses: María Amparo Ruiz de Burton, Resistance Theory, and the Politics of Chicano/a Studies." *American Literature* 70 (September 1998): 551–79.

———. *When We Arrive: A New Literary History of Mexican America.* Tucson: University of Arizona Press, 2003.

Arenas, Reinaldo. *La Loma del Angel.* Miami: Ediciones Universal, 1995.

Badaracco, Claire, ed. "The Cuba Journal," by Sophia Peabody Hawthorne. 2 vols. Ph.D. diss., Rutgers University, 1978.

Basch, Linda, Nina Glick Schiller, and Cristina Szanton Blanc. *Nations Unbound: Transnational Projects, Postcolonial Predicaments, and Deterritorialized Nation-States.* Langhorne, Pa.: Gordon and Breach, 1994.

Belnap, Jeffrey, and Raúl Fernández, eds. *José Martí's "Our America": From National to Hemispheric Cultural Studies.* Durham: Duke University Press, 1998.

Benítez Rojo, Antonio. "Cirilo Villaverde, the Seeker of Origins." In *Coded Encounters: Writing, Gender, and Ethnicity in Colonial Latin America*, edited by Francisco Javier Cevallos-Candau, Jeffrey A. Cole, Nina M. Scott, and Nicomedes Suárez-Araúz, 255–62. Amherst: University of Massachusetts Press, 1994.

———. "Power/Sugar/Literature: Toward a Reinterpretation of Cubanness." *Cuban Studies* 16 (1986): 9–31.

Benjamin, Walter. *Illuminations.* Edited by Hannah Arendt. New York: Schocken, 1969.

Berlant, Lauren. *The Queen of America Goes to Washington City: Essays on Sex and Citizenship.* Durham: Duke University Press, 1997.

Betancourt Cisneros, Gaspar. *Cartas a Saco.* Edited by Hilda Parets. Havana: Editorial Cuba, 1937.

Bhabha, Homi. *The Location of Culture.* New York: Routledge, 1994.

Binder, Frederick M., and David M. Reimers. *All the Nations under Heaven: An Ethnic and Racial History of New York City.* New York: Columbia University Press, 1995.

Binder, Sarah A., and Steven S. Smith. *Politics or Principle?: Filibustering in the United States Senate.* Washington, D.C.: Brookings Institution, 1997.

Bolaños Geyer, Alejandro. *William Walker: The Gray-Eyed Man of Destiny.* 5 vols. Lake St. Louis, Mo.: A Bolaños Geyer, 1988–91.

Brady, Mary Pat. *Extinct Lands, Temporal Geographies: Chicana Literature and the Urgency of Space.* Durham: Duke University Press, 2002.

Bridges, C. A. "The Knights of the Golden Circle: A Filibustering Fantasy." *Southwestern Historical Quarterly* 44 (January 1941): 287–302.

Brown, Charles H. *Agents of Manifest Destiny: The Lives and Times of the Filibusters.* Chapel Hill: University of North Carolina Press, 1980.

Bueno, Salvador, ed. *Costumbristas Cubanos del Siglo XIX.* Caracas, Venezuela: Biblioteca Ayacucho, 1985.

Burdette, Franklin L. *Filibustering in the Senate.* Princeton: Princeton University Press, 1940.

Cairo, Ana. "Emilia Casanova y la Dignidad de la Mujer Cubana." In *Mujeres Latinoamericanas: Historia y Cultura, Siglos XVI al XIX*, edited by Luisa Campuzano, 1:231–41. Havana and Mexico City: Casa de las Américas and University Autónoma Metropolitana-Iztalapa, 1997.

Caldwell, Robert Granville. "The López Expeditions to Cuba, 1848–1851." Ph.D. diss., Princeton University, 1915.

Campuzano, Luisa. "A 'Valiant Symbol of Industrial Progress'?: Cuban Women Travelers and the United States." In *Women at Sea: Travel Writing and the Margins of Caribbean Discourse*, edited by Lizabeth Paravisini-Gebert and Ivette Romero-Cesareo, 161–81. New York: Palgrave, 2001.

Capra, Frank. *Mr. Smith Goes to Washington.* VHS. New York: Columbia Pictures, 1979.

Carbonell, José Manuel. *La Poesía Revolucionaria en Cuba.* Havana: El Siglo XX, 1928.

———. *Los Poetas de "El Laúd del Desterrado."* Havana: Imprenta Avisador Comercial, 1930.

Cardenal, Ernesto. *Antología.* Nicaragua: Ediciones Monimbó, 1983.

Casanova de Villaverde, Emilia. "Cartas de la Correspondencia, 1869–1876." In Villaverde, *Apuntes Biográficos*, 37–224.

Cervantes Saavedra, Miguel de. *The Adventures of Don Quixote.* Translated by J. M. Cohen. New York: Penguin, 1950.

Chaffin, Tom. *Fatal Glory: Narciso López and the First Clandestine U.S. War against Cuba.* Charlottesville: University Press of Virginia, 1996.

Corominos, Joan, and José A. Pascual, eds. *Diccionario Crítico Etimológico Castellano e Hispano.* 6 vols. Madrid: Editorial Gredos, 1980.

Cortina, Rodolfo J. "Cuban Literature of the United States, 1824–1959." In *Recovering the U.S. Hispanic Literary Heritage*, edited by Ramón Gutiérrez and Genaro Padilla, 69–90. Houston: Arte Público, 1993.

Crane, Stephen. *Prose and Poetry.* Edited by J. C. Levenson. New York: Library of America, 1984.

"Cuba." *Putnam's Monthly Magazine* 1 (January 1853): 3–16.

"Cuba." *United States Magazine and Democratic Review* 25 (September 1849): 193–203.

Dalton, Roque. *Poems.* Translated by Richard Schaaf. Willimantic, Conn.: Curbstone, 1984.

Dana, Richard Henry, Jr. *To Cuba and Back: A Vacation Voyage.* Edited by C. Harvey Gardiner. Carbondale: Southern Illinois University Press, 1966.

———. *Two Years before the Mast.* Edited by Thomas Philbrick. New York: Penguin, 1981.

Darnton, Robert. "What Is the History of Books?" In *Books in Society and History,* edited by Kenneth E. Carpenter, 3–26. New York: Bowker, 1983.

De la Cova, Antonio Rafael. "Ambrosio José Gonzales: A Cuban Confederate Colonel." Ph.D. diss., West Virginia University, 1994.

———. *Cuban Confederate Colonel: The Life of Ambrosio José Gonzales.* Columbia: University of South Carolina Press, 2003.

———. "Filibusters and Freemasons: The Sworn Obligation." *Journal of the Early Republic* 17 (Spring 1997): 95–120.

De la Cruz, Manuel. "*Cecilia Valdés.*" In *Acerca de Cirilo Villaverde,* edited by Alvarez García.

———. "Cirilo Villaverde." In *Acerca de Cirilo Villaverde,* edited by Alvarez García.

Delany, Martin. *Blake; or, The Huts of America.* Edited by Floyd Miller. Boston: Beacon, 1970.

———. *The Condition, Elevation, Emigration, and Destiny of the Colored People.* New York: Arno, 1968.

De la Torriente, Loló. *La Habana de Cecilia Valdés.* Havana: J. Montero, 1946.

Deleuze, Gilles, and Félix Guattari. *Kafka: Toward a Minor Literature.* Translated by Dana Polan. Minneapolis: University of Minnesota Press, 1986.

Deschamps Chapeaux, Pedro. "Autencidad de Algunos Negros y Mulatos de *Cecilia Valdés.*" In *Acerca de Cirilo Villaverde,* edited by Alvarez García.

Diner, Hasia R. "'The Most Irish City in the Union': The Era of the Great Migration, 1844–1877." In *The New York Irish,* edited by Ronald H. Bayor and Timothy J. Meagher, 87–106. Baltimore: Johns Hopkins University Press, 1996.

Duany, Jorge. "Reconstructing Cubanness." In *Cuba, the Elusive Nation,* edited by D. J. Fernández and Cámara Betancourt, 16–42.

Fernández, Alfredo Antonio. *Lances de Amor: Vida y Muerte del Caballero Narciso.* Havana: Editorial Letras Cubanas, 1994.

Fernández, Damián J., and Madeline Cámara Betancourt, eds. *Cuba, the Elusive Nation: Interpretations of National Identity.* Gainesville: University Press of Florida, 2000.

Ferrer, Ada. *Insurgent Cuba: Race, Nation, and Revolution, 1868–1898.* Chapel Hill: University of North Carolina Press, 1999.

———. "Rethinking Race and Nation." In *Cuba, the Elusive Nation,* edited by D. J. Fernández and Cámara Betancourt, 60–76.

Figarola-Caneda, Domingo. *Diccionario Cubano de Seudónimos.* Havana: Imprenta "El Siglo XX," 1922.

"Filibustering." *Putnam's Monthly Magazine* 9 (April 1857): 425–35.

Foner, Philip S. *The Spanish-Cuban-American War and the Birth of American Imperialism, 1895–1902.* Vol. 1. New York: Monthly Review Press, 1972.

Fornet, Ambrosio. "The Cuban Literary Diaspora and Its Contexts: A Glossary." *boundary 2* 29 (Fall 2002): 91–103.

——. *El Libro en Cuba.* Havana: Editorial Letras Cubanas, 1994.

Franco, Jean. *The Modern Culture of Latin America: Society and the Artist.* New York: Praeger, 1967.

Galeano, Eduardo. *Open Veins of Latin America.* Translated by Cedric Belfrage. New York: Monthly Review Press, 1973.

García Carranza, Josefina, and Miguelina Ponte. *Catálogo de Publicaciones Seriadas Cubanas de los Siglos XVIII y XIX.* Santiago, Cuba: Editorial Oriente, 1984.

Gay Calbó, Enrique. "La Bandera y El Escudo." In *Los Primeros Movimientos*, edited by Roig de Leuchsenring, 119–30.

"General Lopez, the Cuban Patriot." *United States Magazine and Democratic Review* 26 (February 1850): 97–112.

Gerassi-Navarro, Nina. *Pirate Novels: Fictions of Nation Building in Spanish America.* Durham: Duke University Press, 1999.

Gilroy, Paul. *The Black Atlantic: Modernity and Double Consciousness.* Cambridge: Harvard University Press, 1993.

Gómez de Avellaneda, Gertrudis. *Obras de Doña Gertrudis Gómez de Avellaneda.* Edited by José María Castro y Calvo. 2 vols. Madrid: Ediciones Atlas, 1974.

González Curquejo, Antonio, ed. *Florilegio de Escritoras Cubanas.* 3 vols. Havana: La Moderna Poesía, 1910.

Greene, Laurence. *The Filibuster: The Career of William Walker.* New York: Bobbs-Merrill, 1937.

Gruesz, Kirsten Silva. *Ambassadors of Culture: The Transamerican Origins of Latino Writing.* Princeton: Princeton University Press, 2002.

Guier, Enrique. *William Walker.* San José, Costa Rica: s.n., 1971.

Gutiérrez, Ramón, and Genaro Padilla, eds. *Recovering the U.S. Hispanic Literary Heritage.* Houston: Arte Público, 1993.

Handley, George. *Postslavery Literatures in the Americas.* Charlottesville: University Press of Virginia, 2000.

Hardt, Michael, and Antonio Negri. *Empire.* Cambridge: Harvard University Press, 2000.

Harter, Hugh A. *Gertrudis Gómez de Avellaneda.* Boston: Twayne, 1981.

Henríquez Ureña, Max. *Panorama Histórico de la Literatura Cubana.* Vol. 1. Puerto Rico: Ediciones Mirador, 1963.

Heredia, José María. *Poesías de José María Heredia.* New York: Behr y Kahl, 1825.

——. *Selected Poems in English Translation.* Edited by Angel Aparicio Laurencio. Miami: Ediciones Universal, 1970.

Hicks, D. Emily. *Border Writing: The Multidimensional Text.* Minneapolis: University of Minnesota Press, 1991.

Hietala, Thomas. *Manifest Design: Anxious Aggrandizement in Late Jacksonian America*. Ithaca: Cornell University Press, 1985.

Hijuelos, Oscar. *A Simple Habana Melody*. New York: HarperCollins, 2002.

Hillgarth, J. N. *The Mirror of Spain, 1500–1700: The Formation of a Myth*. Ann Arbor: University of Michigan Press, 2000.

Horrego Estuch, Leopoldo. *Emilia Casanova: La Vehemencia del Separatismo*. Havana: Imprenta el Siglo XX, 1951.

Horsman, Reginald. *Race and Manifest Destiny: The Origins of American Racial Anglo-Saxonism*. Cambridge: Harvard University Press, 1981.

Howe, Julia Ward. *A Trip to Cuba*. Boston: Ticknor and Fields, 1860.

"How They Live in Havana." *Putnam's Monthly Magazine* 1 (March 1853): 288–98.

Hudson, Linda S. *Mistress of Manifest Destiny: A Biography of Jane McManus Storm Cazneau, 1807–1878*. Austin: Texas State Historical Association, 2001.

Huete, Angel. Introduction to *Poesías Completas*, by Luisa Pérez de Zambrana, xvi–xvii.

Hurlbert, William Henry. *Gan-Eden; or, Pictures of Cuba*. Boston: John P. Jewett, 1854.

———. "The Poetry of Spanish America." *North American Review* 58 (1849): 129–59.

Ianes, Raúl. "Metaficción y 'Elaboraciones al Vapor': La Novela Histórica de Gertrudis Gómez de Avellaneda." *Letras Peninsulares* 10 (Fall 1997): 249–62.

Instituto de Literatura y Lingüística de la Academia de Ciencias de Cuba. *Perfil Histórico de las Letras Cubanas: Desde los Orígenes hasta 1898*. Havana: Editorial Letras Cubanas, 1983.

Jay, Gregory. *American Literature and the Culture Wars*. Ithaca: Cornell University Press, 1997.

Jefferson, Thomas. *The Writings of Thomas Jefferson*. 20 vols. Washington, D.C.: Jefferson Memorial Society, 1905.

Jensen, Larry R. *Children of Colonial Despotism: Press, Politics, and Culture in Cuba, 1790–1840*. Tampa: University of South Florida Press, 1988.

Kanellos, Nicolás. "A Brief History of Hispanic Periodicals in the United States." In *Hispanic Periodicals*, edited by Kanellos and Martell, 3–136.

———. *Thirty Million Strong: Reclaiming the Hispanic Image in American Culture*. Golden, Colo.: Fulcrum, 1998.

Kanellos, Nicolás, and Helvetia Martell. "A Comprehensive Bibliography of Hispanic Periodicals in the United States." In *Hispanic Periodicals*, edited by Kanellos and Martell, 137–277.

———, eds. *Hispanic Periodicals in the United States: Origins to 1960*. Houston: Arte Público, 2000.

Kanellos, Nicolás, et al., eds. *Herencia: The Anthology of Hispanic Literature of the United States*. Oxford: Oxford University Press, 2002.

Kaplan, Amy, and Donald Pease, eds. *Cultures of United States Imperialism*. Durham: Duke University Press, 1993.

Kaplan, Caren. "Deterritorializations: The Rewriting of Home and Exile in Western Feminist Discourse." *Cultural Critique* 6 (1987): 187–98.

Kennedy, Paul, and Victor Roudometof, eds. *Communities across Borders: New Immigrants and Transnational Cultures*. New York: Routledge, 2002.

Kirk, John M. *José Martí, Mentor of the Cuban Nation*. Tampa: University Presses of Florida, 1983.

Knight, Franklin W. *Slave Society in Cuba during the Nineteenth Century*. Madison: University of Wisconsin Press, 1970.

Kutzinski, Vera. *Against the American Grain*. Baltimore: Johns Hopkins University Press, 1987.

———. *Sugar's Secrets: Race and the Erotics of Cuban Nationalism*. Charlottesville: University Press of Virginia, 1993.

"The Late Cuba State Trials." *United States Magazine and Democratic Review* 30 (April 1852): 307–19.

Lauter, Paul, et al., eds. *The Heath Anthology of American Literature*. 4th ed. Vol. 2. Boston: Houghton Mifflin, 2002.

Lazo, Raimundo. "Estudio Crítico." In *Cecilia Valdés*, by Cirilo Villaverde, ix–xxxvii. Mexico: Editorial Porrúa, 1972.

Leal, Luis, and Rodolfo J. Cortina. Introduction to *Jicotencal*, by Félix Varela, vii–xlvii. Houston: Arte Público, 1995.

Lee, J. J. "Daniel O'Connell." In *Daniel O'Connell: Political Pioneer*, edited by Maurice O'Connell. Dublin: Institute of Public Administration, 1991.

Levine, Robert S. *Martin Delany, Frederick Douglass, and the Politics of Representative Identity*. Chapel Hill: University of North Carolina Press, 1997.

Lezama Lima, José, ed. *Antología de la Poesía Cubana*. 3 vols. Havana: Consejo Nacional de Cultura, 1965.

———. *La Cantidad Hechizada*. Madrid: Ediciones Jucar, 1974.

Lufriu, Rene. *Letras y Nacionalismo*. Havana: Libreria de José Albela, 1925.

Lugo-Ortiz, Agnes. *Identidades Imaginadas: Biografía y Nacionalidad en el Horizonte de la Guerra (Cuba 1860–1898)*. San Juan, Puerto Rico: Universidad de Puerto Rico, 1999.

Luis, William. *Literary Bondage: Slavery in Cuban Narrative*. Austin: University of Texas Press, 1990.

Mann, Mary Peabody. *Juanita: A Romance of Real Life in Cuba Fifty Years Ago*. Edited by Patricia M. Ard. Charlottesville: University Press of Virginia, 2000.

Martí, José. *Lucía Jerez o Amistad Funesta*. Havana: Editorial Letras Cubanas, 1997.

———. *Obras Completas*. 21 vols. Havana: Editorial Nacional, 1963.

———. *Selected Writings*. Edited and Translated by Esther Allen. New York: Penguin, 2002.

———, ed. *Los Poetas de la Guerra*. 1893. Havana: Universidad de la Habana, 1968.

Martí de Cid, Dolores. "Comparación Estilística de 'Fidelia' y 'La Vuelta al Bosque.'" *Circulo* 10 (1981): 57–67.

Mather, Cotton [C. Mathero, pseud.]. *La Fe del Christiano*. Boston: n.p., 1699.

Mathews, Mitford. *A Dictionary of Americanisms on Historical Principles.* Chicago: University of Chicago Press, 1951.

May, Robert. *Manifest Destiny's Underworld: Filibustering in Antebellum America.* Chapel Hill: University of North Carolina Press, 2002.

———. *The Southern Dream of a Caribbean Empire, 1854–1861.* Baton Rouge: Louisiana State University Press, 1973.

———. "Young American Males and Filibustering in the Age of Manifest Destiny: The United States Army as Cultural Mirror." *Journal of American History* 78 (December 1991): 857–86.

McCadden, Joseph, and Helen McCadden. *Father Varela, Torch Bearer from Cuba.* New York: U.S. Catholic Historical Society, 1969.

McDonald, Forrest. *States' Rights and the Union: Imperium in Imperio, 1776–1876.* Lawrence: University Press of Kansas, 2000.

Meléndez, A. Gabriel. *So All Is Not Lost: The Poetics of Print in Nuevomexicano Communities, 1834–1958.* Albuquerque: University of New Mexico Press, 1997.

Méndez Rodenas, Adriana. *Gender and Nationalism in Colonial Cuba: The Travels Of Santa Cruz y Montalvo, Condesa de Merlin.* Nashville: Vanderbilt University Press, 1998.

Meyer, Doris. *Speaking for Themselves: Neomexicano Cultural Identity and the Spanish Language Press, 1880–1920.* Albuquerque: University of New Mexico Press, 1996.

Montes-Huidobro, Matías, ed. *El Laúd del Desterrado.* Houston: Arte Público, 1995.

Montgomery, Cora [pseud.]. *Eagle Pass; or, Life on the Border.* New York: Putnam, 1852.

Morales y Morales, Vidal. *Iniciadores y Primeros Mártires de la Revolución Cubana.* 3 vols. Havana: Cultural, 1931.

Mott, Luther. *American Journalism: A History, 1690–1960.* 3d ed. New York: Macmillan, 1962.

Oboler, Suzanne. *Ethnic Labels, Latino Lives: The Politics of (Re)Presentation in the United States.* Minneapolis: University of Minnesota Press, 1995.

An Officer in the Service of Walker. *The Destiny of Nicaragua: Central America as It Was, Is, and May Be.* Boston: Bent, 1856.

Ojito, Mirta. "Best of Friends, Worlds Apart." *New York Times.* 5 June 2000.

Olivera, Otto. *Cuba en Su Poesía.* Mexico City: Ediciones de Andrea, 1965.

———. *Viajeros en Cuba (1800–1850).* Miami: Ediciones Universal, 1997.

Opartny, Josef. *U.S. Expansionism and Cuban Annexationism in the 1850s.* Lewiston, N.Y.: Mellen, 1993.

Owsley, Frank Lawrence, Jr., and Gene A. Smith. *Filibusters and Expansionists: Jeffersonian Manifest Destiny, 1800–1821.* Tuscaloosa: University of Alabama Press, 1997.

Padilla, Genaro. *My History, Not Yours: The Formation of Mexican American Autobiography.* Madison: University of Wisconsin Press, 1993.

Paine, Thomas. *Collected Writings.* Edited by Eric Foner. New York: Library of America, 1995.

Paquette, Robert. *Sugar Is Made with Blood: The Conspiracy of La Escalera and the Conflict between Empires over Slavery in Cuba*. Middletown, Conn.: Wesleyan University Press, 1988.

Pease, Donald. "C. L. R. James, *Moby-Dick*, and the Emergence of Transnational American Studies." *Arizona Quarterly* 56 (Autumn 2000): 93–123.

Pérez, Louis A., Jr. *Cuba and the United States: Ties of Singular Intimacy*. Athens: University of Georgia Press, 1990.

———. *Cuba: Between Reform and Revolution*. 2d ed. New York: Oxford University Press, 1995.

———, ed. *Slaves, Sugar, and Colonial Society: Travel Accounts of Cuba, 1801–1899*. Wilmington, Del.: Scholarly Resources, 1992.

Pérez de Zambrana, Luisa. *Elegias Familiares*. Havana: Secretaría de Educación, 1937.

———. *Poesías Completas*. Edited by Angel Huete. Havana: P. Fernández, 1957.

Pérez Firmat, Gustavo, ed. *Do the Americas Have a Common Literature?* Durham: Duke University Press, 1990.

———. *Life on the Hyphen: The Cuban American Way*. Austin: University of Texas Press, 1994.

Pickens, Lucy Holcombe. *The Free Flag of Cuba: The Lost Novel of Lucy Holcombe Pickens*. Edited by Orville Vernon Burton and Georganne B. Burton. Baton Rouge: Louisiana State University Press, 2002.

Piñeyro, Enrique. *Vida y Escritos de Juan Clemente Zenea*. Paris: Garnier Hermanos, 1901.

Pollard, Edward. *Historia del Primer Año de la Guerra del Sur*. Translated by Cirilo Villaverde. New York: Imprenta de L. Hauser, 1863.

Portell Vilá, Herminio. *Narciso López y Su Época*. 3 vols. Havana: Cultural and Compañía Editorial, 1930–58.

Poyo, Gerald. *"With All and for the Good of All": The Emergence of Popular Nationalism within the Cuban Communities of the United States, 1848–1898*. Durham: Duke University Press, 1989.

Pratt, Julius W. "John O'Sullivan and Manifest Destiny." *New York History* 14 (1933): 213–34.

Pratt, Mary Louise. *Imperial Eyes: Travel Writing and Transculturation*. New York: Routledge, 1992.

Rahe, Paul A. *Republics Ancient and Modern*. Chapel Hill: University of North Carolina Press, 1992.

Ramos, Julio. "The Repose of Heroes." *Modern Language Quarterly* 57 (June 1996): 355–67.

Rauch, Basil. *American Interest in Cuba, 1848–1855*. New York: Octagon, 1974.

Read, J. Lloyd. *The Mexican Historical Novel, 1826–1910*. New York: Instituto de las Españas en los Estados Unidos, 1939.

Remos y Rubio, Juan. *Historia de la Literatura Cubana*. 2 vols. Cuba: Cárdenas y Compañia, 1945.

Rizal, José. *El Filibusterismo*. 3d ed. Barcelona: Imprenta de Henrich, 1908.

———. *The Subversive*. Translated by León M. Guerrero. Bloomington: Indiana University Press, 1962.

Rocafuerte, Vicente. *Ideas Necesarias a Todo Pueblo Americano Independiente, Que Quiera Ser Libre*. Philadelphia: D. Huntington, 1821.

Roig de Leuchsenring, Emilio, ed. *Los Primeros Movimientos Revolucionarios del General Narciso López*. Havana: Municipio de la Habana, 1950.

Rosengarten, Frederic. *Freebooters Must Die!: The Life and Death of William Walker*. Wayne, Pa.: Haverford House, 1976.

Rowe, John Carlos. "Nineteenth-Century U.S. Literary Culture and Transnationality." *PMLA* 118 (January 2003): 78–89.

Saco, José Antonio. "Análisis por Don José Antonio Saco de Una Obra Sobre el Brasil, Intitulada, *Notices of Brazil in 1828 and 1829 by Rev. Walsh, Author of a Journey from Constantinople, etc.*" In *José Antonio Saco, Acerca de la Esclavitud y Su Historia*, edited by Eduardo Torres-Cuevas and Arturo Sorhegui, 173–205. Havana: Editorial de Ciencias Sociales, 1982.

———. *La Situación Política de Cuba y Su Remedio* (1851), in *Folletos Escritos por Don José Antonio Saco, contra la Anexión de la Isla de Cuba a los Estados Unidos de América*, 151–78. New York: Lockwood, 1856.

Said, Edward. *Culture and Imperialism*. New York: Vintage, 1993.

———. *Representations of the Intellectual*. New York: Vintage, 1994.

Saldívar, José David. *The Dialectics of Our America*. Durham: Duke University Press, 1991.

Sánchez, Joseph P. *The Spanish Black Legend: Origins of Anti-Hispanic Stereotypes*. New Mexico: Spanish Colonial Research Center, 1990.

Sánchez, Rosaura. *Telling Identities: The Californio Testimonios*. Minneapolis: University of Minnesota Press, 1995.

Sánchez-Boudy, José, ed. *Diccionario Mayor de Cubanismos*. Miami: Ediciones Universal, 1999.

Santacilia, Pedro. *El Arpa del Proscripto*. New York: Durand, 1864.

———. *Lecciones Orales sobre la Historia de Cuba, Pronunciadas en el Ateneo Democrático de Nueva York*. New Orleans: Luis Eduardo del Cristo, 1859.

Santovenia, Emeterio S. *La Bandera de Narciso López en el Senado de Cuba*. Havana: Ediciones Oficiales del Senado, 1945.

Scott, Rebecca J. *Slave Emancipation in Cuba: The Transition to Free Labor, 1860–1899*. Princeton: Princeton University Press, 1985.

Shell, Marc, and Werner Sollors, eds. *The Multilingual Anthology of American Literature*. New York: New York University Press, 2000.

Sollors, Werner, ed. *Multilingual America: Transnationalism, Ethnicity, and the Languages of American Literature*. New York: New York University Press, 1998.

Sommer, Doris. *Proceed with Caution, When Engaged by Minority Writing in the Americas*. Cambridge: Harvard University Press, 1999.

Stimson, Frederick S. *Cuba's Romantic Poet: The Story of Plácido*. Chapel Hill: University of North Carolina Press, 1964.

Stowe, Harriet Beecher. *La Cabaña del Tio Tom*. Translated by Andrés Aveline de Orihuela. Paris: Libreria Española y Americana de Boix, 1852.

Suárez y Romero, Anselmo. *Francisco*. Edited by Mario Cabrera Saqui. Havana: Ministerio de Educación, 1947.

Sundquist, Eric. *To Wake the Nations: Race in the Making of American Literature*. Cambridge: Harvard University Press, 1993.

Thomas, Hugh. *Cuba: The Pursuit of Freedom*. New York: Harper and Row, 1971.

Tolón, Miguel T. *The Elementary Spanish Reader and Translator*. New York: Appleton, 1853.

——. *Leyendas Cubanas*. New York: Mesa and Familton, 1856.

——. *Lola Guara: Novela Cubana*. Matanzas, Cuba: Imprenta de Gobierno y Marina, 1846.

Valdez, Gabriel de la Concepción [Plácido, pseud.]. *Poesías Completas de Plácido*. 1862. Reprint, Nendl, Germany: Kraus, 1970.

Van Alstyne, R. W. *The Rising American Empire*. 5th ed. Chicago: Quadrangle, 1965.

Varela, Félix. *El Habanero: Papel Político, Científico, y Literario*. Miami: Ediciones Universal, 1997.

——. *Jicoténcal*. Edited by Luis Leal and Rodolfo J. Cortina. Houston: Arte Público, 1995.

Villaverde, Cirilo [Un Contemporáneo, pseud.]. *Apuntes Biograficos de Emilia Casanova de Villaverde*. New York, 1874.

——. *Cecilia Valdés o La Loma del Angel*. Edited by Jean Lamore. Madrid: Cátedra, 1992.

——. *Homenaje a Cirilo Villaverde*. Havana: UNESCO, 1964.

——. *La Joven de la Flecha de Oro y Otros Relatos*. Havana: Editorial Letras Cubanas, 1984.

——. Prologue to *Cecilia Valdés*. Edited by Iván Schulman. Caracas, Venezuela: Biblioteca Ayacucho, 1981.

——. *The Quadroon; or, Cecilia Valdés: A Romance of Old Havana*. Translated by Mariano Lorente. Boston: Page, 1935.

Vitier, Cintio. *Lo Cubano en la Poesía*. Santa Clara, Cuba: Universidad Central de Las Villas, 1958.

Walker, William. *The War in Nicaragua*. Mobile, Ala.: Goetzel, 1860.

Warner, Michael. *The Letters of the Republic: Publication and the Public Sphere in Eighteenth-Century America*. Cambridge: Harvard University Press, 1990.

Weinberg, Albert K. *Manifest Destiny*. Baltimore: Johns Hopkins University Press, 1935.

Wells, William. *Walker's Expedition to Nicaragua; a History of the Central American War; and the Sonora and Kinney Expeditions, Including All the Recent Diplomatic Correspondence, Together with a New and Accurate Map of Central America, and a Memoir and Portrait of General William Walker*. New York: Stringer and Townsend, 1856.

Wenders, Wim, and Donata Wenders. *The Buena Vista Social Club: The Companion Book to the Film*. New York: Neues, 2000.

Whittier, John Greenleaf. *The Complete Poetical Works.* Cambridge: Riverside, 1892.

Widmer, Edward L. *Young America: The Flowering of Democracy in New York City.* New York: Oxford University Press, 1999.

Williams, Raymond. *Keywords: A Vocabulary of Culture and Society.* New York: Oxford University Press, 1983.

Williams, Stanley T. *The Spanish Background of American Literature.* 2 vols. New Haven: Yale University Press, 1955.

Yun, Lisa, and Ricardo René Laremont. "Chinese Coolies and African Slaves in Cuba, 1847–74." *Journal of Asian American Studies* 4 (June 2001): 99–122.

INDEX